GW00983062

Revitalising the Silk Road

China's Belt and Road Initiative

RICHARD T. GRIFFITHS

Copyright © 2017 Richard T. Griffiths.

All rights reserved. No part of this book may be reproduced, stored, or transmitted by any means—whether auditory, graphic, mechanical, or electronic—without written permission of the author, except in the case of brief excerpts used in critical articles and reviews. Unauthorized reproduction of any part of this work is illegal and is punishable by law.

ISBN: 978-9-4924-3902-4 (sc)
ISBN: 978-9-4924-3903-1 (e)

Library of Congress Control Number: 2017905809

HIPE Publications
PO Box 1005
2302 BA Leiden
The Netherlands
00.31.640974999
HIPE Publications

Because of the dynamic nature of the Internet, any web addresses or links contained in this book may have changed since publication and may no longer be valid. The views expressed in this work are solely those of the author and do not necessarily reflect the views of the publisher, and the publisher hereby disclaims any responsibility for them.

Any people depicted in stock imagery provided by Thinkstock are models, and such images are being used for illustrative purposes only.
Certain stock imagery © Thinkstock.

Rev. date: 5/2/2017

To Wendy

CONTENTS

LIST OF FIGURES

LIST OF TABLES

PREFACE

Since, as reader and author respectively, we will be spending some time together, a few words may not come amiss over why I have written this book. As an economic historian, the subject matter certainly interests me, but neither China nor Asia are my recognised fields of expertise. I am specialised in 19th and 20th century Western European history with a concentration on European integration. Ironically it was that interest in Europe that first got me involved with China.

At the turn of the century the European Union decided that China's economic development had reached a level that disqualified it from receiving further development aid from the EU Budget. To mark the end of this phase of EU–China relations, the EU decided to use the remaining funds to establish a network of EU Studies Centres throughout Chinese universities. It was in this context that I was approached in 2005 to see whether Leiden University, where I was the director of the MA programme in European Union Studies, would become the lead European partner in establishing one of the new Study Centres. The centre would create a network of four universities in the cities of Xi'an, Lanzhou and Urumqi. It did not register with me at the time that the distance between Xi'an and Urumqi was about 2500 kms, about the same as that between Oslo and Rome nor that the three cities lay on the route of the old Silk Road from the ancient capital of Xi'an to the border in the North Western province of Xinjiang. Indeed, one of the aims of the project was to concentrate 'on issues of sustainability in the process of EU integration with relevance to the revitalisation of the Silk Road'. This, by the way, explains the title of the book.

In August 2006 I first travelled to China in connection with the project. My first hours in Beijing completely dispelled any preconceptions I had held over the role of bicycles in the city's transport system. I had seen more bicycles in half an hour in Leiden than I did throughout my short stay in Beijing. My destination, however, was Urumqi, the capital of Xinjiang province and home to over two million inhabitants. The city was surprisingly modern. It reminded me much of Istanbul and I would have guessed that its level of real per capita income was about the same. But the comparison did not stop there. As I wrote in my report, 'it reminded me a lot of Turkey with its oven-baked nan bread, its markets and its lamb kebabs cooked over charcoal fires in the streets'. I stayed for a week lecturing and talking to staff and students. I also had a little time to explore the region. At Bezeklik I visited the hundreds of caves hewn into the stone by Buddhist monks some fifteen centuries ago. In the middle of the desert, I strolled under the vines in the oasis town of Turpin, its waters still fed by the irrigation system constructed two thousand years earlier linking the town to the mountains in the distance. Slowly, I was being affected by the dust of the ancient Silk Road. In the year that followed, over fifty teachers and researchers came to Leiden for short periods to talk with staff and to use the library resources. The first phase of the project was concluded with a conference in Xi'an, the ancient capital of a unified China and the start of the Silk Road. I found the walled town utterly charming and, of course, I took the opportunity to visit the tomb of the first Qin emperor and its guard of terracotta warriors. By now the Silk Road was firmly lodged in my consciousness. The Combined Silk Road European Studies Centre still exists. It continues to prosper and I have met friends and colleagues from those times at various academic conferences. After the violence in Xinjiang in 2009 I gradually lost touch with my friends in Urumqi. Email contact was broken and letters elicited no replies.

It was not until the summer of 2013 that I returned to China for any length of time. I had been invited to teach for a month in the international summer school at Renmin University in Beijing. While I was in Beijing, I visited the Forbidden City and had the privilege to see the recently (re-) discovered 'Mongolian Map'. This had been taken by the Japanese during the first Sino-Japanese War (1894-5) and had been mistakenly filed as a landscape painting. It was, in fact, an early 16th century map of the Silk Road. It is 59 centimetres high and slightly over 30 metres long. The last part, covering the entry into Europe, has been lost. The map was purchased by Chinese businessmen in the year 2000 and a team of scholars spent the next seven years locating the 211 names recorded on the map. The original map itself is now back in a private collection.[1]

As usual, when I am abroad I try to keep abreast of the news by reading the English-language newspapers, in this case the *China Daily.* While I was there the paper was featuring was the progress being made in constructing the high speed rail link from Hami to Urumqi that lay 530 kms to the south-west. It showed how wind-screens had to be built that would protect the trains from the desert storms and how the track had to be laid so that it would not damage the millennia old irrigation system lying just below the surface. It also boasted of the travel time saved once the route had been completed. The journey from Beijing would be sliced from forty hours to twelve. I was inspired. That August I wrote,

> Two millennia ago began the old 'silk-road' that had once linked Europe and Chinese civilisations. It could do so again. Since 2012 freight-trains have been trundling along the 11,179 kms of railway linking Chongqing in the East to the Dutch border, in the West. Already these have cut the transport times from five weeks by sea to three weeks by rail and, for the moment, they have eliminated the dangers of piracy. Rail transport is seven times cheaper than air freight and is far less polluting. During my stay, the newspaper headlines were celebrating the heroic work in building the new high-speed rail line for the 1176 kms Lanzsu-Xinjiang section that, when opened in 2014, would slash the total journey time to sixteen days.
>
> At a time when the new "iron silk road" is promising to reduce physical barriers to increased commerce, it would be short-sighted indeed to allow the invisible barriers to trade and finance remain in place. Only the EU can initiate

[1] For the background of the map see http://www.hq.xinhuanet.com/fukan/2013-05/06/c_115649626.htm and for videos (commentary in Chinese) see http://v.youku.com/v_show/id_XNTUxNTc0NTU2.html?tpa=dW5pb25faWQ9MTAyMjEzXzEwMDAwMl8wMV8wMQ andhttp://v.youku.com/v_show/id_XNTU1NzI3MjI0.html?spm=a2h0j.8191423.module_basic_relation.5~5!2~5~5!4~5~5~A&from=y1.2-1-91.3.2-1.1-1-1-1-0 (to 14.00)

> and conduct such negotiations. The Netherlands, as a founder-member, should nudge it in that direction.

The article was published in the Dutch online magazine *The Diplomat* on 1 September 2013.[2] Seven days later President Xi Jinping gave his speech in Kazakhstan's Nazarbayev University in which he called for the construction of a "Silk Road Economic Belt", the opening up of a transportation channel from the Pacific to the Baltic and the gradual formation of a transport network that connecting East, West and South Asia. With that speech, the revitalisation of the Silk Road had become part of China's official foreign policy.

The mystery of ancient legends[3] and the lure of long train journeys through foreign lands are a powerful combination. The reality is more prosaic – bilateral government dealings, massive investment plans and geo-political speculation. I hope you will join me in our journey. I have first to thank those who have helped make it possible, starting with Zhu Guichang, the director of the Confucius Centre in Leiden and Charlie Parton from the European External Action Service in Beijing. Li Xin was of the Confucius Centre was kind enough to translate some of the Chinese texts for me. Elizabeth Stone undertook the valiant and unforgiving task of proof-reading my original text. I would also like to thanks Frans-Paul van der Putten and the staff at the Clingendael Institute for their weekly Silk Road Headlines[4] and I also benefitted from the discussions in the Think-tank preparing the Dutch government's response to the Chinese initiative. The maps and figures for the book have all been drawn by Clémence Overeem. Finally, I dedicate this book to Wendy Asbeek Brusse, my companion on so many journeys both intellectual and physical including, of course, this one.

Leiden, 25 March 2017

---

[2] R.T.Griffiths, 'Europe's ABC?', *The Diplomat*, 1.9.2013.

[3] For the romantics among you, there is a twelve-part series on the Silk Road in China following a joint Chinese-Japanese expedition that was first broadcast in 1980. It is available free on Youtube at this address https://www.youtube.com/watch?v=8qer5yTyYvI&list=PLILRQ_uVCaoOtZ6Q6egVvUyEMhbN7OG9y

[4] These are always an interesting read and they are archived at https://www.clingendael.nl/publication/silk-road-headlines-archive

ABBREVIATIONS

ADB Asian Development Bank
AH Asia Highway
AIIB Asian Infrastructural Investment Bank
ALTID Asian Land Transport Infrastructure Development
ASEAN Association of Southeast Asian Nations
BCIM Bangladesh–China–India–Myanmar Economic Corridor
BCM Billion cubic metres
BCP Border crossing point
B-O-T Build-Operate-Transfer
BRICS Grouping of Brazil, Russia, India, China and South Africa
CAREC Central Asian Regional Economic Cooperation Programme
CEPC China–Pakistan Economic Corridor
CHEC China Harbour Engineering Company
CIS Commonwealth of Independent States
CITIC China International Trust Investment Corporation
CNPC China National Petroleum Corporation
COPHC China Overseas Ports Holding Company
COSCO China Ocean Shipping Company
CRRC China Railway Rolling Stock Corporation
CREC China Railway Engineering Corporation
EAEC Eurasian Economic Community
EACU Eurasian Customs Union
EAEU Eurasian Economic Union
EFSI European Fund for Strategic Investments
EIU Economist Intelligence Unit
EU European Union

FEU Forty-foot Equivalent Unit, container size. Usually carrying 26 tons of cargo or 67m3
GATT General Agreement on Tariffs and Trade
GDP Gross Domestic Product
GMS Great Mekong Sub-region
HSR High-speed rail
JICA Japan International Cooperation Agency
Km Kilometre
MFN Most favoured nation
MPAC Masterplan on ASEAN Connectivity
MSR Maritime Silk Road
OBOR 'One Belt, One Road'
ODA Overseas Development Assistance
OECD Organisation for European Cooperation and Development
QR Quantitative restriction
SKLR Singapore–Kunming rail link
SOE State-owned enterprise
TAR Trans-Asian Railway
TEU Twenty-foot Equivalent Unit, container size
TIR Transports Internationaux Routiers
TTP Trans-Pacific Partnership
WTO World Trade Organisation
UNECAFE United Nations Economic Committee for Asia and the Far East
UNESCAP United Nations Economic and Social Committee for Asia and the Pacific
UNESCO United Nations Educational, Scientific and Cultural Organization
US(A) United States (of America)

Throughout the text all dollar figures ($) refer to US dollars calculated at the prevailing exchange rate at the time

INTRODUCTION

The rise of China will be one of the stories of the 21st century. For almost thirty years its unprecedented economic growth has transformed the international economy shifting centres of production and stimulating a commodity boom that has lifted the fortunes of many lesser developed countries. As China became the 'factory of the world' it has accumulated massive foreign exchange reserves with which it has fuelled a boom in foreign direct investment and in mergers and acquisitions. Many assumed that it would be only a matter of time before Beijing translated this increasing economic clout into political power. The only question that remained was 'what form would it take?'. The answer was not long in coming. First China tried to reform existing international financial institutions. When that failed it created new ones, better to meet the perceived needs of its clients. Then, in September 2013, President Xi Jinping launched an idea of monumental ambition and breath-taking vision – Beijing would help revive the old trade routes between China and Europe, and China and Asia, and in the process it would help transform all the economies lying in their paths. The sums involved are staggering. Already it is claimed that there are 900 projects envisaged with a combined price tag of $890 billion. Eventually China plans to invest $4 trillion in the economies involved in the project.[1] Not since the Marshall Plan has there been a scheme of such dimensions. Many Western commentators have looked for hidden motives behind the scheme. Others have highlighted the risks involved and cast doubts on its success. Few have analysed it as a development project, admittedly one that benefits China as well as the recipients. This volume intends to help fill this gap in the literature.

[1] *The Economist*, 2.7.2016.

The book reconstructs what is actually happening in those countries benefiting from the development loans being advanced by China in the name of the 'one belt, one road' initiative (or OBOR, as it has become known). It will examine the nature of the problems that OBOR is intended to address. It will review the experience from which the Chinese authorities have drawn their development model. It will explore the scale and scope of the infrastructural projects in the different countries. It will study the patchwork of existing rivalries and alliances that help condition international responses to China's advances. And it will draw some tentative conclusions and offer some lessons from the experience to date. This volume does not pretend to be the definitive book on the subject. No book can claim that since the entire OBOR project is in a state of flux. Regimes change. Circumstances alter. Individual projects get delayed or cancelled. Right to the moment of publication, amendments were being made in the text to incorporate the latest developments. For this reason the book is accompanied by its own website which will update developments. After that, if there is sufficient demand, there will be a second, revised edition. The website's name is http://www.silkroadtextbook.com

It is hard to resist the lure of trains travelling through empty and often hostile landscapes and the romance of ancient maps tracing the millennia-old camel trains loaded with exotic produce. OBOR's headline project is almost just as romantic – the construction of a network of high-speed rail links from Beijing all the way to the cities of Europe. However it will be decades before that particular project becomes a reality. Meanwhile a more prosaic endeavour is already underway involving power stations and power lines, road improvements, container ports, industrial zones and some upgrading of railways. Central to most of these projects is the aim of improving connectivity and reducing trade costs. Even now, OBOR is leaving its imprint on places as far away as Indonesia and Bulgaria, Chongqing and Duisberg, Colombo and Piraeus. From the beginning the Chinese authorities have claimed that the initiative covers 65 countries (including China) with a combined population of 4.4 billion people, but without specifying what they were. However the more detailed OBOR planning has concentrated on several corridors and it is upon these that this book will concentrate. Table 0.1 lists all the OBOR countries and those that are indicated in bold are the focus of this text.

Table 0.1 Countries recognised as participating in the OBOR initiative

China	**China**
Central and West Asia	Afghanistan, Armenia, Azerbaijan, Georgia, Iran, **Kazakhstan**, **Kyrgyzstan**, **Mongolia**, **Tajikistan**, **Turkmenistan**, **Uzbekistan**.
Central and Eastern Europe	Albania, **Belarus**, Bosnia, Bulgaria, Croatia, Czech Republic, Estonia, Hungary, Latvia, Lithuania, Macedonia, Moldova, Montenegro, Poland, Romania, **Russ**ia, Serbia, Slovakia, Slovenia, Ukraine
Middle East	Bahrain, Egypt, Iraq, Israel, Jordan, Kuwait, Lebanon, Oman, Palestine, Qatar, Saudi Arabia, Syria, Turkey, UAE, Yemen.
South Asia	**Bangladesh**, Bhutan, **India**, Maldives, Nepal, **Pakistan**, **Sri Lanka**.
South-East Asia	Brunei, **Cambodia**, East Timor, **Indonesia**, **Laos**, **Malaysia**, **Myanmar**, Philippines, **Singapore**, **Thailand**, **Vietnam**.

Source: PRC, National Development and Reform Commission, 一带一路大数据报告, Beijing, 2016 (One Belt One Road. Big Data Report)

If all the projects involved in the OBOR initiative are completed, it will completely change the economic face of the world, and it will lead to dramatic shifts in the centres of political power and influence. If OBOR fails, some countries will be enjoying the benefits of their infrastructural investments, others will be struggling to pay off enormous debts and China could be left with one big financial hangover.

Figure 0.1 Outline of the Book

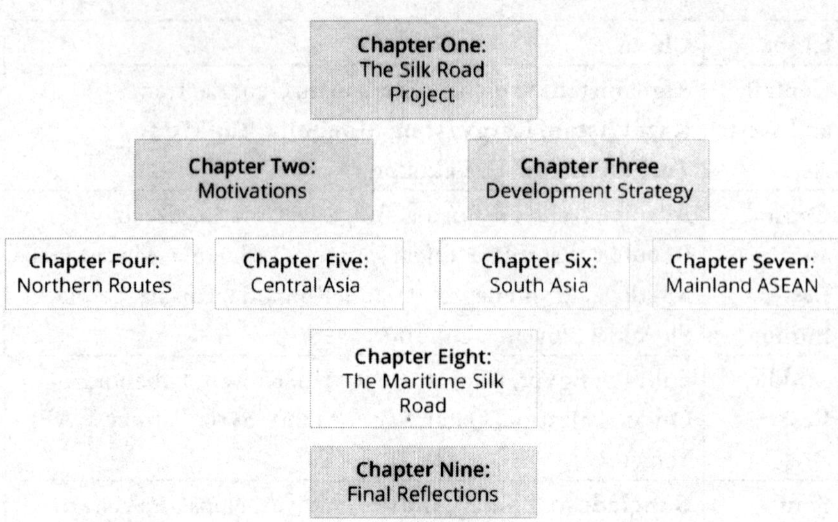

The book starts with three introductory chapters. Chapter One describes the history of the Eurasian trade routes that emerged two millennia ago and shows how these histories were employed in two speeches made by President Xi Jinping in September and October 2013 to signal a new direction in China's foreign policy. In the year and a half that emerged before more details emerged of the new initiative, China proposed the creation of an Asian Infrastructural Investment Bank (AIIB). Although this was initially viewed as a challenge to Western Institutions, it has since been joined by many Western nations. OBOR itself is revealed as one more step in China's gradual engagement with the international community since 1990. Whilst the Chinese leadership has stressed the country's peaceful intentions there are 'realist' scholars that view these developments as a veneer to cover more nationalistic motives. Neither the attempts to revive overland Eurasian trade routes nor the use of the 'silk road' as a foreign policy metaphor are new. What sets China's initiative aside from the rest is the means and the determination to give it form. The chapter concludes by looking at an Index constructed by the authorities to monitor the policy's reception among the 64-country target audience.

Chapter Two will study the motivations for OBOR. This will start with an examination of the decision-making structure in China, especially in the wake of the changes in the leadership that occurred with Xi Jinping's rise to power, and how this could help determine the priorities and distribution of resources. The chapter then turns its attention to debate over the original motivations for the policy both in China and among Western commentators, but we will leave the final choice for the reader to decide and for political scientists, and later, historians to debate. The complexity of the settings and their novelty for China makes the outcomes more than usually difficult to plan for and to anticipate. These are circumstances that are familiar to foreign development aid donors, and they will also condition the success of the OBOR initiative.

Chapter Three will address the development model implicit in the OBOR initiative. It will explore the similarities between China's own development and the development model adopted in China's own aid offensive in Africa. It will then explore the OBOR development strategy more systematically, looking at the effects of investments on the donor and on the recipient country and examining both the construction and implementation phases of investment projects. It will focus specifically on investments in railways and highways, power plants, pipelines and enterprise zones, and end by assessing the financial and operating risks (for the Chinese) and development risks (for the recipient). Finally, it will turn its attention to the barriers that exist to international trade in the region.

The chapters that follow will all concentrate on the different regions involved in the OBOR initiative. Chapter Four will concentrate on the overland rail freight route between China and Europe. It will concentrate on the relations between China and Russia and China and Mongolia, also briefly touching on those with Belarus. Chapter Five will turn to Central Asia where China's ambitions in the region have to accommodate those of Russia as well as the demands and preferences of the Central Asian states themselves. Chapter Six will look at Southern Asia and will focus on two specifically designated corridors. The first is between China and Pakistan and the second is a development corridor stretching from Kolkata in India, through Bangladesh and Myanmar before reaching into China. Here China has to accommodate its policy to the decades' long antagonism between India and Pakistan. Chapter Seven will focus its attention on the mainland states of South East Asia, and particularly on the ambition to construct a railway from Kunming in China through to Singapore. In this region

China has to take account of its own maritime dispute with several of the individual countries, as well as the ambitions of ASEAN, the institutional body promoting regional integration. Finally, Chapter Eight will look at the ambitious investment plans that China is executing for the construction of sea-ports that will shorten the trade routes from Southern China to the Indian Ocean, and reduce the possible security risks. This survey ends with the Chinese take-over of the Greek port of Piraeus.

The Final chapter will examine the response of the European Union to the OBOR initiative and its own initiative for improving the region's transport network. The chapter will end by offering some tentative suggestions for improving OBOR's efficiency and for enhancing its attractiveness for potential partners.

CHAPTER ONE

The Silk Road Project

This chapter begins by sketching the development of the ancient Silk Road[1] from its origins over 2000 years ago until its eclipse by the early 16th century. Even today the legend lives on in public memory. In autumn 2013 President Xi Jinping revived the concept as a powerful metaphor for a new and ambitious foreign policy initiative that would become known as 'one belt, one road', occasionally reduced to the acronym OBOR. The chapter then explores the extent to which the OBOR initiative represents an extension of Chinese foreign policy in gradually increasing the country's engagement with the international community. However the peaceful rhetoric is seen by some observers as a cloak for more ambitiously nationalistic intentions. These people always look for balance of power explanations behind public utterances so it is not surprising that they should do so in the case of China's 'rise'. Chinese scholars can be equally scathing about the wicked intentions of US foreign policy, and this was long before the inauguration of the Trump presidency. The idea of enhancing overland trade in the Eurasian landmass is not new, and neither is the use of the Silk Road as a metaphor. What is new is the firm sense of purpose and the considerable financial backing behind the initiative. However not all countries have been equally receptive to China's initiative and the chapter concludes by introducing a 'country cooperation

---

[1] P. Frankopan, *The Silk Roads. A New History of the World*, London, New York, New Delhi, Sydney, 2015; V. Hansen, *The Silk Road. A new history*, Oxford, 2013; J.A. Millward, *The Silk Road. A very short introduction*, Oxford, 2013; F. Wood, *The Silk Road. Two thousand years in the heart of Asia*, Berkley and Los Angeles, CA, 2002.

index' constructed by the Chinese authorities for measuring the reception of the OBOR initiative among the 64 target countries.

The Ancient Silk Road

In 138 BC, so the story goes, Emperor Wu, the seventh emperor of the Han dynasty that had first unified the core of territory that we know as modern China, sent his envoy Zhang Qian at the head of a large delegation to establish an alliance with the Yuezhi nation, in what is now modern Tajikistan. Unfortunately for him, Zhang Qian was captured by the Xiongnu, a people in the Northern steppes against whom the alliance was to be directed, and was kept as a slave by them for ten years. Eventually he was able to escape and find his way to the Yuezhi nation, only to discover its rulers were disinclined to disrupt their comfortable lives for military adventure. Zhang Qian spent the best part of a year with the Yuezhi people before setting off on his return journey, only to be recaptured by the Xiongnu. After a further two years in captivity he managed again to escape, and in 125 BC he returned to the Imperial Court without the desired alliance but with stories of the existence of vast sophisticated trading economies to the west of the Chinese empire. The news he brought prompted the emperor to start establishing commercial as well as military alliances with his neighbours, and to tie the Empire to the trading routes that stretched infinitely westward to lands and cultures then unknown.[2]

At the other side of the world, the Roman Empire was expanding into the Middle East and North Africa and stretching its frontiers in the North to embrace much of modern France and Germany and across the North Sea into Britain. As the tentacles of Empire expanded so they tapped into trade routes stretching further to the East, through Persia, Northern India and into Central Asia. Already the wealth of Rome and Egypt was attracting trade in exotic luxury items from the East, including silks from China. By AD 60 these had become so common among wealthy Roman ladies that Seneca was drawn to comment upon how a lady could be both dressed and naked at the same time.[3] The trade routes that spanned the distance between

[2] X. Lui, *The Silk Road in World History*, Oxford, 2010, 1–19.

[3] Cited by Frankopan, *The Silk Roads*, 17–18.

the ancient capitals of Rome and China were never primarily devoted to silk: the 'silk routes' name was first coined by the German explorer and archaeologist Ferdinand von Richthofen in 1877, but he had intended to apply it only to the period of the Han dynasty.[4] Even then, silk was not the main product of the trade but the image has proved stronger than the reality and the name has stuck.

Silk is in many ways a mysterious product. The process of silk-making is some 8000 years old. Biomolecular evidence of silk and weaving tools and needles have recently been discovered in three tombs in Jiahu Province in China.[5] Ancient silk, probably from China, has been discovered on Egyptian mummies dating from 1000 BC.[6] Silk is made from thread harvested from the dead pupae of the silk moth. A single pupa can yield a single thread of over 1.5 km in length, and five to ten such strands are twisted to make a single thread. It takes the thread from 3000 worms to yield a kilogram of material.[7] Little wonder that by the time it had reached ancient Rome it was the most highly priced luxury item one could buy. But it was not the only product traded along the long and difficult routes that linked the various markets and trading towns along its route. High value manufactured goods, precious stones and metals, rare perfumes and oils, herbs and spices made their way from town to town. The tentacles of the trade routes did not simply stretch laterally across the Eurasian continent. Trade routes also reached southwards into South East Asia and the Indian subcontinent. The recently excavated remains of the bronze-age 'Shu' civilisation (1500–500 BC) in the South of China have uncovered shells from the Indian Ocean that had probably been used as currency.[8] Although the direct route from Xi'an in the east to Antioch in the west is 6461 km, the shortest feasible route was closer to 7250 km. Indeed, when all the alternative roads and tracks were included and the various spurs, a recent geographical survey estimates that there were

---

[4] Millward, *The Silk Road*, 4–5.

[5] Y. Gong, L. Li, D. Gong, H.Yin and J. Zhang, 'Biomolecular Evidence of Silk from 8,500 Years Ago', *PLoS ONE* 11/12, 2016.

[6] G. Lubec, J. Holaubek, C. Feidl, B. Lubec and E. Strouhal, 'Use of silk in Ancient Egypt', *Nature*, 362/25, 1993, 25.

[7] P. Scott, *The Book of Silk*, New York, 1999.

[8] D. Yu, 'Sino-Foreign Communication in Southwestern China via the Southern Silk Road during the Pre-Qin/Han Dynasty period', *Historical Research*, 2009-01.

75,000 km of road in the corridors constituting the Silk Road.[9] Many of the spices that gradually spread throughout the area came from sea routes that reached deep into the Indonesian archipelago, along the coast of India and into the lands of Persia, Arabia and, eventually, the Mediterranean.[10]

Ironically, it was not people who moved along the routes but goods. Very few traders emulated the feats of Marco Polo whose travels took him to the court of Kublai Khan, the Mongol ruler of China and the founder of the Yuan dynasty, on a journey lasting twenty-four years from 1271 to 1295. Even the shorter journeys were lengthy, hard and dangerous. Caravans of traders had to wait until the summer before timing their journeys over the mountain chains that crossed the continent, and to wait for the cooler winter months before skirting the deserts that lay in between. Sailors had to wait in distant harbours before the prevailing winds guided them home. Yet as goods moved further from their points of origin, so their scarcity and their value increased. However, as the value of the trade increased, so too did the temptation for piracy and robbery, and wars of pillage and conquest. Indeed over the centuries wars did ravage the area and many famous cities were destroyed and rebuilt, but in between all the fighting powerful states were concerned to regulate (and profit from) the increased wealth and prosperity that flourishing commerce allowed. The volume of trade ebbed and flowed in inverse relation to the political stability along the routes. The first high point in the overland Silk Road spanned the period from 200 BC to AD 200. A second peak of activity occurred in the 8th and 9th centuries AD, but further development was checked by an increase in trading by sea. The final period of prosperity and welfare was under the so-called 'Pax Mongolia' in the 13th and 14th centuries and it lasted until the break-up of the Timurid Empire in the early 16th century. The end of hegemonic power in Central Asia and the eastward spread of Islam helped to sever the overland routes linking Europe to the rest of Asia. The death blow was provided by the penetration by the European powers into the long-distance ocean routes to the treasures of the Far East. The merchant fleets of the Dutch and English East

---

9 T. Williams, *The Silk Roads. An ICOMOS Thematic Study*, Charenton-le-Pont, 2014, 12–14, 31.

10 P. Beaujard, 'The Indian Ocean in Eurasian and African World-Systems before the Sixteenth Century', *Journal of World History*, 16/4, 2005, 411–65.

India Companies shipped their cloths and spices from the Indian Ocean and the Java seas to their respective homelands. The Silk Road became the stuff of legend and the sites along its routes the object of study by historians and archaeologists.[11]

In 2006 China, Kazakhstan, Kyrgyzstan, Tajikistan, Turkmenistan and Uzbekistan agreed to make a joint application to UNESCO (the United Nations Educational, Scientific and Cultural Organization) to have the Silk Road registered as a World Heritage Site. After advice from UNESCO it was decided to split the bid into two. In June 2014 China, Kazakhstan and Kyrgyzstan won recognition for the 5000 km corridor from Xi'an to the Tianshan Mountains, covering thirty-three sites in the three countries.[12] It is still possible to see the news item made by the Chinese English language broadcaster CNTV. Rather incongruously, underneath the evocative film of some of the sites a news-line beneath broadcast headlines emanating from a distinctly more troubled world. The second news item read, '13 rioters killed while attacking police stations in Kashgar, Chinese Xinjiang'.[13]

The Belt and Road Policy Initiative

The framing of Chinese foreign policy changed dramatically on 7 September 2013 when President Xi Jinping of China gave a speech to Central Asian leaders at Nazarbayev University in Kazakhstan. He started by recalling that 'the imperial envoy Zhang Qian was sent to Central Asia twice to open the door to friendly contacts between China and Central Asian countries as well as the transcontinental Silk Road linking East and West, Asia and Europe'.[14] Xi had left Beijing on 3 September 2013 with a small delegation to attend a G20 summit in St Petersburg (Russia) and a Heads of State meeting of the Shanghai Cooperation Organisation in Bishkek (Kyrgyzstan) on 11 September. Into this tight schedule he managed to include state visits to Turkmenistan, Kazakhstan and Uzbekistan and to squeeze in high-level

[11] *Wood, The Silk Road.*

[12] *Beijing News*, 23.6.2014.

[13] *CNTV News*, 21.6.2014.

[14] J Xi, *Promote People-to-People Friendship and Create a Better Future*, speech at Nazarbayev University, Kazakhstan, 11.9.2013.

talks with the President of Tajikistan.[15] In addition, Turkmenistan agreed to increase gas supplies and, together with Uzbekistan, Kyrgyzstan and Tajikistan, to start the construction of the fourth China–Central Asia natural gas pipeline. Kazakhstan agreed to complete its section of the third pipeline within the year. Together, the contracts were worth over $60 billion.[16]

President Xi's speech observed that for 2000 years the Silk Road 'had proved that countries with differences in race, belief and cultural background can absolutely share peace and development as long as they persist in unity and mutual trust, equality and mutual benefit, mutual tolerance and learning from each other, as well as cooperation and win-win outcomes'. China, he stated, wanted to work together with the peoples of Central Asia to strengthen development and prosperity in the region. He suggested that during the preceding twenty years, the rapid development of China's relations with Asian and European countries had given the ancient Silk Road a 'new vitality'. He reminded his audience that China's foreign policy had always been based on respect of countries' chosen development paths and non-interference in their internal affairs. The new Silk Road Economic Belt would be a step-by-step operation. The main steps were:

- Improved communication of national policies,
- Improved transport connectivity,
- Improved trade facilitation,
- Improved currency convertibility,
- Improved people-to-people exchanges.

He exhorted his audience, 'We should turn the advantage of political relations, the geographical advantage, and the economic complementary advantage into advantages for practical cooperation and for sustainable growth, so as to build a community of interests. We should create new

[15] In the space of eight days, China established a strategic partnership with Turkmenistan and Kyrgyzstan, deepened the comprehensive strategic partnership with Kazakhstan and signed the Treaty on China–Uzbekistan Friendly and Cooperative Partnership.

[16] PRC, MFA, Statement Wang Yi, 14.9.2013; M. Alymbekov, 'Kyrgyzstan and the Great Silk Road: Compatibility of Concepts', *Kabar*, 6.10.2013.

brilliance with a more open mind and a broader vision to expand regional cooperation.'[17]

One month later President Xi was due to attend an Asia-Pacific Economic Cooperation (APEC) summit in Bali. On the way to the meeting he paid state visits to Indonesia and Malaysia. Both visits were accompanied by announcements that China had upgraded its ties with each to that of a 'comprehensive strategic partnership'. This is not quite the achievement it appears; by June 2014 China had already amassed no less than fifty such partnership agreements.[18] On 3 October President Xi addressed the Indonesian parliament. He started by reflecting that, despite the sea separating them, Indonesia and China have enjoyed long and peaceful relations. He then evoked the memory of the seven large naval expeditions made in the 15th century by Admiral Zheng, recalling that on each occasion he had visited Indonesia. The sea, he argued, had linked the two countries, not separated them, and he described at length the mutual support they had enjoyed in development projects and in disaster relief. He then branched out to cover the relations between China and the ASEAN countries (members of the Association of Southeast Asian Nations) as a whole, and urged them to work together 'to ensure that China and ASEAN are good neighbours, good friends and good partners who would share prosperity and security and stick together through thick and thin' and to build a 'community of common destiny'. The pillars of this policy were:

- The building of trust and good neighbourliness,
- The improvement of mutual assistance and security,
- The enhancement of understanding and friendship,
- The maintenance of openness and inclusiveness,
- The striving to achieve win-win cooperation.

To achieve win-win success, he proposed using the China-ASEAN Maritime Cooperation Fund to 'vigorously develop maritime partnership

---

[17] Xi, *Promote People-to-People Friendship.*

[18] Z. Feng and J. Huang, *China's Strategic Partnership Diplomacy: Engaging with a Changing World*, ESP Working Paper 8, June 2014. It now has 75.

in a joint effort to build the Maritime Silk Road of the 21st century'.[19] This fund had been established by China in 2011 with a capital of $0.5 billion to enhance maritime cooperation with ASEAN.[20] And that was the only mention at that time of what would become the second strand in China's new policy.

The concept of the maritime Silk Road deliberately invoked the seven voyages made by Admiral Zheng to the region during the Ming dynasty between 1405 and 1433. Each voyage involved up to 300 vessels accompanying several 'treasure ships' each over 120 metres long and 50 metres wide. Every voyage visited the main port cities of South East Asia and those on the east coast of the Indian subcontinent. From the fourth voyage onwards the fleet also visited ports on India's west coast, the Persian Gulf and the coast of East Africa. On each voyage new alliances were formed, treasures were traded, pirates were defeated and such exotic animals as giraffes were brought back to China.[21] However, Zheng He's epic voyages were for diplomacy rather than for trade. Indeed, long-distance maritime trade had been active between India and China for over 1000 years earlier. For example in the second half of the 4th century AD a Buddhist monk named Faxian had returned from a study visit to India by boat, stopping off in Sri Lanka and Sumatra on his way. The ships had to battle through horrendous storms. On the final leg of the trip, while he prayed to the Buddhist goddess of mercy for intervention, his 200 Indian fellow passengers decided that Faxian was the cause of the problem. Only the intervention of a fellow Buddhist passenger stopped them from abandoning him on an island and continuing without him. Three hundred years later, voyages like this had almost become routine. The monk Yijing, who also visited India to collect documents, made the trip three times in his lifetime, and always by boat. Over half of the fellow monks whom he met in India had travelled the same way.[22]

These two speeches by President Xi, one month apart, signalled the

---

[19] J. Xi, Speech to the Indonesian Parliament, 2.10.2013. Full text of speech released by ASEAN–China Centre, 2.10.2013.

[20] P. Cai, 'China-ASEAN Maritime Cooperation: Process, Motivation, and Prospects', China Institute of International Studies, 25.9.2015.

[21] Y. Wei, 'Admiral Zheng He's Voyages to the "West Oceans"', *Education about Asia*, 19/2, 2014, 26–30.

[22] V. Hansen, *Silk Road. A New History*, Oxford, 2013, 160–1, 164–5.

inauguration of the OBOR policy initiative of the Chinese government, but for a long time little else appeared. In May 2014 and again in October 2014 the Chinese news agency published maps showing the routes of the belt and the road. The most interesting feature in the two maps was that whereas the first seemed almost deliberately to exclude any route through Russia, the second featured an elegant but implausible arm swinging from Istanbul back to Moscow and from there continuing to Europe. The illustration of the sea routes confined itself to showing the ports or harbours where Chinese firms already held an interest or were planning to do so, and ending at the port of Piraeus in Greece and through to Venice in Italy.

In China, scholars and officials started working on outlines and proposals, whilst observers in the West speculated on the motivation behind it all and the possible implications. Meanwhile Beijing added some financial muscle to the Silk Road skeleton. Already, during the visit where he made the 'maritime silk road' speech President Xi mentioned to Indonesia's president that China was considering the creation of an Asian Infrastructure Investment Bank (AIIB). This would exploit some of China's huge financial resources and employ its expertise to boost development in the region.[23] In April 2014 the Chinese Prime Minister Li Keqiang announced that China was ready to talk with partners both in and outside Asia about the AIIB. He also mentioned that OBOR plans now included provisions for building the Bangladesh–China–India–Myanmar Economic Corridor (BCIM) and the China–Pakistan Economic Corridor (CPEC).[24]

The AIIB was the result of China's disillusion with the World Bank and the Asian Development Bank (ADB) and its frustration with its limited influence in shaping their strategies. The Western powers had written their rules, provided the leadership, dominated the voting and set the agenda – and continued the provide the bulk of the funding. When the US Congress blocked proposals agreed by G20 in 2010 that would have increased the funding (and voting power) of the BRICS countries (Brazil, Russia, India, China and South Africa) to the International Monetary Fund (IMF), it was clear that the Western powers seemed determined to keep things that

[23] *The Economist*, 4.10.2013.

[24] *China Daily*, 11.4.2014. The speech addressed the Bo'ao Forum (an annual meeting of businessmen from Asia often known as the Asian Davos).

way.[25] Exasperated by the lack of progress China had chosen to create a new institution rather than trying to buy in to an increased share in the vote in the old ones. Already in February 2014 the BRICS signed an agreement to create their own development bank with an initial capital of $50 billion. At the same time, they issued a statement that took a swipe at the high running costs of the World Bank and pledged to keep the new development bank small and efficient.[26] Now China signalled its intention to create a second financial institution, this time in service of its OBOR initiative. Within one year twenty-one countries had signed a memorandum of understanding on the creation of the new bank. Although membership of the AIIB was open, the USA stayed aloof and, behind the scenes, tried to persuade its allies to do likewise, with no success. In March 2015 the UK applied for 'founder member' status, joined within the week by France, Germany and Italy. A US spokesperson reacted by warning against 'the trend toward constant accommodation of China, which is not the best way to engage a rising power'.[27] By the time the AIIB was created fifty-seven countries had joined. The USA and Japan are both missing from the list of members. But while the USA remained frosty in its reaction (intoning the need for high administrative standards and a good human rights record) the Japanese-led ADB was broadly welcoming in its reaction and Japan was even rumoured to be considering membership itself.[28] There can be little doubt that the US handing of the AIIB initiative had been an unmitigated disaster – firstly by failing to prevent its allies from joining and secondly, that having failed, making it almost impossible for itself to join. It is instructive that when the AIIB announced its first four projects in July 2016 they were all in developing countries covered by the OBOR initiative, but they were also all projects that were to be completed in collaboration with other international institutions, such as the ADB and the World Bank.[29]

The creation of the AIIB was followed, in November 2014 by the announcement of the creation of a separate Silk Road Fund to which China

---

[25] *Bloomberg*, 10.4.2014, *The Economist*, 11.11.2014.

[26] M. Troyjo, 'The Brics Development Bank is More than Welcome', *Financial Times*, 10.6.2013.

[27] *Financial Times*, 13.3.2015

[28] *The Economist*, 21.3.2015; *Forbes Magazine*, 23.3.2015.

[29] *The Economist*, 2.7.2016.

would contribute $40 billion. The aim of the Fund would be to 'break the bottleneck in Asian connectivity by building a financing platform', and would be open to other countries.[30] The first investment project it announced was $1.65 billion for the construction of the Karot hydropower project in Pakistan.[31] The subsequent activity of the Fund has shown an oblique relation to the original Silk Road vision. Its resources have been used to buy a 9.9% stake in Russia's liquefied natural gas project Yamal LNG, to help finance the takeover of the Italian Pirelli tyre company and, most recently, to acquire a 10% stake in SIBUR Holding, Russia's largest gas processing and petrochemicals company.[32]

Throughout this period the dominant theme employed in China's exposition of its relations with its neighbours was that of a 'community of common destiny'. The apogee of this phase came in the Conference on Interaction and Confidence-Building Measures in Asia (CICA) held in Shanghai in May 2014. The USA is a full member of CICA, but President Obama was conspicuous by his absence. As a result, when it was his turn to speak, President Xi was able to project a vision for Asian security that was specifically Asian. Security, he argued, should be on the basis of four principles – it should be common, comprehensive, cooperative and sustainable. He elaborated this by explaining that common security should benefit all countries. No country should attain its security at the expense of others. Relations between states should respect sovereignty, independence and territorial integrity, and non-interference in internal affairs. Comprehensive security should cover both traditional and non-traditional threats. It should enhance regional cooperation and show zero tolerance for terrorism, separatism and extremism. A cooperative security should build on dialogue and cooperation, promote peace and security through cooperation, and show a commitment to resolve disputes through peaceful means. Finally, security should become sustainable by narrowing the wealth gap between nations through regional cooperation and integration. He then proclaimed that 'China's peaceful development begins here in Asia, finds its support in Asia, and delivers tangible benefits to Asia ... the Chinese people, in their pursuit

30 Xinhua News Agency, 8.11.2014.

31 Xinhua News Agency, 21.4.2015.

32 *China Money Network*, 16.12.2016.

of the Chinese dream of great national renewal, stand ready to support and help other peoples in Asia to realize their own great dreams.'[33] Just as security was to be specifically Asian, so too was the dream. There seemed to be little room reserved for the Western economies in sharing it.

The Asian dream harks back to an age when Asian civilisations were equal to, if not more advanced than, the West in terms of size, wealth, power and economic development. It was from the East that the fine silks, exotic spices, rare jewels and splendid work originated that were traded along the old overland and maritime trading routes. It is projected as an era of peace and prosperity, cooperation and harmony across the region before the intrusion of Europeans with their navies, guns and thirst for conquest.

Despite the power of the metaphor, and its re-evocation in innumerable speeches in the months that followed, the project remained shrouded in mystery. It was not until the spring of 2015 that any real details emerged.[34] It now became clear that what the Chinese authorities had in mind was to create several international development corridors spanning the Eurasian land mass and reaching down into South and South East Asia. These were:

- China-Mongolia Russia Economic Corridor,
- New Eurasian Land Bridge Economic Corridor,
- China-Central Asia-West Asia Economic Corridor,
- China-Pakistan Economic Corridor,
- Bangladesh-China-India-Myanmar Economic Corridor,
- China-Indochina Peninsula Economic Corridor,
  and, of course,
- Maritime Sea Route.

Meanwhile, analysis of the motives and the possible consequences continued apace despite a numbing absence of tangible information. On one

[33] PRC, MFA, *The 4th Conference on Interaction and Confidence Building Measures in Asia (CICA) Summit Held in Shanghai Xi Jinping Presides over the Summit and Delivers Important Speech, Advocating Common, Comprehensive, Cooperative and Sustainable Security in Asia for New Progress in Security Cooperation of Asia* 21.5.2014 (henceforth Xi, *Asian Dream*)

[34] PRC, National Development and Reform Commission, *Vision and Actions on Jointly Building Silk Road Economic Belt and 21st-Century Maritime Silk Road*, 28.3.2015.

point, however, most commentators were agreed; we were witnessing a more assertive foreign policy that represented a radical departure in the tradition of Chinese foreign policy.

China's New Foreign Policy

One reason why OBOR has attracted so much attention is that it seems to be part of a radical departure in Chinese foreign policy. For over twenty years since its launch in 1990, the world has become acquainted with the practice, if not the principles, of Deng Xiaoping's '24 Character' foreign policy. Basically, these urged that China should remain patient and concentrate on domestic development until the country was ready to play a constructive role in promoting and maintaining a harmonious world development.[35] Some have even argued that the 24 Characters was a reflection of the fact that China did not actually have a foreign policy – it had a domestic policy, and that had implications abroad. In this sense its 'foreign policy' behaviour was essentially realist, in that it reflected the pursuit of national interest. It dealt with issues as they arose, preferably on a bilateral basis, and it eschewed international or multilateral forums, certainly for dispute settlement. As leaderships came and went, and as the international economic balance slowly shifted in China's favour, there were modifications in the strategy. For example, under Jiang Zemin (1992–2002) the overriding slogan was 'peace, development and national interest'. It was also under Jiang Zemin's regime, in 1999, that China articulated a 'go out' which encouraged Chinese firms to seek opportunities for foreign direct investment abroad.[36] At that time the stock of China's outward foreign direct investment (FDI) was $26.9 billion or 0.37% of the world total. Ten years later it had risen to $245.8 billion, or 1.31% of the world total.[37]. By the time of Hu Jintao (2001–12) it

---

[35] Z. Chen, 'International responsibility and China's foreign policy' in M. Iida (ed) *China's Shift: Global Strategy of the Rising Power,* Tokyo, 2009, 7-28.

[36] A.L Friedberg, *" Going Out": China's Pursuit of Natural Resources and Implications for the PRC's Grand Strategy,* National Bureau of Asian Research, 17/3 2006.. A. Yelery, 'China's 'Going Out' Policy: Sub-National Economic Trajectories', *ICS Analysis 24,* 2014, Delhi; Y. Zhang, *China Goes Global,* London, 2005.

[37] UNCTADSTAT database. http://unctad.org/en/Pages/DIAE/FDI%20Statistics/FDI-Statistics.aspx. The latest figure (2014) is $729.6 billion, or 2.97% of the world total.

was emphasised that China's own peaceful rise should be accompanied by a renewed emphasis on cooperation and participation in a multipolar world.[38]

China's entry into the existing international economic order began in 1986 when it joined the General Agreement on Tariffs and Trade (GATT) though it was to take a further fifteen years before it fully satisfied the criteria for membership of its successor organisation, the World Trade Organisation (WTO). China's participation in the new liberal trade regime had contributed to the country's economic boom which saw years of double-digit growth and led to China becoming the world's second largest economy. Many scholars thought that China's increasing dependence on the persistence of a globalised world order would lead first to an acceptance of its liberal democratic precepts and later to a change the policy preferences within China itself.[39] This peaceful assimilation of China into a liberal world order has been continued with the creation of the BRICS Development Bank and the AIIB. Observers could have been forgiven for interpreting China's new approach to foreign policy as an endorsement for a form of multilateral institutionalism, with new and fairer rules. On the other hand, the hoped for democratisation of domestic politics clearly lagged behind.

The closed nature of policy-making and the slow development of popular democracy in China has helped reinforce an alternative view of the implications of China's economic rise. Some observers have always held that state behaviour are a reflection of relative power. They predict that as China's power resources increased, it would eventually challenge the established hegemonic position of the United States. At present China's economic power is not matched by its military power, but when that moment arrives, some predict

[38] B.S. Glaser and E.S. Medeiros 'The Changing Ecology of Foreign Policy-Making in China: The Ascension and Demise of the Theory of "Peaceful Rise"', *The China Quarterly*, 190, 2007,291-301; Y. Zheng and S.K.Tok, *Harmonious society and harmonious world: China's policy discourse under Hu Jintao.* Nottingham University, China Policy Institute Briefing Series, 26, 2007.

[39] D.H. Bearce and S. Bondanella, 'Intergovernmental organizations, socialization, and member-state interest convergence', *International Organization*, 61/4, 2007, 703-733; A. Kent, 'China's International Socialization: The Role of International Organizations', *Global Governance*, 8/3, 2002, 343-364; M. Lanteigne, *China and International Institutions: Alternate Paths to Global Power.* London, New York, 2005; J.W. Legro, 'What China will want: the future intentions of a rising power', *Perspectives on Politics*, 5/3, 2007, 515-534.

that a military conflict will occur, especially if there is dissatisfaction with the existing order.[40] Seen in this light, the OBOR initiative and the construction of new financial institutions would be a prelude towards a more aggressive foreign policy. Meanwhile China has challenged US hegemony more directly through its approach to the settlement of territorial disputes. In September 2012 the disputes with Japan in the East China Sea reached a new height of antagonism when the Japanese government purchased the disputed Diaoyu/ Senkaku islands from their private (Japanese) owner. China responded by declaring an air identification zone over the area, which elicited a US statement to the effect that the islands were covered by the joint USA–Japanese security treaty, though it did not pronounce on the eventual sovereignty over the islands.[41] In the South China Sea, China had territorial disputes with several South East Asia nations which, in 1984 and 1988, had escalated as far as naval engagements with Vietnam, resulting in numerous casualties. In January 2013, the government of the Philippines referred its dispute to arbitration by the UN Convention Law of the Sea. From the first, China refused to participate. It argued that the Convention had no jurisdiction over territory and insisted that the individual disputes be resolved by bilateral negotiations. When the Arbitration Court ruled in the Philippines favour in July 2016, the Chinese response was incandescent with rage. Long before then, however, the situation in the South China Sea had changed. Possibly in response to the US intervention on the side of Japan in the East China Sea, the government began converting several of the reefs to which it had laid claim into artificial islands, equipped with landing strips and military defence forces. China was replacing lines on a map with land in the sea[42]

[40] C. Glaser 'Will China's Rise Lead to War? Why Realism Does Not Mean Pessimism' *Foreign Affairs*, 90/2, 2011, 80-91; J. Kirshner, 'The tragedy of offensive realism: Classical realism and the rise of China', *European Journal of International Relations*, 18/1, 2012, 53–75; J.J. Mearsheimer, 'Can China rise peacefully?', *The National Interest*, 25, 2014, 23–37; R.L. Tammen and J. Kugler, 'Power transition and China–US conflicts', *The Chinese Journal of International Politics*, 1/1, 2006, 35-55.

[41] R. Bendini, The struggle for control of the East China Sea, European parliament, DG EXPO/B/PolDep/Note/2014_158, Brussels, 2014; B. Chapman (2016)'Geopolitical Implications of the Sino-Japanese East China Sea Dispute for the US.' *Geopolitics, History, and International Relations*, epublication.

[42] M.T. Fravel, "US Policy Towards the Disputes in the South China Sea Since 1995". In E. Feis and T-M. Vu (eds.) Power Politics in Asia's Contested Waters, Heidelberg,

There appear to be at least two streams existing in parallel in the new foreign policy.[43] The first is an apparent increased engagement in international arrangements in the world economy, but with an increased room for manoeuvre and an increased Chinese character. This has been promoted with high-level personal diplomacy unmatched in post-war Chinese history.[44] The second as exemplified by the approach to the disputes over islands, harks back to a stark pursuit of national interest. It is characterised by an uncompromising statement of the national position and an insistence on bilateral negotiations where China's stronger military and strategic influence could be employed to the full.

Eurasian Road and Rail Routes

One noticeable feature in the analysis of the OBOR initiative in Western literature is that the commentators write as though before September 2013 no one had conceived of railways and highways stretching from the Atlantic to the Pacific, far less had done anything to help realise such ambitions.[45] It is as though China's policy initiatives are a completely new development. This is simply not true. China's policy builds upon and extends development efforts by individual donors and by established international organisations. It locks into national development plans drafted and approved by individual counties, or groups of countries, lying along the development corridors and routes identified by the OBOR plans. Where China's initiative differs from existing schemes lies in the scale envisaged for the realisation of various projects, and the provision of the means to realise them. Indeed, projects

---

New York, Dordrecht, London, 2016, 389-402. S. Rolf and J. Agnew, "Sovereignty regimes in the South China Sea: assessing contemporary Sino-US relations", *Eurasian Geography and Economics*, 57/2, 2016, 249-273;

[43] R.D. Blackwill and K.M. Campbell, *Xi Jinping on the Global Stage*, New York, 2016.

[44] Since he became President, Xi Jinping has personally visited more than fifty countries Reported by *China Vitae*, counted to January 2017.

[45] Some of the recent academic literature has been more alert to the historical antecedents. See G. Xing, "Understanding China's One-Belt-One-Road Initiative. A New Pattern for Deepened Interaction between China and the World' in B. Shao (ed.) *Looking for a Road. China Debates its and the World's Future*, Leiden, Boston, 2017, 152-154.

undertaken under the OBOR umbrella have to be offered, and eventually approved, by the recipient governments and the fact that these may be part of an existing international framework should be recognised as a strength rather than a weakness of the entire project.

The idea of roads and railways spanning the Eurasian continent, linking trading centres and peoples together, has a long history. More to the point, however, there have been consistent international efforts to turn these dreams into practical reality. The original Trans-Siberian Railway was completed in 1916.[46] The idea of further linking the railway networks of East-Central Asia with those of the Middle East and Europe was first suggested to the UN Economic Committee for Asia and the Far East (UNECAFE) in 1960. The plans envisaged a 14,000 km railway connecting Singapore to Istanbul through the shortest route, taking it through Malaysia, Thailand, Myanmar, India, Pakistan and Iran. There were several reasons why the idea never really started. First, the project floundered on technical problems involved in connecting national systems. For example, there were four different gauges of track in the different countries along the line. Second, many segments of the planned routes were missing. It was estimated that the completion of the routes would require the construction of an additional 2000 km of track. Third, the question of how all of this was to be financed was never resolved and this problem, in its turn, was made more difficult because of intense regional rivalries, many of which stemmed from the Cold War. Indeed, it was only at the end of the Cold War, in April 1992 at a meeting in Beijing, that the UN Economic and Social Committee for Asia and the Pacific (UNESCAP, the successor to UNECAFE) started again to look seriously at the possibilities and it launched the Asian Land Transport Infrastructure Development (ALTID). This move was also prompted by the rapid growth in intra-area trade, and therefore the need to improve the physical means to conduct it. One of the first feasibility studies it ordered was for connecting the networks of China, Kazakhstan, Mongolia, Russia and the Korean Peninsula (TAR-1).[47] In 2006 eighteen countries, including

[46] C. Wolmar, *To the Edge of the World: The Story of the Trans-Siberian Railway*, London, 2013.

[47] UN, ESCAP, *Trans-Asian Railway Route Requirements: Developments of the Trans-Asian Railway in the Indo-China and ASEAN Sub-Region*, Volume One, 1996, New

China and Russia, signed an agreement to study the harmonisation of standards and practices that would facilitate the construction of an integrated transport network, aimed at reducing both costs and times. A further ten countries joined later. The priorities required for improving the main transport arteries intended to connect European and Asian trade were quickly identified.[48]

International cooperation in transport development was not confined to railways. In 2003 thirty-two countries agreed to the creation of the Asian Highway. The signatories identified eight major highway networks spanning the Eurasian landmass from east to west and north to south, and fifty road networks of regional significance. They agreed a scheme for classifying road conditions and committed themselves to upgrading the network.[49] The entire network spanned 142,000 km, and in 2011 it included 11,570 km of what could basically be called 'tracks'. By 2005 the members had committed $25 billion to the project, and they later agreed that finding $18 billion to upgrade roads in the worst condition should be a priority. Somewhat over 20% of the costs were being carried by the Asian Development Bank.[50]

In both rail and road transport, the Chinese initiative could build on existing infrastructure and plans for its improvement. The design of the connectivity network already existed. The real work lies in its realisation. Many of the individual schemes contained in the development of the OBOR initiative that have attracted sneers of derision and disbelief among some commentators have been the targets for development and investment for years or even decades.

York; K. Kasuaga, 'Trans-Asian Railway', *Japan Railway and Transport Review*, June 1997, 31–5.

[48] UN, ECE/ESCAP, *Joint Study on Developing Euro-Asian Transport Linkages*, 2008, New York.

[49] UN, ESCAP, *Intergovernmental Agreement on the Asian Highway Network*, 2003, no location.

[50] M.D. Regmi, *Experience in the Development of the Asian Highway*, PowerPoint Presentation to High Level Expert Group Meeting on Trans-African Highway Addis Ababa, 19–20.9.2011.

Silk Road as a Metaphor

Many of the transport developments described in the preceding paragraphs are unknown outside a small circle of experts and policy-makers. UNESCAP publications and pronouncements rarely attract banner newspaper headlines, or much academic attention for that matter. Yet scarcely had President Xi's announcements in September and October2013 had been made than they began to attract the attention of the international press. Of course, this was partly because the initiative was seen as a major departure in China's foreign policy. However part of the reason was that the initiative had been framed in a powerful metaphor. The new Silk Road promised the revival of a legendary trade route, whose past had been studded with exotic locations. Now it was mixed in with that boyhood fantasy of a railway stretching into the distance to unknown destinations. Well, it certainly got me hooked!

However, the Silk Road has been employed before as a foreign policy metaphor. In 1997 the Japanese government employed the term 'Silk Road Diplomacy' to describe its intensified development efforts in Central Asia and the adoption of a more active policy towards both Russia and China. The Ministry of Foreign Affairs formulated 'three principles' which underpinned Japan's relations in the area, and these were promulgated in a speech by the prime minister, Hashimoto Ryutaro, to a group of businessmen in July 2007. Towards Russia, he formulated the principles in terms of trust, mutual benefit and long-term perspective. Towards Central Asia he described them as political dialogue, economic cooperation and efforts to promote democratisation and security.[51] In the wake of the speech, Japan increased its diplomatic representation in the area, and with the space of a few years it had become the largest provider of overseas development assistance (ODA) to Kazakhstan, Kyrgyzstan and Uzbekistan. Most of the aid was in the form of loans, because the Japanese believed that the recipient government would be more careful in the selection and implementation of projects if the sums involved had to be repaid. The loan projects tended

[51] R. Hashimoto, *Address by Prime Minister Ryutaro Hashimoto to the Japan Association of Corporate Executives* (provisional translation).

to focus on connectivity – improvements in roads, rail, air and telephone infrastructure.[52]

The idea of a 'new Silk Road' was also employed by the USA. It was conceived as a metaphor and a proposal for action by S. Frederick Starr, in a series of articles published between 2000 and 2007 as part of a policy prescription for the region after the American withdrawal from Afghanistan.[53] The idea was taken up in September 2011 by the then Secretary-of-State, Hillary Clinton, who suggested that an Afghanistan at peace would have to re-establish its normal economic relations with its neighbours. Then, in a burst of lyricism, she continued:

> For centuries, the nations of South and Central Asia were connected to each other and the rest of the continent by a sprawling trading network called the Silk Road. Afghanistan's bustling markets sat at the heart of this network. Afghan merchants traded their goods from the court of the Pharaohs to the Great Wall of China. As we look to the future of this region, let's take this precedent as inspiration for a long-term vision for Afghanistan and its neighbours. Let's set our sights on a new Silk Road – a web of economic and transit connections that will bind together a region too long torn apart by conflict and division.[54]

Subsequent details that emerged indicated that the plan would involve both the construction of new infrastructure such as highways, railways, electricity networks and pipelines (the so-called 'hardware' portion) and the reduction of legal barriers to trade (the 'software'). In addition to aiding Afghanistan, the plan seemed intent on orienting Central Asia away from the North (and its historical orientation on Russia) and towards India and

[52] K. Akio, 'What is Japan up to in Central Asia?' in C. Len, U. Tomohiko and H. Tetsuya (eds.), *Japan's Silk Road Diplomacy: Paving the Road Ahead*, Washington, 2008, 15–29.

[53] S.F. Starr (ed.), *The New Silk Roads. Transport and Trade in Greater Central Asia*, Washington, 2007. He was the founding chairman of the Central Asia-Caucasus Institute and Silk Road Studies Program of Johns Hopkins University.

[54] US Department of State, *Remarks at the New Silk Road Ministerial Meeting*, 22.9.2011.

Pakistan. However, India and Pakistan were never symbols for cross-border cooperation, and with potential investors likely to baulk at the risks, and without substantial external government financial backing, the scheme seemed doomed from the start.[55] When hostilities in Afghanistan did not die out, the project perished, though it still gets a page on the State Department's website.

The Silk Road, of course, was never a single road, but a series of paths and tracks along which people and goods travelled at a pace dictated by geography and season. Boundaries and borders are strangely absent, though there were always tolls and taxes – how else did the magnificent cities of the ancient Silk Road get built? The metaphor goes deeper. It was not only goods that passed along its routes, but languages and cultures, technology and knowledge, food, spices and cuisines. The Silk Road evokes thoughts of an open and welcoming spirit; a mutually beneficial meeting and exchange of peoples and ideas. It is also a very Asian story, representing epochs when their civilisations equalled or surpassed the levels attained in Europe. It was from Asia to Europe that the treasures and knowledge largely flowed. It was an epoch in which space was not primarily defined by 'states', though it was often anchored by looser 'empires', and it evokes a largely borderless world in which all places along its route could benefit from the advantages that exchanges could offer. Moreover, although the entire route was often convulsed by warfare and savagery, the highest flowering of trade and the peaks of its prosperity coincided with periods of peace.

Country Cooperation Index

In September 2016 China's National Development and Reform Commission published its first annual 'big data' report. It also contained a 'country cooperation index'. On the basis of the index, the authors concluded that of the 64 countries included under the OBOR umbrella, 2 were 'deeply cooperative', 13 were 'rapidly advancing' and 17 were 'expanding'. The other half were labelled 'to be strengthened'. Since such indices are often used to classify countries, possibly as a prelude to policy-making, it is worth examining them in more detail. This is especially the case since we will view a similar type of index in Chapter Three.

[55] J. Kucera, 'The New Silk Road?', *The Diplomat*, 11.11.2011.

The Index is what is called a 'composite index'. It combines different and often diffuse perspectives into a single number. The first task in compiling such an index is to decide what it should contain. The second is to compress the different types of raw data, often compiled on different criteria, into a number that can be compared with data collected for the other categories. The compilers then have to decide what weight to give to each separate part of the index. Finally, they need to decide the cut-off points in the results that, in this particular case, tilt a county from one degree of cooperation to another.

In this case the Index is made up of five dimensions, each weighted equally (20%). The five dimensions are policy cooperation, facility relevance (transport connectivity), trade openness (trade facilitation), financial integration and popularity (people-to-people exchanges). The first point to note is that all of these dimensions refer back directly to China. They take no account of bilateral or regional arrangements among the other countries, unless they include China. The second point is that several of the items are in the form of a check-list which allows little or no nuance in the experience. For example, either one has a highway connection with China or one has not (2 points); either one has signed a memorandum of understanding or one does not (3 points). Fully 82% of the index is comprised of items with either a yes/no response or with a limited range of options. The third point is whether the individual components of a sub-index really capture the phenomenon reported. Surely the achievement of policy coordination is reflected by the actual record of achievement rather than the signing of documents of intent. Equally 'culture and talent exchange' (a subcategory of popularity) is more than the sum of city twinnings, joint festivals, the existence of tourist visas and the establishment of a Confucius Institute (a cumulative 12 points). The final point lies in the weighting given to individual items. Is a meeting between heads of state (possibly at an international junket) and a declaration (which belongs to the fluff of diplomacy) (worth jointly 10 points) really equal to the existence of rail, highway, port, power and pipeline connectivities? Is the existence of a Confucius Institute really equal to the importance of Chinese FDI in a country?

These criticisms are not made to be facetious. The dangers revealed are inherent in all such composite indices. Moreover policy-makers use much more refined data in making decisions than the headline numbers produced by such indices. On the other hand, the fact that numbers are not perfect does not mean that they are completely useless. Therefore we will return to this index when analysing the individual OBOR corridors in Chapters Four-Seven, but then concentrating on the subcomponents rather than on the index as a whole.

Reflections

When I was writing this book, I decided to end this chapter by returning to the two basic approaches to the analysis of China's foreign policy. They occur in almost all international relations analyses. One the one hand there are '(liberal) institutionalists'. Institutionalists believe that institutions can modify state behaviour, and that since the dominant ethos of such institutions is liberal, states joining them will evolve more liberal perspectives to their own approach to foreign policy and also to their own domestic development. On the other side are 'realists' who believe that states will always fight to secure their own survival and, in the most extreme version, this involves enhancing their own position at the expense of that of their rivals. Realists assume that military and economic power, and the ability to use it, are more important determinants of a country's behaviour on the international scene After some reflection I have kept that format. But this is no longer a part of game that academics play. The inauguration of the Trump administration in the United States in January 2017 has pushed these different approaches right to the front of US policy towards China and has framed placed China's policy towards its neighbours in a far more critical light.

This chapter has tried to place the OBOR initiative within the context of the evolution of China's foreign policy, or rather, China's foreign policy rhetoric. We have seen that the overlying discourse is one of engagement and peaceful cooperation. In this analysis, China's increasing economic power has been linked to an emergence from isolationism to responsible leadership. So-called 'institutionalists' view these developments as part of a process by which China's experience with liberal international institutions, and the economic benefits that have come with the country's internationalisation, will modify its foreign policy behaviour. The OBOR initiative and the creation of the AIIB represent an increased engagement, all be it in a different regional context and shaped more to incorporate China's interests. Policy pronouncements, however, are not the same as policy intent and action.

Looked at from a realist perspective, OBOR is a smoke-screen. Behind the declarations of noble intentions lies a modernisation of armed forces and an accumulation of currency reserves. Both of these developments represent a change in the regional and international balance of power. China's approach to bilateral disputes and the way in which the country is exercising pressure on its neighbours are seen as the first symptoms of increased intransigence, that will eventually lead to a war with the United States.[56] Moreover, military might is not the only route to power. China's trade surplus is not the benefit to consumers implied by neo-classical economic thinking, but a predatory tool to aquire technological knowledge and to destroy productive capacity elsewhere. 'Death by China' is a realist perception of the impact of China's rise on the US economy.[57] In December 2016 its author, Peter Navarro was appointed director of the National Trade Council in the Trump administration.

The fact that divining China's intentions on the world stage have now become a factor 'great power' politics makes it all the more important unravel what factors originally motivated the adoption of OBOR and what has been driving it ever since. This will not be easy. One reason is that realist and institutionalist approaches are not the outcome of empirical analysis but normative perspectives chosen in advance by analysts and commentators. The second reason is that the foreign policy-making process is almost always complex and opaque, and that of China particularly so. This is the topic that will be discussed in the next chapter.

---

[56] This is the stated belief of Steve Bannon, appointed Chief White House strategist to the Trump Administration.

[57] P. Navarro, *Death by China: Confronting the Dragon – A Global Call to Action*, Upper Saddle River, NJ, 2011.

CHAPTER TWO

Motivations

In the previous chapter we touched briefly on how changes in China's foreign policy have been interpreted in the West through realist and through institutionalist perspectives. Realists tend to emphasise the threat posed by China's rise as a global power world. Liberal institutionalists tend to look for signs of hope in China's increased engagement in international arrangements. In this chapter we will see how these same divergent perspectives influences the interpretation of the OBOR initiative. Before starting that analysis it is important to examine the decision-making structure in China's policy-making, especially against the background of the changes in the top of the Chinese leadership that accompanied President Xi's choice as chairman of the Communist party and the country's president. Unfortunately, the outcome of this analysis will suggest that the opaque nature of policy-making means that it is unlikely that we will ever know for certain why or how the OBOR initiative came about. What tends to happen instead is that analysts surmise what the likely effects of the policy will be and transform these probable consequences into hypothetical intentions. However assessing which of the many dimensions of a policy are important often depends of the choice of institutionalist/realist perspective chosen in advance. This is not unusual in journalism, political science or even policy-advice. However, it is particularly inappropriate for interpreting the OBOR initiative for two reasons. First, China does not have complete control over the policy. It cannot determine the degree of participation of individual countries along the route or the choice of the individual projects. If policy-makers themselves do not know where the policy is heading, it is difficult to determine the intention from the direction in which it develops. Second, OBOR is not a policy that employs traditional military or diplomatic instruments. The economic nature of the OBOR instruments - development loans and infrastructural investment – and their impact both on China and on the recipient countries allows for a greater range of possible outcomes than is the case with military or diplomatic initiatives. Many of these cannot be perceived in advance.

The Policy-Making Setting

The influence of the Communist Party of China (CPC) is pervasive in all top levels of decision-making in China.[1] It has over 82.6 million members and a strict internal promotion system that sees individual members gradually rise in terms of responsibility in their work and also in the political hierarchy, towards the upper echelons of party decision-making. The decision-making hierarchy is shown in Figure 2.1. The Party itself is run by a Politburo consisting of twenty-five members, from which is chosen a seven-man Standing Committee. The Standing Committee is the main policy-making body in the country and it acts by consensus. The Politburo itself is nominated by the Central Committee whose membership, in its turn is determined by the Party Congress. Although the Party Congress holds a pivotal position in the hierarchy, the compliance of the membership means that it largely endorses decisions already taken, including membership of the Politburo.

The Party, in its turn, controls the armed forces. Unlike the situation in other countries, the armed forces are not an agent of the state but the armed wing of the party itself. Their top political boss is appointed from the ranks of the Standing Committee, and is usually its highest ranking member, the General Secretary. In the past there has been a wait of two years before this merging of functions, but Xi Jinping assumed this position immediately, possibly because of his earlier function as minister of defence.

---

[1] K.E. Brødsgaard and Y. Zheng (eds.), *Bringing the Party Back In: How China Is Governed*. Singapore, 2004; K. Dumbaugh and M.F. Martin, *Understanding China's Political System*, Washington, 2009; J. Fewsmith, 'The 18th Party Congress: Testing the Limits of Institutionalization', *China Leadership Monitor*, 40, 2013; S.V. Lawrence and M.F. Martin, *Understanding China's Political System*, Washington, 2013; R. McGregor, *The Party: The Secret World of China's Communist Rulers*, London, 2012; D. Shambaugh, China's Communist Party: Atrophy and Adaptation, Washington, 2008.

In theory there is a division of responsibility between the party and the civil administration, but in practice the National People's Congress that nominally oversees the State Council, and the State Council itself, are subservient to the Party. The 2900 delegates are dominated by party members, state officials and civil servants, who together hold approximately 85% of the seats. Whatever limited separation of powers there may have been under Zhao Ziyang (Secretary-General of the party 1987–9), those days have long passed. The State Council nominally controls the ministries of commerce, finance, foreign affairs and of national development and reform, as well as the China Export-Import Bank, the China Development Bank and the body supervising the administration of state-owned assets. It also formally controls the various layers of local government; but with the leaders of provinces often being powerful political figures (and party members) in their own right there is considerable tension in the relationship.

Figure 2.1 The Formal Decision-Making Hierarchy in China's Policy-Making

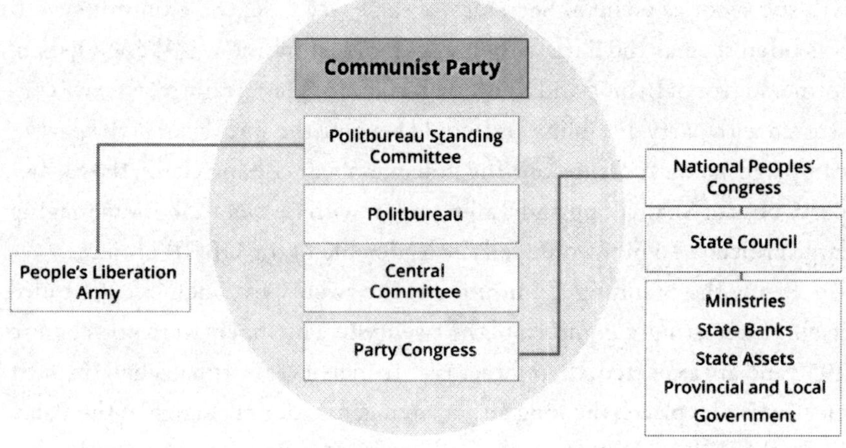

The launching of the OBOR initiatives coincided with a major change at the top of the Chinese leadership, the Politburo Standing Committee.[2] In November 2012 Xi Jinping was elected General Secretary of the Central

[2] M. Badkar, 'Meet The New Politburo Standing Committee—China's 7 Most Powerful Men', *Business Insider*, 14.11.2012; S.V. Lawrence, *China's Political Institutions*

Committee of the Chinese Communist Party and he also assumed the chairmanship of the Party's Central Military Commission. In March 2013 he assumed what was probably seen as the least important of his posts, when he became President of the People's Republic of China. Xi Jinping's reputation stemmed from his success in creating Special Economic Zones and introducing economic liberalization when he was party chief in Shanghai. His military background, having served earlier as minister of defence, also helped. China's vice-president, Li Keqiang, was also a leading reformer. His efforts in promoting economic development in Henan had succeeded in transforming several poor areas in the province into profitable, investment-attractive cities. These were the only two survivors from the previous Politburo Standing Committee. They were also its youngest members.

All the other members of the Standing Committee had been elevated from the Politburo of the CPC. The third in the rank order was Zhang Dejiang, who had previously been vice-premier and had held responsibility for energy, telecommunications and transport. The fourth member in order of importance was Yu Zhengsheng, who had been Xi Jinping's successor as party boss in Shanghai. The fifth member was Liu Yunshan, who had been Xi's successor as General Secretary of the Party's Central Committee and was often seen as the Party's theoretician. Next in line was Wang Qishan, former mayor of Beijing and a powerful voice for liberal reform, who was entrusted with party discipline and would become the spearhead of the party's campaign against corruption. The final member is Zhang Gaoli, the former party boss of Shangdong and Taijin, a man with a reputation for managing large projects. To him would fall the leadership of the OBOR project.

Below the Standing Committee is the twenty-five-member Politburo itself.[3] Interestingly, eighteen of the twenty-five members were born before 1950 and are expected, therefore, to retire in five years' time, when the next elections take place. The long anticipated generational change in the Party leadership will evidently have to wait. It is easy to analyse the new leadership

---

and Leaders in Charts, Washington, 2013; S. Miller, 'The New Party Politburo Membership', *China Leadership Monitor*, 2013.

[3] In addition to the seven members of the Standing Committee, the current Politburo comprises six provincial party secretaries, two military officers, five heads of Central Committee departments, four state officials and one official of the national People's Congress.

in terms of factional politics and their allegiance to one of the two previous party chiefs, but perhaps more important is the growing influence of provincial politics: 52% of the current Politburo obtained their position while party secretaries of provincial administrations, up from 40% five years earlier and 20% ten years before that. The proportion with provincial experience at some time in their careers is a stunning 76%. The reverse side of this development is the rapid decline of the 'technocratic leadership' that had been encouraged in the 1990s. Their share of the membership has fallen to 16%, down from 76% ten years earlier.[4]

The ten-member State Council, elected in March 2013, comprises Le Keqiang and Zhang Gaoli from the Standing Committee, three members of the Politburo, two ministers (national defence and public security) the chairman of the state-owned assets administration, a member of the party secretariat and the former foreign minister, Yang Jeichi.[5]

The Policy-Making Setting and OBOR

Now that we have sketched the main governance structures and their composition, it is time to return to the question of the OBOR policy. Here we will make a distinction between the policy formulation and its subsequent elaboration. President Xi was dissatisfied with the effectiveness of the decision-making structures he had inherited, especially in the field of foreign policy. He was particularly concerned to achieve better policy coordination between domestic, foreign and security policy. To this end he created new 'small leading groups' (SLGs) and a National Security Council, all directly under his control.[6] By deciding the composition of the National Security Council, and by reducing the importance of the existing groups on foreign

[4] C. Li, 'A Biographical and factional Analysis of the Post-2012 Politburo', Brookings *China Leadership Monitor,* 41, 1-17, 6.6.2013

[5] S.V. Lawrence and M.F. Martin, *Understanding China's Political System,* Congressional Research Service, R41007, Washington, 2013, 26-30.

[6] D.M. Lampton, 'Xi Jinping and the National Security Commission: Policy Coordination and Political Power'. *Journal of Contemporary China* 24/95, 2015, 1–19; *South China Morning Post,* 20.1.2014 (leading small group, hidden power).

policy and security policy,[7] Xi could hope both to reform decision-making and to impose his personal stamp on the new policies emerging under his rule. There is a saying in politics that ideas do not shape political decisions, but that politicians seize on ideas that best articulate the direction in which they want to move.

Around this time Professor Wang Jisi[8] published a paper in which he urged the reconstruction of the old silk routes to South East Asia, to South Asia and to Central Asia. Wang had been worrying that the US formulation of its own geo-strategic interests was proving incapable of embracing China's rise and that the space for strategic cooperation was being squeezed. He added that only by being able to manage its domestic development better would China be able to meet the challenge of improved Sino–US relations.[9] In a later paper, he argued that although the USA was pivoting to the East, China should not restrict its focus on the Asia-Pacific region but should instead 'march towards the West'. He suggested that such a move might actually help reduce tensions with the USA since both parties wanted stability in the region (and especially Afghanistan and Pakistan) and would therefore be able to cooperate.[10] This message obviously fell on fertile ground. At which point it received Xi Jinping's support is not known and what happened next is unclear. The initiative probably passed through the Policy Research Office and the Office of Foreign Affairs of the CPC Central Committee. We do not know whether it passed through the SLG on foreign policy or possibly the National Security Council. Certainly the State Council would also have had to approve such an important measure. All that was needed was an occasion and a forum at which to present it, and that was the visit to Kazakhstan in September 2013.

---

[7] L. Jakobson, 'Domestic Sectors and the Fragmentations of China's Foreign Policy' in R.S. Ross and J.I. Bekkefold (eds.), *China in the Era of Xi Jinping. Domestic and Foreign Policy Challenges*, Washington DC, 2016, 155.

[8] At the time he was director of Peking University's Center for International and Strategic Studies.

[9] J. Wang, 'Strategic Conflict Inevitable Between China and US', *Global Times*, 5.8.2010.

[10] A. Bondaz, 'Rebalancing China's Geopolitics', in F. Godement (ed.), *'One Belt, One Road': China's Great Leap Outward*, European Council on Foreign Relations, London, 2015, 7.

The next phase was rather unusual from a Western perspective. Having made two important announcements, the Chinese themselves were urged to give the new policy some substance. On the surface it immediately produced a swathe of publications and rash of conferences, one or two of which I attended. Beneath the surface, the call to action led to a jockeying for position by ministries and provinces to secure for themselves a favourable position in the final policy, and to justify their claim to a share of the funds that would become available. Not for nothing did it take another eighteen months before even a rudimentary blueprint for the new policy appeared.[11]

Figure 2.2 Sources of Influence in Policy-Making in China

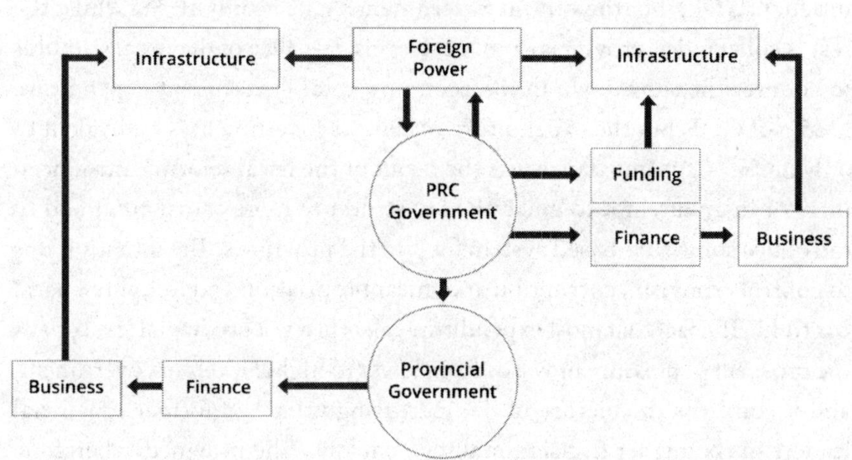

The CPC may appear all powerful and its policy-making processes are most certainly opaque, but that does not mean that the decision-making processes are not porous and open to external influence.[12] Some of these

[11] C. Parton, 'China's Foreign Policy as Domestic Policy', paper presented at Chatham House, 29.9.2015.

[12] N. Ahrens, *China's Industrial Policy-Making Process*, Washington, 2013; G. Anderson, How Policies are Made in China, Hong Kong, 2013; Z. Chen, 'Coastal Provinces and China's Foreign Policy-Making', in. Y. Hao and R. Ho (eds.), *China's Foreign Policy Making: Societal Forces and Chinese American Policy*, Routledge, 2005, 187–207; G. Fan and N.C. Hope, 'The Role of State-Owned Enterprises in the Chinese Economy', *China–US Focus*, 2013; R. McGregor, 'Chinese Diplomacy 'Hijacked' by Big Companies', *Financial Times*, 16.3.2008; C.J. Yu, *Firms with Chinese Characteristics:*

sources of influence are shown in Figure 2.2. The following paragraphs will examine in more detail the transmission belts of influence over policy managed by (local) government funding, the banking system and state-owned enterprises.

In the case of OBOR, we are examining a government that formulates, and starts implementing, a major international infrastructural project, or set of projects. One of the main ways in which a government can influence decision-making in the economy is through the funds it commands via its fiscal policy. In this respect, the central government is less monolithic than one would expect from the degree of central political control that it exercises. Total government revenues in 2013 amounted to 22.7% of gross domestic product (GDP), but the central government's take is only 10.6% whilst the rest is collected at provincial and local levels. Because of the fiscal stimulus to counter the slow-down in the economy, total government expenditure is 25% of GDP, but the expenditure of central government is equivalent to only 3.6%.[13] This imbalance was the result of the fiscal reforms introduced in 1994 in an attempt to make the tax structure more transparent and to introduce some rule-based system for it in the provinces. The intention was to control cronyism, corruption and misappropriation and to tighten fiscal control.[14] The fact that most expenditure takes place at provincial level opens the prospect of pressure upwards from lower to higher levels of government, and it confirms the picture of the increasing weight of former provincial leaders in the higher decision-making echelons. The provinces, therefore, are not merely policy-takers; they will also have been active in fine-tuning the strategy and in trying to obtain central funding for themselves.

The state also impacts on the economy through its influence on the banking system. Since the liberalisation of the banking sector from 1978 onwards, China has developed a multi-tiered commercial banking system. In addition to state-owned banks, there are also 'equitized banks' in which the state is still the major shareholder. Below that there are a variety of local

---

The Role of Companies in Chinese Foreign Policy, LSE Working Paper, London; C. Zhang, *The Domestic Dynamics of China's Energy Diplomacy*, Singapore; Y. Zheng, *De Facto Federalism and Dynamics of Central–Local Relations in China*, Nottingham, 2006.

[13] *China Statistical Yearbook 2014*, Tables 3.1, 7.2, 7.3.

[14] C. Shen, J. Jin and H-F. Zou, 'Fiscal Decentralization in China: History, Impact, Challenges and Next Steps', *Annals of Economics and Finance*, 31/1, 2012, 1–51.

banks, in which provincial and local governments are the main shareholder and finally a number of joint-stock banks, where government agencies also hold shares. Whatever the ownership profile, all banks are frequently asked to comply with government directives, though there is no evidence that this extends down to individual projects. There are three wholly state-owned policy banks, namely the Agricultural Development Bank of China, the China Development Bank and the Export–Import Bank of China. Four of the largest equitized banks belong among the five largest in the world. In rank order and with their share of state ownership and their capitalisation in brackets they are the Industrial and Commercial Bank of China (first, 71% state owned, capitalisation $274.4 billion), the China Construction Bank (second, 57% state owned, capitalisation $220 billion), Bank of China (fourth, 68% state owned, capitalisation $198.1 billion) and the Agricultural Bank of China (fifth, 83% state owned, capitalisation $185.6 billion).[15] All these banks have their directors appointed by the State Council, all report directly to it and all frequently rely on and follow State Council directives in establishing their operational priorities. The inclination to do so stems from the fact that they are all high-ranking positions in the Party. Moreover, their further career development relies also upon assessment of their performance.[16] The state-owned and equitized banks together account for 52% of the asset value of the banking sector, still substantial but down from over 65% a decade ago.[17]

The chief regulatory body boasts in its annual report that it 'encouraged banking institutions to strengthen financial cooperation with the countries or regions along the Belt and Road and devise appropriate means and measures in business expansion and branch establishment, to support the Initiative'. In response, it argued, the China Development Bank had built the repository of major projects along the Belt and Road and set out preferential credit policies. The Export–Import Bank of China has also made active efforts to promote infrastructure projects of host countries and support the development of interconnectivity projects.[18]

[15] M.E. Martin, *China's Banking System: Issues for Congress*, Congressional Research Service, R42380, Washington, 2012; The Banker, *Top 1000 Global Banks*, 2016.

[16] Martin, *China's Banking System*.

[17] China Banking Regulatory Commission, *Annual Report, 2014*, 2015, 24.

[18] China Banking Regulatory Commission) *Annual Report, 2014*, 57–8.

Because of the way in which statistics are compiled in China, it is difficult to estimate the size of the state-owned business sector in the economy. In 2009 the OECD (the Organisation for Economic Co-operation and Development) wrestled with the fragmentary data and suggested that state-owned enterprises (SOEs) contributed 35.8% to industrial value-added and about 30% to the urban labour force.[19] China has about 150,000 SOEs, holding more than 100 trillion yuan ($15.7 trillion) in assets and employing over 30 million people.[20] *The Economist* recently suggested that 80,000 were in the 'economic lowlands: they run hotels, build property developments, manage restaurants and operate shopping malls'.[21] Even so, state-owned enterprises are dominant in so-called 'strategic industries and certainly in those industries expected to contribute most (and benefit most) from the OBOR initiative. Table 2.1 lists the shares of largest SOEs in the total sales of each sector:

Table 2.1 Share of State Owned Enterprises in Total Sales, by sector

Sector	Percent	Sector	Percent
Telecommunication Services	96.2	Shipping	60.7
Petrol and Petroleum	76.6	Coal	59.2
Automobile	74.0	Construction	20.1
Air Transport	73.2	Non-ferrous Metal	19.5
Power	70.6	Crude Steel	17.65

Source: A. Szamosszegi and C. Kyle, An Analysis of State-Owned Enterprise and State Capitalism in China, US–China Economic and Security Review Commission, Washington DC, 2011, 22–43.

All these enterprises benefit from close relations with the national and provincial banks. This tends to take the form of easier access to credit, cheaper loans and debt forgiveness (either in the form of write-offs or in

[19] OECD (2009) *State Owned Enterprises in China: Reviewing the Evidence,* OECD Working Group on Privatisation and Corporate Governance of State Owned Assets, Occasional Paper, Paris.

[20] Xinhua, 24.9.2015.

[21] *The Economist,* 30.8.2014.

rolling-over loans). Similarly, government departments will tend to favour them when it comes to offering contracts, which it might have done anyway because of their size. It has been estimated that some 61% of government expenditure, including the fixed investment of the SOEs themselves, is provided by SOEs.[22] If the government continues to reorient the economy away from investment and towards consumption, away from heavy industry and towards light industry, these firms are likely to be at the losing end of the deal. And if these shifts are accompanied by falling prices, the impact will be greater still. Even before the most recent slow-down in Chinese growth rates, and even before the launch of OBOR, these were the firms that were active in China's 'going global' strategy (*zouchaqu*) that had been launched in 2000. By the end of 2013 non-financial SOEs had accounted for 55.2% of the total stock of China's outward non-financial FDI (and 43.9% of the flow in that year).[23]

It does not take much imagination to see how a mutually reinforcing triangle of interest can emerge. Industry seeks investment and development opportunities abroad, either to gain access to energy and raw materials or to maintain output. Banks seek to at least defend their investments and use their lending policies to promote these ventures. And the government wants new opportunities for its foreign currency reserves and promotes a go global policy. It too wants to keep state enterprises viable and to secure more reliable sources of energy and raw materials. Add to this mix a high degree of interpenetration between the three sectors and an overlapping membership of the Communist Party. Put it all behind a cloak of opaque policy-making processes and it becomes difficult to say how the details for OBOR took shape. If we then replicate this triangle at the level of the twenty-two provinces (excluding Taiwan), the five autonomous regions and the four municipalities (Beijing, Chongqing, Shanghai and Tianjin) that report directly to the state, bearing in mind the increased representation of experience in provincial government in the CPC Politburo, then the work of untangling the web of decision-making becomes more difficult still.

---

[22] Szamosszegi and Kyle, *An Analysis of State-Owned Enterprise*, 51–9.

[23] Ministry of Commerce, People's Republic of China, *Joint Report on Statistics of China's Outbound FDI 2013*, released 12.9.2014.

Motivations ascribed by Chinese Scholars

An early survey of explanations for the origins of OBOR among Chinese elite opinion, between the original announcement and the revelation of the main contours in the 'Vision and Action' document[24], was published by Michael D. Swaine, an Asia expert working for the Carnegie Endowment in Paris. The survey showed that elite opinion generally stayed close to the public pronouncements. It endorsed the view that OBOR represented a positive contribution to the development of an open world economy, coupled with a more in-depth regional cooperation that would ultimately benefit all parties. Many of the early commentators used the metaphor of a 'symphony' to capture the open and inclusive nature of the scheme. The benefits for China itself were also specified in more detail – the development of the western provinces, the provision of energy and raw materials and a rebalancing of the economy by shifting factories away from the over-industrialised eastern provinces. Only occasionally did they refer to geo-strategic factors as part of the motivation. In this context OBOR was seen as a reaction to moves by other major powers such as the USA, Japan and India and observers contrasted the positive nature of China's cooperative win-win approach to international relations with the aggressive foreign policies of the others. Slightly removed from Chinese officialdom, some 'non-authoritative' sources suggested that OBOR represented the international face of an increasing openness in economic relations that mirrored the reforms and transformation within China itself. Still others saw OBOR in terms wider than purely economic and emphasised the spill-over into cultural and security cooperation. Finally, a few military observers dared to mention that enhanced military and naval security played a part in the greater geographical range and commitment of Chinese interests. But these were very much isolated voices addressing their own areas of expertise.[25]

One year after Swaine's survey, Zhoa Hong published a review of Chinese academic opinion on the motivations for the OBOR initiative. With little

[24] PRC, National Development and Reform Commission, *Vision and Actions on Jointly Building Silk Road Economic Belt and 21st-Century Maritime Silk Road*, 28.3.2015.

[25] M.D. Swaine ' Chinese Views and Commentary on the 'One Belt, One Road' Initiative', *China Leadership Monitor*, 47, 2015, 4-10.

extra information available it is not surprising that their commentary has still remained close to the official narrative. Some economists suggested that the current Chinese growth model has exhausted its potential and that the growth frontiers have shifted to other low income areas, both inside the country and abroad. OBOR was seen as allowing China to couple its economic restructuring to the promotion of growth in these areas and, at the same time, to assist other more advanced regions to shift their output structure towards more high-value production. All of these efforts would rebound onto China in the form of higher demand for its goods. Other commentators have embellished the security elements. They suggested that the Chinese export and investment drives have created negative backwash effects and that, by emphasising cooperation and mutual benefits, OBOR can help recalibrate relations with the periphery as well as providing a new model of international relations. It was also argued that OBOR is a response to the current fixation with free trade and the removal of trade barriers. In this vision, the Asian economies are too diverse and isolated to benefit from such a trade liberalisation without measures to improve the physical and institutional infrastructural arrangements designed to response to the needs of individual countries or groups of countries.[26]

An 'official' review of 1600 papers on OBOR produced by Chinese think-tanks up to and including November 2015 confirmed that 95% were positive towards the initiative. The 2% which were judged to be negative expressed doubts only over whether China's economy was strong enough to carry the burden on investments that OBOR implied. The review lambasted Chinese scholarship for lacking in depth, staying wedded to theory and failing to offer much help to practice. It suggested that academics started talking with businesses and policy-makers, acquiring more real data to analyse real questions and to move away from generalisations and start investigating actual case studies.[27] One cannot blame Chinese scholars from following the official rhetoric which emphasises the idea that China is contributing positively to the provision of international 'public goods' – growth, trust,

---

[26] Z. Hong, *China's One Belt One Road: An Overview Of The Debate*, ISEAS – Yusof Ishak Institute, Trends in South Asia, 2016, 6, 11-17. See also W.X. Lim, 'China's One Belt One Road Initiative: A Literature Review' in T.W. Lin, H. Chan, K. Tseng and W.X. Lim (eds.) *China's One Belt One Road Initiative*, London, 2016, 133-147.

[27] PRC, National Development and Reform Commission, 一带一路大数据报告, Beijing, 2016 (One belt One Road. Big Data Report), 237, 241-2.

cooperation. However, public pronouncements made by politicians rarely offer explanations in the sense of a set of plausible factors that prompted a course of action. Mostly, they are justifications – a set of plausible factors that are recognised as such by the audience to which the pronouncements are directed. Occasionally they are rationalisations – a set of plausible factors that fit the subsequent course of events. It is possibly also unreasonable to expect a public motivation that accurately translates the varied inputs into a complex decision-making process that is itself under pressure to produce some acceptable outcome, and that is underlain by all the hopes, fears and ambitions of the individuals and institutions involved.

Motivations ascribed by Western Scholars

In the following paragraphs we will examine how the motivations behind the OBOR initiative have been perceived in Western literature.[28] Chapter One ended by reviewing the evolution of China's foreign policy and it suggested that there were two streams that seemed to diverge. On the one hand there was an engagement with international organisations, some of its own creation, whilst on the other hand there was a more strident pursuit of national interests in territorial disputes. These two experiences coincided with two competing schools of foreign policy analysis – the liberal/internationalist school and the realist school. This section will follow these two schools of interpretation as they wrestle with explaining the motivation behind OBOR.

Realists are predisposed to start their analysis from the assumption that all states follow policies in their own best interests. The first priority of states is their own survival. Having achieved that aim, states employ a mixture of military, economic and diplomatic means to advance their standing against others. At its most extreme, realists have always seen an expansionist China stretching its military and financial muscles entirely of its own volition.[29] In this light, the intention of OBOR and its development corridors would be to

[28] See also S. Djankov and S. Miner (eds.) *China's Belt and Road Initiative. Motives, Scope, and Challenges*, PIIE Briefing, 16-2, 2016; Y. Huang, 'Understanding China's Belt & Road Initiative: Motivation, framework and assessment', *China Economic Review*, 40, 2016, 314-321.

[29] J.J. Mearsheimer, 'China's Unpeaceful Rise', *Current History*, 105, 160-163; S.M. Walt, 'China's new strategy', *Foreign Policy*, 26.4.2010.

create a series of links and entanglements that would tie the client states to a Chinese-centric agenda. The infrastructural projects would literally speed connections with China, stimulate trade with China and create an asymmetric dependence on China that could be employed as leverage in other fields.[30] One commentary points to the irony that whereas a liberal institutionalist perspective sees increased economic integration as contributing to a reduction in geo-political tensions, the opposite is now occurring and geo-political rivalries are spilling over into economic interactions.[31] In addition to bilateral leverage, OBOR could be seen as a step towards creating an area of regional hegemonic power that would counter the possible encroachments of other powers, whether they be India, Russia or the USA. The increasing interdependence inherent in the intensification of economic relations could be employed to influence their policies in other directions.[32] On the other hand, China could be pursuing those same goals with a less aggressive intent and motivation. It may simply be developing a pro-active foreign policy within an environment that is more aligned with its own interests and that enhances its central position in a developing Asian spatial economy.[33] However, the structure of the Chinese economic system, with its prevalence of state-owned enterprises and state-owned banks, has given the country more instruments for pursuing a geo-economic strategy than its more liberal western rivals. Beijing is moving consciously or unconsciously into policy areas where they find it difficult to compete and, therefore, challenges their leadership.[34]

---

[30] S.L. Kastner, 'A Few Thoughts on the Motivations and Consequences of the One-Belt-One-Road Initiative' in S. Binhong (ed.) *Looking for A Road. China Debates Its and the World's Future*, 2017, 254-257.

[31] C. Bajpaee 'Japan and China: The Geo-Economic Dimension', *The Diplomat*, 28.3.2016.

[32] A. Viehe, A. Gunasekaran, and H. Downing, 'Understanding China's Belt and Road Initiative: Opportunities and Risks' Center for American Progress, 22.9.2015.

[33] H. G. Hilpert and G. Wacker, *Geoeconomics Meets Geopolitics China's New Economic and Foreign Policy Initiatives*, SWP Comments 33, June 2015. They comment "To brand the new Chinese initiatives from the outset as anti-Western attempts to dismantle the existing system will only feed into the widely held Chinese belief that the US and the West are trying to keep the country down and imposing a policy of containment".

[34] R.D. Blackwill and J.M. Harris, *War by Other Means: Geoeconomics and Statecraft*, Cambridge MA, 2016; A. Panda, 'Geoeconomics and Statecraft in the Asia-Pacific', *The Diplomat*, 21.5.2016.

Other realist scholars are more inclined to see the OBOR initiative as part of a Chinese response to strategic challenges from other countries, particularly the USA. One early, but oft-repeated, motivation appeared in the influential US magazine *Foreign Policy.* It described the OBOR initiative as being a response to the Trans-Pacific Partnership (TPP) promoted by the USA. The TPP was designed to weaken China economically and politically, to 'contain' its influence and power. OBOR was designed better to reflect Beijing's priorities and diplomatic approach.[35] The TPP started life as a small but interesting intergovernmental regional discussion forum embracing Brunei, Chile, Singapore and New Zealand). It was turned into a potential economic powerhouse through a US declaration in 2008 to use it as a framework for the discussion of trade liberalisation of financial services, negotiations for which were stalled within the WTO. The ambition of the TPP later expanded to become an all-encompassing trade agreement in the Asia pacific region, but one that excluded China.[36] It was suggested at the time that the unstated aim of the initiative had been specifically to exclude China from a trade agreement among a group of countries representing 40% of world GDP. This was supposed to be a 'punishment' for what was seen as China's currency manipulations, industrial subsidies and the flouting of intellectual property rights while benefiting from the market access afforded by the WTO. On the other hand, the prospect of TPP access might act as an incentive for China to improve its behaviour. Moreover, the fact that it was an 'anyone but China' club acted as an incentive for other countries, such as Japan, to join.[37]

In the event, China did remain aloof, wary of the impact on its economic

---

[35] B.R. Deepak, *Trans Pacific Partnership (TPP): Responses from China and Options for India*, SAAG, Paper 6020, 2015; A.H. Hearn and M. Mayers, *China and the TPP: Asia–Pacific Integration or Disintegration*? China–Latin America Report, June 2015; P. Mendis and D. Balázs, 'When the TPP and One Belt, One Road Meet', *East Asia Forum,* 26.4.2016; J. Ross, 'Realities behind the Trans-Pacific Partnership', *China.org,* 18.11.2011; M. Ye, 'China's Silk Road Strategy. Xi Jinping's Real Answer to the Trans-Pacific Partnership', *Foreign Policy,* 10.11.2014.

[36] T. Rajamoorthy, 'The Origins and Evolution of the Trans-Pacific Partnership (TPP)', *Global Research,* 10.11.2013.

[37] D. Pilling, 'It Won't be Easy to Build an 'Anyone But China' Club'', *Financial Times,* 22.5.2013.

structure and suspicious of American intentions. Other prospective partners also had their doubts and the proposals met strong resistance in the US Congress, perhaps persuaded by the argument that the attraction of the deal to the USA relies very much on the fact that China is not included.[38] One of the first acts of the Trump Administration was to kill off the entire project. At the time of writing it was still unclear what the implications for China and OBOR would be.[39] However it seems unlikely that OBOR was ever conceived as a response to the TPP. For a start, the timing is wrong. Negotiations towards the TPP started in 2008. Even if like the Chinese you have a historical perspective stretching back over centuries, it seems implausible to wait five years to respond to something perceived as a serious threat. Moreover, if the loss of equal access to large markets in the Asia-Pacific region constitutes a problem, switching the focus to small land-locked countries in Central Asia scarcely constitutes an adequate solution. Furthermore, OBOR is not an alternative to the TPP. China could go ahead with all its Silk Road infrastructural investments and ancillary policy initiatives, and still join the TPP if it so wished.

Another American event to which OBOR was supposed to be a response was the so-called 'Pivot to Asia' initiated by the then Secretary-of State Hillary Clinton, in 2011.[40] Initially her stance was warm in its embrace of China as a possible partner in establishing new framework of collaboration in the region. However, within the space of two years this even-handed

---

38 A.J. Tellis, *Balancing without Containment. An American Strategy for Managing China*. Carnegie Endowment, 2014, Washington DC.

39 There are several possible options. The TTP countries could continue their efforts but without the USA, but this is unlikely. Another option would be for countries to try to obtain similar concessions in bilateral negotiations with the USA, but given the protectionist stance of the current administration this is unlikely to yield good results. A third option would be to redesign TTP to include China, but this is likely to meet resistance from japan and Korea. A final option would be for China to offer new trade deals with its neighbours and to add this to the OBOR framework.

40 K.A. Abbasi, 'Changing Security Dynamics in Asia Pacific Region', *CISS Insight: Quarterly News & Views*, 2016; European Parliament, *One Belt, One Road (OBOR): China's Regional Integration Initiative*, EPRS Briefing, June 2016; M.D. Swaine, 'Chinese Leadership and Elite Responses to the U.S. Pacific Pivot', *China Leadership Monitor*, 38; J. Szczudlik-Tatar, 'China's Response to the United States' Asia–Pacific Strategy', *PISM Policy Paper*, 41, 2012.

approach was already beginning to fray as the reaffirmation of US commitment towards the its traditional allies in the region involved taking sides in regional maritime disputes involving China and Japan.[41] While the rhetoric of the Obama administration continued to talk about cooperation with China (while still remaining vigilant)[42] the foreign policy establishment in Washington was urging 'less emphasis on support and cooperation and more on pressure and competition ... less hedging and more active countering'.[43] Against this background, the USA started building up its military capacity and demonstrating its presence in the Asia-Pacific.[44] By 2020, 60% of naval assets will be stationed in the Pacific (up from 50%) and a contingent of US marines will be stationed in Darwin, Australia.[45] This has provided a potential threat to China's maritime trade routes both through the disputed South China Sea and through the Malacca Straits, off the Malay coast. Ironically, as early as 2005, long before the OBOR initiative had been launched, China's interest in acquiring port facilities overseas, and especially in Africa and the Middle East, were being described as a 'string of pearls'. A US Defence Department report was quoted as claiming that 'China is building strategic relationships along the sea lanes from the Middle East to the South China Sea in ways that suggest defensive and offensive positioning to protect China's energy interests, but also to serve broad security objectives'. China was accused of wanting to use its power to project force and undermine US and regional security and of employing its commercial ports to exert control over strategic 'chokepoints'. The report continued to suggest that Chinese military leaders want an ocean-going navy and 'undersea retaliatory capability to protect the sea lanes' and to 'counter any attempt by the USA to blockade the country in the event of a conflict'.[46]

In my opinion, the trouble with geo-strategic experts is that if you put

---

[41] H. Clinton, 'America's Pacific Century', *Foreign Policy*, 11.10.2011.

[42] White House, *National Security Strategy*, 2015, Washington DC.

[43] R.D. Blackwill and A.J. Tellis, *Revising U.S. Grand Strategy Toward China*, Council on Foreign Relations, Special Report, 72, Washington DC, 2015, viii.

[44] *Wall Street Journal*, 27.4.2014; 12.5.2015.

[45] R.G. Sutter, M.E. Brown and T.J.A. Adamson, *Balancing Acts: The U.S. Rebalance and Asia-Pacific Stability*, Washington DC, 2013.

[46] *Washington Post*, 17.1.2005.

two points on a map, they will find a way in which they encircle someone.[47] The ports foreseen in OBOR are commercial ports, some deep harbour container ports, others terminals for the transmission of oil or liquefied natural gas. Owned or controlled by China, they are still part of another country's sovereign territory and would require an alliance or an invasion, and some considerable investment, to transform them into military assets. Some commentators have thought it likely that any build-up of a military presence in the Indian Ocean (note not the South China Sea) would advance only slowly, since effective control could only be achieved by a much larger navy than that being planned. These commentators have construed China's efforts as directed at maintaining sea-lane security (as a common good) rather than national domination.[48] There are several reasons to explain a limited naval ambition, not least being the anticipation of a likely US reaction to any dramatic naval build-up. It also has to take account of the reluctance of most countries to host Chinese military bases. Finally, it has to take into account that 'For any nation, obtaining actual military bases overseas is an expensive, time-consuming, politically and diplomatically fraught process involving real costs and risks'.[49]

Still others have suggested that the OBOR is part of a general struggle for power and influence in Central Asia, replaying, as it were, the 'great game' of the 19th-century imperial powers. In this version, China is seeking to use its economic power to establish a sphere of influence in Central Asia, a new empire.[50] The opportunity might have been afforded by the run-down of

[47] For discussion on this issue see V. Marantidou, 'Revisiting China's "String of Pearls" Strategy: Places "with Chinese Characteristics" and their Security Implications', *Pacific Forum CSIS, Issues and Insights*, 14/7, 2014; F.P. van der Putten and M. Mijnders, *China, Europe and the Maritime Silk Road*, Clingendael Report, The Hague, 2015; P.K. Shee, 'An Anatomy of China's "String of Pearls" Strategy' *The Hikone Ronso*, Spring 2011, 22–37; S. Tiezzi, 'The Maritime Silk Road vs. the String of Pearls', *The Diplomat*, 13.2.2014; B. Zhou, *The String of Pearls and the Maritime Silk Road*, China-US Focus, 11.2.2014.

[48] M. Clemens, 'The Maritime Silk Road and the PLA: Part One', *China Brief*, 15/6, 19.3.2015.

[49] M Clemens, 'The Maritime Silk Road and the PLA: Part Two', *China Brief*, 15/7, 3.4.2015.

[50] C. Clover and L. Hornby, 'China's Great Game. Road to a New Empire', *Financial Times*, 12.10.2015.

American troop presence in Afghanistan and the closure of its air bases in Karshi-Khanabad (Uzbekistan) and Manas (Kyrgyzstan) in November 2005 and June 2014 respectively. But it is not the USA that is challenged in this scenario, but 'an aggressive but weary Russia' which had long ruled over the entire area. Now it seems to be Central Asia facing the same kind of challenge that the EU posed in the Ukraine, but now with China assuming that role and Central Asia playing the part of Russia's back yard.[51] One reason given for China's interest in Central Asia is a drive for energy security,[52] but one does not need the whole framework of OBOR just to build pipelines.

I would like at this juncture to stake out a position for OBOR not being a foreign policy response to anything. I do this for two reasons. The first reason lies in the nature of OBOR itself – a series of (uncoordinated?) long-term investment projects agreed individually with Asian governments; a mixture of development assistance and hard business united by a silken banner of high rhetoric, higher principles and a jolly good yarn. It does not really seem to be the stuff of an appropriate reply to the various foreign policy challenges for which it is supposed to be a response. The second reason lies in the curious absence of a foreign minister in much of the story. Most of the actual policy-making is done in executive sub-committees, where party hierarchy matters more than formal functions. The advisors upon whom Xi relies on his foreign trips rank more highly that the most senior foreign policy official present. The foreign minister is rarely in attendance. Indeed, he does not even make it to the standing committee of the CPC (putting his rank at thirty or less, with another twenty holding equal rank to him). Within such a hierarchy he is expected to take orders rather than give them. The Politburo also has study sessions, twenty-two so far under the new leadership, of which five are on foreign policy. All of these, including those on foreign policy, are headed by Xi Jinping. These tend also to be attended by officials from the propaganda department, who usually outrank any foreign

---

[51] K. Kirişci and P. Le Corre, 'The Great Game that Never Ends: China and Russia Fight over Kazakhstan' *Brookings Brief*, 18.12.2015.

[52] C. Brugier, 'China's Way: The New Silk Road', *European Union Institute for Security Studies Brief*, May 2014; A.C. Kuchins and J. Mankoff, *Central Asia in a Reconnecting Eurasia: U.S. Policy Interests and Recommendations*, 2015; E. Rumer, R. Sokolsky and P. Stronski, *U.S. Policy Toward Central Asia 3.0*, Carnegie Endowment for International Research, 2016.

office official represented.[53] Moreover, as already stated, the OBOR initiative is not under the control of China's foreign affairs apparatus but under a department run under Zhang Gaoli. He is the seventh-ranking official in the Chinese Communist Party. He is also the deputy to Premier Li Keqiang and second-in-charge of China's government and economic sector. Directives from his officials usually describe OBOR as 'economic strategy'.[54]

At the 'soft end' of the spectrum of realist interpretations, or the start of liberal/institutionalist interpretations, OBOR could be viewed as an investment in the provision of 'public goods' that would also help protect its own security. That public good is stability. In this view by increasing the region's economic development OBOR can help hold back the tide of radical Islamic and other separatist groups that threaten not only the stability of governments in the region, but also the restive region of Xinjiang, in the northwest of China, which is one of the poorest regions in China (twenty-fourth out of twenty-nine provinces) and the scene of religious-related unrest and violence. In order to keep the region in check the Chinese government has made the combating of what it calls the 'three evils' (religious extremism, separatism and terrorism) a priority in the region. To achieve these aims and reduce discontent in Xinjiang, Beijing has engaged in a policy of regional economic development. Since 78% of Xinjiang's exports already go to Central Asia, developing neighbouring economies would consolidate the demand and guarantee further development. In order to improve trade flows between Xinjiang and Central Asian countries, Beijing has already invested more than $91 billion in trade-related infrastructure in the western province (including in roads, hydropower plants and primary industry facilities).[55] The OBOR strategy is aimed at turning the western interior into the new frontier as it opens up to the world,. In so doing, development opportunities will increase and new growth points will emerge.[56] Whereas previously China's development had been dependent on the eastern and coastal cities, OBOR would reinforce growth of the inland regions, thereby

---

53 L. Jakobson and R. Manuel, 'How are Foreign Policy Decisions Made in China?', *Asia and the Pacific Policy Studies*, 3/1, 2016, 101–10.

54 R. Manuel, 'One Belt, One Road, Many Mixed Messages', *Nikkei Asian Review*, 1.9.2015.

55 Brugier, 'China's Way'.

56 Swaine, 'Chinese Leadership and Elite Responses'.

contributing to the formation of 'one body and two wings'.[57] This scenario brings the explanation closer to home, and closer to the core of the policy's emphasis. However, it is far from certain whether the OBOR strategy, with its emphasis on modernisation and with its increased visibility of (Han) Chinese construction projects and businesses will dampen militancy in the region rather than inflame it.

At this point the debate abandons the realist/institutionalist schools and turns towards domestic economic factors to explain on OBOR's motivation. One large body of thought attributes OBOR to the need to find an outlet for over-capacity in several of China's basic industries such as steel, cement and construction materials. Local businesses, with the support of provincial governments and the financial backing of local banks, are planning to employ OBOR to absorb output that will not be used domestically.[58] However, the country's National Development and Reform Commission condemned a similar strategy that was adopted after the 2008 financial crisis. It suggested that such a policy would exacerbate over-investment and contribute to wasteful expenditure. It argued that state controls were inadequate to prevent overspending, and the system whereby provinces were rewarded for growth would only amplify the distortions. The dangers would be worse still if the strategy were wheeled out as part of a cross-border grand strategy.[59] Moreover the likely demand generated by OBOR is unlikely to be sufficient to alleviate current levels of over-capacity. For example, if the demand for steel were equivalent to the entire demand for one year of domestic railway construction (an impressive 21 million tons) it would only amount to less than 5% of the estimated overcapacity.[60]

---

[57] H. Gao, *Deepen Economic, Trade Cooperation, Co-Create New Brilliancy*, original in *People's Daily*, 2.7.2014, translation supplied by Ministry of Commerce website.

[58] Economist Intelligence Unit, *Prospects and Challenges on China's One Belt One Road: A Risk Assessment Report*, London, 2015; M. Fulko, *Solving the Prickly Issue of Overcapacity in China*, CKGBS Knowledge, 14.6.2016; E. Ng, '"One Belt" infrastructure investments seen as helping to use up some industrial over-capacity', *South China Morning Post*, 2.11.2015; J. Zhang, 'What's Driving China's One Belt One Road Initiative?' East-Asia Forum, 2.6.2016; J. Zhou, K. Hallding and G. Han, 'The Trouble with China's "One Belt One Road" Strategy', *The Diplomat*, 26.6.2015.

[59] National Development and Reform Commission, 防止低效与无效投, 20.11.2014 (Prevent Inefficient and Ineffective Investment).

[60] Hong, *China's One Belt, One Road*, 20-21.

On the other hand, it has been argued that OBOR is less an escape route for China to revive its investment-led growth model than a temporary relief valve in the country's efforts to rebalance the economy in the direction of increased consumption. In this scenario, investment cannot be allowed to fall too quickly, for fear that the negative shock would crush growth before consumer spending could catch up and become the principal motor of growth. OBOR can help rebalance China towards consumption-led growth by preventing investment from falling too fast during the country's structural reforms. From China's perspective, however, economic growth is key to its national security, as it legitimises the Communist Party's rule and OBOR is part of its survival tactics.[61]

Other commentators have suggested that the surplus provided by OBOR had less to do with industrial over-capacity than with the accumulation of foreign exchange, much of which was tied up in low interest-bearing American Treasury bonds. In order to alleviate the symbiotic financial dependence of US monetary policy, and to at least have the prospects of higher returns, OBOR acts as a vehicle for diversifying (foreign) direct investment, providing a boost for domestic industry and, in the process, helping the Renminbi to become an international currency.[62] Seen in this light OBOR is nothing more than a continuation of the 'go global' strategy in a more ambitious format.

Reflections

It is not my intention to choose from among these contending motivations behind the OBOR initiative. As I suggested earlier, much of the motivations identified have been a back projection of the probable consequences. For example, it is certain that the extension of Chinese infrastructural investment abroad, and the government-to-government agreements that underpin it, will alter the balance of power throughout Asia. Trade and investment may bring a greater sympathy and support for Chinese policies in international

[61] L. Chi, 'China's "One Belt One Road": "One Stone Kills Three Birds"', *Paribas*, 24.6.2015.

[62] J. Kynge, ''One Belt, One Road' set to turbocharge renminbi usage', *Financial Times*, 30.11.2015.

fora, but it may also provoke a reaction from those countries that see their influence and control to be waning as a result. Equally it is inevitable that OBOR will stimulate demand not only for the Chinese goods required for the initial projects, but also from the induced demand that will follow. It is interesting, however, that in all the foreign commentary, hardly any take the official explanation at its face value – that OBOR is a development strategy, sharing Chinese expertise and finance to produce a win-win situation for the greater prosperity and stability for the region as a whole. This is curious because the entire OBOR initiative will have development consequences for the regions most affected. The increased connectivity between centres of population and the accessibility of rural areas lying in between will stimulate increased traffic and stimulate regional economies. The improved access to energy will promote a new chances for industry and create a demand for new consumer goods. Whether these gains outweigh the initial investment costs is a different question, but here at least is a direct connect between policy intent and policy instrument. The official Chinese arguments on OBOR do actually fit the roll-out of the policy itself. However, accepting this line of reasoning does not mean that one has to abandon other any or all of the explanations advanced in this chapter. There is no reason to view these as mutually exclusive. It is possible, indeed likely, to enjoy promoting a foreign development programme while promoting domestic providers, finding an more outlet for foreign currency reserves, stimulating exports and enjoying better relations with one's neighbours all at the same time. However the core of OBOR lies in its infrastructural expenditure abroad, and this will have consequences for the economic development in the countries affected. In the next chapter, therefore, I will explore the development strategy (explicit or implicit) underpinning the OBOR initiative and the implications for its success.

CHAPTER THREE

Development Strategy

In September 2013 President Xi Jinping launched a vision of staggering breadth and ambition of a development corridor stretching from China to Europe and transforming all the economies that lay across its path. Vast sums of money were mentioned. By mid-2016 it was claimed that 900 projects were envisaged, including many in China, with a combined price tag of $890 billion. Eventually, it was suggested that China would invest $4 trillion in the economies of the OBOR countries but no specification has yet appeared.[1] Details of the scheme have emerged only slowly, country by country. Even then it is never clear whether the funds are loans or grants, and the extent to which the figures include private investment. Since OBOR was launched, the value of foreign Chinese-backed projects announced has averaged over $100 billion a year (though the dispersion of the funds will be spread over years into the future). The pattern of this expenditure is shown in Figure 3.1.

[1] *The Economist*, 2.7.2016.

Figure 3.1 Dollar value of Projects announced in OBOR countries (million $)

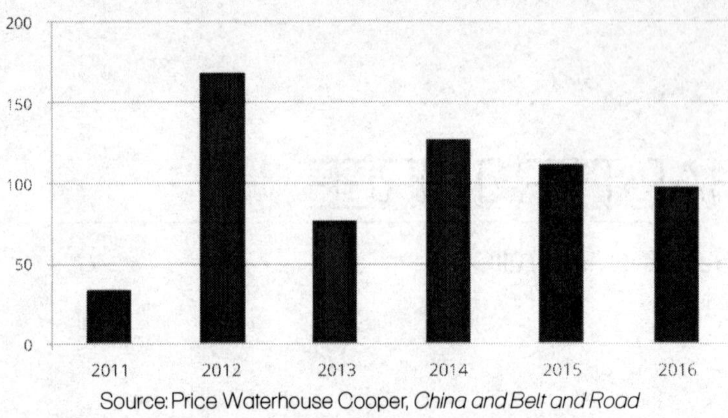

Source: Price Waterhouse Cooper, *China and Belt and Road Infrastructure. 2016 Review and Outlook*, 2017, 8-9.

The projects are funded by a mixture of local funding, Chinese government-government loans and private investment, often backed by Chinese state-owned banks. Since 2013, firms in mainland China have annually invested over $100 billion abroad. In the latest year for which statistics are available (2015), the size of the outward flow reached $128 billion.[2] These figures are probably overstated, since a large proportion of Chinese FDI flows to Hong Kong and overseas tax havens before being repatriated, a practice known as 'round tripping'. Recent re-estimation has reduced the outflow by almost 25%, which would still leave a large amount; but only half of the re-estimated amount stays in Asia.[3] OBOR-related investments in 2015 have been estimated at 36.7% of the total.[4] Reports on OBOR developments rarely specify whether a project has already commenced and, if it had, whether the sums reported are the full sum or the new injection of cash. There is often little indication of the time-scale over which the sums will be dispersed. The progress reports often employ different timescales and different units.

Despite the difficulties in obtaining information that is both comparable and consistent, it is still possible to discern an OBOR development

[2] UNCTAD, *World Development Report, 2016*, 2016.

[3] C. Casanova, A. Garcia-Herrero and X. Li, *Chinese Outbound Foreign Direct Investment. How Much Goes Where after Round-Tripping and Offshoring?* BBVA Working Paper 15/17, Hong Kong, 2015.

[4] *Financial Times*, 30.11.2015.

strategy. As we saw in Chapter One, already in his speech September 2013 President Xi's outlined five steps towards creating silk road economic belt. Two of these steps - improved transport connectivity and improved trade facilitation - also suggest themselves as ways of promoting economic development. Moreover the projects so far undertaken in OBOR's various land corridors also reveal a pattern in the infrastructural investment with projects concentrated in transport, power, pipelines and enterprise zones. In addition the maritime silk road allows us to add seaports to the list, in particular container ports and oil/gas terminals, but these we will examine separately in Chapter Eight. All of these elements could be justified as part of a grand development strategy, but they also derive to some extent from China's own experience. This could be both an advantage and a disadvantage. It could be an advantage in that China is familiar with these kinds of investments and also has the capital equipment and expertise to execute them. On the other hand, the success of the strategy within the Chinese context might contribute to an underestimation of the problems that could arise when the model is transplanted into different settings abroad.

The next section will start by briefly examining the Chinese growth model as it evolved in China and then as it was first transplanted abroad in Africa. After that the chapter will explore the OBOR development strategy more systematically by looking at the effects of investments on both the donor and on the recipient country and both during the construction and implementation phases. It will focus specifically on investments in railways and highways, power plants, pipelines and enterprise zones, and it will conclude with framework for risk assessment. This will distinguish between financial and operating risk (for the Chinese) and development risk (for the recipient). Finally, it will turn its attention to the challenge presented by barriers to international trade in the region.

China's Economic Growth

Since 1990 China's economic growth has been remarkable by any standards, growing annually by a shade under 10% for the best part of thirty years.[5]

[5] E.C. Grivoyannis (ed.), *The New Chinese Economy: Dynamic Transitions into the Future*, New York, 2012; Y. Huang. *Capitalism with Chinese Characteristics:*

In 1980 Deng Xiaoping started the transition from a heavily regulated, planned economy by creating Special Enterprise Zones (SEZs) which would be allowed a greater policy freedom than the rest of the country. They were intended to attract FDI and to stimulate the adoption of new technology. The first four zones were all created in the coastal provinces: Shenzhen, Zhuhai and Shantou in Guangdong Province and Xiamen in Fudan Province. The spectacular success of these early experiments prompted the government to expand the scheme. In 1984 fourteen coastal open cities were created. Hainan was added to the list of SEZs in 1985 and in 1989 Pudong New District was established in Shanghai. With the gradual opening of the economy as a similar enterprise zones were established throughout the land under a series of different titles and with different priorities and different privileges.[6]

One way of explaining economic performance is by 'growth accounting'. This involves estimating the contribution of different factors of production and the efficiency in their use. In the case of China, this exercise would reveal that its growth was fuelled by a high savings/investment rate and an ability to transfer labour from low-productivity sectors (agriculture) to industry and services or, differently put, from the countryside to the cities. Beyond these sources of growth, there was an exogenous contribution to growth from the renewal of industrial capital and from reaping the benefits of economies of scale. Basically this was the result of the optimal use of inward FDI, the market reforms that had been introduced and the access to export markets.[7]

The huge increase in manufacturing that accompanied China's growth

---

Entrepreneurship and the State, Cambridge, 2008; A.R. Kroeber, *China's Economy: What Everyone Needs to Know*, Oxford, 2016; J.Y. Lin, *Demystifying the Chinese Economy*, Cambridge, 2012; B.J. Naughton, *The Chinese Economy: Transitions and Growth*, Cambridge, MA, 2007.

[6] Y. Yeung, J. Lee and G. Kee, 'China's Special Economic Zones at 30', *Eurasian Geography and Economics*, 50/2, 2009, 222–40; D.Z. Zeng (ed.), *Building Engines for Growth and Competitiveness in China: Experience with Special Economic Zones and Industrial Clusters*, Washington, 2010; Idem., *How Do Special Economic Zones and Industrial Clusters Drive China's Rapid Development?* World Bank Policy Research Working Paper 5583, 2011.

[7] B. Bosworth and S.M Collins, 'Accounting for Growth: Comparing China and India', *Journal of Economic Perspectives*, 22/1, 2008, 45–66.

required an enormous increase in the volume of fuel and raw materials that needed to be brought to the factories, and a large volume of finished goods to be transported to domestic (urban) markets and abroad. This demanded a vast investment in infrastructure.[8] Between 1990 and 2013, the length of China's railway network almost doubled to reach 103,000 km (60% electrified) by 2013. Although China possessed the world's third largest railway network, 25% of the world's traffic was carried on just 6% of the total track. This impression of an overstretched network is confirmed when it is realised that 59% of passengers and 35% of freight traffic were carried on only 13% of the tracks. A symbol of China's modernisation is its high-speed rail network, which grew from nothing in 2006 to 19,000 km by 2016. This total was more than the rest of the world combined. Moreover, since 1990 the size of the highway network had quadrupled, not only to carry the increased volume of goods, but also to accommodate the growing number of passenger vehicles as consumer incomes rose.[9]

The insatiable demand for raw materials and the massive export drive also contributed to the development of China's ports and harbours. Seven of the world's largest ports by cargo volume today are located in China. The country's port development was largely driven by local state authorities, which provided much of the investment and oversaw the administration of port-cities, often combining port investment with various development zone incentives. Although this had the advantage of creating synergies, it also led to an over-concentration of manufacturing activities within a relatively restricted area, with all the environmental damage that that incurred. The port itself was often seen as a medium to ensure the profitability or sustainability of local enterprise rather than a venture in its own terms.[10] In terms of efficiency China's container ports can also compete with the world's best,

---

[8] P. Sahoo, R.K. Dash and G. Nataraj, *Infrastructure Development and Economic Growth in China*, IDE Discussion Paper, 261, 2010; Idem., 'China's Growth Story: The Role of Physical and Social Infrastructure', *Journal of Economic Development*, 37/1, 2012, 53–75.

[9] China Statistical Yearbook, 2014; KPMG, *Infrastructure in China. Foundation for Growth*, 2009. H. Chan Hing Lee, 'Prospects of Chinese Rail Export under "One Belt, One Road"' in T.W. Lin, H. Chan Hing Leee, K. Tseng Hui-Yi and W.X. Lim (eds.) *China's One Belt One Road Initiative*, London, 2016, 197-235.

[10] J.J. Wang, *Port-City Interplays in China*, Abingdon, New York, 2014 (2nd ed.).

with the country boasting five of the top ten and eight of the top twenty. However, in other areas there is room for improvement. In coal it has three in the top ten and four in the top twenty. For oil it has none in the top ten but three in the top twenty. For iron ore it has one in the top ten and two in the top sixteen, and for bulk grain harbours it has one in the top twenty.[11]

The ferocious speed of infrastructural improvement has allowed the country to stay ahead of demand for their services, but only just. Many of the transport routes are choked to capacity and seaports are strained to their limits. But the country now has the production capacity, experience and technical knowhow not only to continue expanding its domestic infrastructure, but also to transplant its model abroad.

China's Development Model in Africa

As China's reforms began to reflect themselves in its rapidly rising industrial output the country's demand for energy and raw materials also began to accelerate, and this manifested itself in a renewed interest in Africa. Initially Chinese FDI was concentrated in the oil and extractive industries and, as late as 2007, 85% of China's imports from Africa came from five oil and mineral exporting countries.[12] To help secure these vital supplies, China not only invested on site in mining and excavation, but it also financed a large-scale programme of road and rail construction and port improvement. China's policy in the region, however, went beyond the investment needed for the commercial extraction of minerals and their transport, but also embraced wider infrastructural investment in areas that resembled the pattern of its own development strategy. This infrastructural investment was usually

[11] O. Merk and T. Dang, *Efficiency of World Ports in Container and Bulk Cargo (Oil, Coal, Ores and Grain)*, OECD Regional Development Working Papers, 2012/09, OECD.

[12] S.A. Asongu and G.A.A. Aminkeng, 'The Economic Consequences of China–Africa Relations: Debunking Myths in the Debate', *Journal of Chinese Economic and Business Studies*, 11/4, 2013, 261–77; H.G. Broadman, *Africa's Silk Road. China and India's New Economic Frontier*, Washington DC, 2007: 6–13; J. Eisenman, 'China–Africa Trade Patterns: Causes and Consequences', *Journal of Contemporary China*, 21/77, 2012, 793–810; J.Y. Lin and Y. Wang, *China-Africa Co-Operation in Structural Transformation; Ideas, Opportunities, and Finances*, WIDER Working Paper 2014/046, Helsinki, 2014.

in the form of soft loans. The terms were rarely published and so the sums were excluded from Western definitions of 'official development assistance' (ODA).[13] According to the latest official figures, grants accounted for 36.3% of China's total aid in the years 2010–12 (but this not the same as the OECD calculation). Interest-free loans, which are usually offered where there is a genuine prospect of repayment from the increased output associated with the project, accounted for only 8%. The sources of loan repayment (e.g. by ear-marking revenues from future exports) was sometimes stipulated in the loan agreement itself. However, the bulk of the assistance, fully 55.7%, is in the form of interest-bearing concessional loans. These are common in funding large projects and they usually stipulate a minimum of Chinese content (over 50%) in the project. In this respect they represent a form of tied aid and they are as much a subsidy to a Chinese contractor as aid for the recipient.

These developments were not immediately welcomed in the West. Many security analysts viewed them as a direct threat to Western interests and to the interests of Africa itself. The official rhetoric in China had always stressed its peaceful intentions, but it seemed that a phrase as seemingly innocuous as 'peaceful rise' could be misconstrued. As a consequence there was a subtle shift in the rhetoric.[14] No longer was China simply an emerging power, it was still a developing country as well. Recast in this way, Chinese aid and investment became a mutual experience in which both parties would benefit, producing a win-win situation. The rhetoric also promoted the five principles of peaceful development which underscored mutual respect for sovereignty and territorial integrity, mutual non-aggression, non-interference in internal affairs, equality and mutual benefit, and peaceful co-existence. This all served to contrast China's intent to provide assistance that was beneficial for development with Western interference with internal issues as governance and democracy. It also captured African dissatisfaction with the slowness of Western aid donors in matching aid promises with resources, with the insistence on conditionality and with the cumbersome bureaucracy that

[13] In order to qualify as ODA at least 25% *of each transaction* has to be in the form of a grant and the definition excludes military aid and equipment.

[14] L.J. Corkin, 'China's Rising Soft Power: The Role of Rhetoric in Constructing China–Africa Relations', *Revista Brasileira de Política Internacional*, 57, 2014, 49–71; S. Grimm, 'China-Africa Cooperation: Promises, Practice and Prospects' *Journal of Contemporary China*, 23/90, 2014, 993–1011.

recipients had to construct to satisfy different conditions and different reporting criteria.[15] It also prepared the rhetoric for the OBOR initiatives.

One common accusation levied against China is that its aid effort is primarily directed at securing resources. One way of 'testing this' is to compile various indicators that could be used to describe the economic and political characteristics of recipient nations and to see if any statistically significant relations emerged with the pattern of aid distribution. Such exercises are interesting, but they do have important limitations. One problem lies in the quality of the data assembled, and whether they accurately distinguish between the countries included in the analysis. A second problem is that establishing whether a pattern existed is not the same as establishing that it was intended. Ex-post correlation is not the same as motivation. The handful of such tests that have been conducted for China suggest that there is indeed a close relationship between China's commercial relations with individual countries and the resources received, but not that it is focused on resource rich countries.[16] In addition, aid and investment flows also favour countries with which China has enjoyed a close political relationship[17] but the same is true for most large Western donors. Moreover, despite the accusation that China's aid ignores issues of corruption and governance, the data shows no evidence suggesting any bias in aid allocation towards such regimes. The most recent study, that is better able to distinguish between development assistance and commercially oriented forms of state financing,[18] suggests that China's ODA is primarily motivated by political concerns. 'Social aid', which includes prestige projects

---

[15] N. Woods, 'Whose Aid? Whose Influence? China, Emerging Donors and the Silent Revolution in Development Assistance', *International Affairs*, 84/6, 2008, 1205–21.

[16] J.C. Bethelemy, 'China's Engagement and Aid Effectiveness in Africa' in R. Schiere, L. Ndikumana and P. Walkenhorst (eds.), *China and Africa: An Emerging Partnership for Development?*, Belvédère (Tunisia), 2011, 71-89; D. Brautigam, 'Chinese Development Aid in Africa: What, Where, Why, and How Much?' in J. Golley and L. Song (eds.), *Rising China: Global Challenges and Opportunities*, Canberra, 2011, 203–23; A. Dreher and A. Fuchs, 'Rogue Aid? An Empirical Analysis of China's Aid Allocation', *Canadian Journal of Economics*, 48/3, 2015, 988–1023.

[17] The proxy chosen to measure this is usually voting with China in the UN or the non-recognition of Taiwan.

[18] A. Dreher, A. Fuchs, B. Parks, A.M. Strange. and M.J. Tierney, *Apples and Dragon Fruits: The Determinants of Aid and Other Forms of State Financing from China to Africa*, AidData Working Paper, 15, 2015.

such as palaces and stadiums as well as schools and hospitals, is closely related to diplomatic support for the country. Even so, funds for poverty relief and development assistance do tend to flow towards the poorer African nations, and therefore go to where they are needed most. Such flows also tend to show little relation to perceived standards of governance, thus testifying to China's adherence to its own principles of non-interference. By contrast, other more commercial concessional loans and financing did correlate with the natural resource endowment of the recipient country, and they favoured countries with better governance performance. This may have been coincidental, but it could also reflect obtaining a better prospect that the loans may be repaid at some time in the future.

Linkage Effects

One useful conceptual tool in exploring the potential of OBOR as a development model is to distinguish between two so-called 'linkage effects'. A backward linkage effect deals with the benefits of an investment on the supplier – labour, raw materials, finance, R&D and so forth. The forward linkage deals with the benefits for the operator or the final consumer. If the investment is in the form of an intermediate good (for example a transport facility) the operator will employ labour and resources and hope that revenues will these exceed costs so that he/she can benefit from the profits generated. The purchaser of such intermediate goods will hope that the reduced costs will permit increased sales and investments. The purchasers of final goods, such as food or clothing, will hope to reduce spending on such items, allowing them to increase demand for other products. The greater the backward and forward linkage effects, the greater is the potential of investment for economic growth.[19]

Backward Linkage Effects

The first input is money. The OBOR process starts with China offering to finance a particular project. However, China alone cannot alone decide which project it will fund, but nor can the recipient country. What usually follows

[19] The concept was first developed by A.O. Hirschman, *The Strategy of Economic Development*, New Haven CT, 1958.

is a bargaining process between two governments where project suggestions on the one side are reconciled with capacities on the other. Occasionally, a recipient government will offer a project to open tender, allowing interested parties from other countries to bid. In this process the conditions for funding will represent an important part of the package. Chinese finance for OBOR projects usually takes the form of an interest-bearing loan. The interest charged is usually (but not always) a fraction above the prevailing LIBOR rate. This is far below what an infrastructural project in a less developed country would usually warrant and must be lower than would have been charged if it had been determined by a commercial assessment of the risks involved. However the risk does not disappear. What follows, therefore, is a bargaining process over who should carry that risk. The lender (i.e. China) will try to tie the loan to the government, assuming that governments will offer better prospects of repayment (or some other compensatory advantage) than a commercial enterprise. The borrower will try to avoid this if possible. This could be done by leaving the running of the project in Chinese hands or in some form of mixed enterprise, but this will involve some sacrifice of the forward linkage benefits that come with the operational profits. We will return to this conundrum a little later on.

A second input into the project is land. New projects often add value to land, especially if it had previously been of little value (marginal agriculture or low value housing). However this importance for economic development depends on the circumstances of acquisition. If the process is one of sequestration or forced sale with low compensation, the effects will be muted. This question is especially important for transport infrastructure, especially for railways or highways where continuous lines of land along the route are required as well as and large areas at the sites of major stations for commercial development. In theory, anyone holding land along the route is in a quasi-monopoly position and can employ a threat of non-sale to boost the price to stratospheric heights. For this reason, most states establish rules of compulsory purchase and fair compensation or some other form price controls in attempts to curb speculation. However 'fair' compensation allows land holders of otherwise marginal land to obtain some extra economic benefits and thereby help raise income levels in the area. In Chongqing an experiment has been conducted whereby land use and land ownership are separated and developers must buy development certificates, transferring cash that can allow peasants to obtain land-use rights elsewhere, though most used the cash to ease their move into the city.[20] By de facto allowing an upward revaluation of property and guaranteeing its subsequent disposal, railway construction can inject mobile capital into the local economy and thus enhance its development.

Labour is also required for the laying of the for the construction of the project. Nowadays very little of this requires unskilled or semi-skilled labour track and most operations require the use of advanced machinery. Unless there is already a large and sustained transport infrastructural programme in operation in the country, and one that can release the necessary personnel, it is likely that much of the labour would come from the investing country, in this case China. Moreover the common nature of language and culture would also help ease the burden of project supervision. On other hand recipient countries will try to limit the ' loss' of this injection of income into domestic economies by stipulating local content quotas. Turkmenistan, for example, requires that a project's workforce consists of 70% local employees, and Uzbekistan stipulates that Chinese companies send only management personnel, not labourers. Whether these are strictly observed is doubtful.[21]

Some of the raw materials and semi-manufactures can be supplied locally, but even here most of the value-added might still accrue to the local provider. For example, high(er) speed Chinese railways tend to build track on pre-fabricated concrete viaducts that are produced in mobile factories build near the point of construction. Similarly much of the equipment for coal-fired power stations comes from dismantled (polluting) power stations in China itself. Indeed the fact that Chinese loans stipulate the use of a Chinese contractor reinforces a tendency to subcontract to members of familiar networks at home. The same consideration also applies for the logistical infrastructure, the locomotives and the rolling stock. However there are examples where local companies have kept contracts for rolling stock and even one occasion where German firms have secured contracts for some of the logistical work in the transport hubs. Thus, although there

---

[20] R. Lafarguette, 'Chongqing: Model for a New Economic and Social Policy?' *China Perspectives*, 2011/4, 2011, 62–4. M. Keith, S. Lash, J. Arnoldi and T. Rooker, *China Constructing Capitalism: Economic Life and Urban Change*, London, New York, 2014.

[21] S. Lain, 'China's Silk Road in Central Asia: Transformative or Exploitative?', *Financial Times*, 27.4.2016.

are definitely backward linkages associated with railway construction, it is far from certain in what proportion in the recipient country.

Forward Linkage Effects

Once the investment has been made, there are two possible options. There is either 'turn-key' investment, where the entire project is handed over to the recipient upon completion or there is build-operate-transfer (B-O-T) where the operational control will remain with Chinese firms for periods ranging from twenty to fifty years, after which it is handed over to the recipient. The recipient will prefer the turn-key option when there are reasonable prospects of making a profit. Remember there is still the principal of the loan and the interest to pay off, and maintenance and depreciation costs to be borne. The recipient will prefer the B-O-T option if it is uncertain of the profit or if it lacks the expertise to run the project. For many infrastructural projects uncertainty stems from the anticipated demand for the services supplied, since idle capacity will raise average production costs.

For China, the B-O-T option may also be attractive for several reasons. First, it may have the necessary management expertise to minimise the risks of making a loss. Second, the management of a project may facilitate a rationalisation of the supply chain in such a way as to reduce risks. These two factors help explain China's willingness to run some of the container ports that it is building. Chinese container ports rank among the most efficient in the world, and by managing the port facilities themselves allows the port authorities more easily to form alliances with Chinese shipping companies. Finally, China may have security concerns that override commercial considerations. This is particularly the case in LPG and oil pipelines, designed primarily to enhance China's energy flow security.

Looking again at the linkage effects, at this operational stage it is difficult to judge in which direction positive linkage effects may flow. In managing projects themselves, recipient countries may reap the profits of the enterprise, but this assumes that they are capable of making profits. In many cases the provision of infrastructural services already run at a loss, whether it be the running of railways or the provision of electricity. In other cases they have no experience in managing the type of enterprise envisaged. For example, most of the sea-ports in the region are undercapitalised, over-bureaucratic and inefficiently run. The task of organising large-scale container traffic or multi-modal 'dry ports' is simply beyond the scope of local management.

Let us now turn to the forward linkage effects starting with transport improvements. One of the most prominent items is the investment in railways. In particular, the public imagination has been captured by the investments in HSR which can travel at speeds of over 300 km/h and can slice travelling times to fractions of what they had been. The latest HSR covering the 2252km between Kunming and Shanghai has cut the travel time from 34 to 11 hours.[22] However, HSR will probably be the last piece of the jigsaw to be slotted into place, for several reasons. First, they are very expensive to build - costing as much as ten times the price of a conventional railway. Tickets are therefore relatively expensive. The rule of thumb is that relative advantage lies in distances between 500 and 1000 kms. Below 500 kms and conventional rail and roads offer a better alternative and above that the airlines do. All of this assumes that along the line there are sufficient people to transport. For example, on the first regular freight route between China and Europe for the best part of 4500 kms (roughly speaking from Lanzhou to Kazan) there are on average fewer than ten inhabitants per km^2. The studies of the impact of HSR in China on economic development show no impact on the location of manufacturing industries, but a small effect on the concentration of service industries. The main advantage of moving passengers onto HSR is that it releases track for freight services. However, there are plenty of other ways of raising the average speed of freight than employing HSR. Many improvements in rail freight speeds can be achieved by employing more powerful locomotives, straightening bends, creating longer sidings and more regular sidings for overtaking and improving connections between carriages. It is interesting that most of the passenger lines already agreed under the banner of OBOR are slower (and cheaper) than the latest Chinese HSR lines.

However, there is some evidence to suggest that even conventional rail expansion has delivered few long-term economic benefits. A group of Oxford scholars have suggested that large infrastructural projects are prone to systematic underestimation of costs and overoptimistic assessment of potential

---

22 *ECNS*, 28.12.2016.

benefits. Analysing 21 conventional rail projects constructed between 1984 and 2008 in China, they found that 90% had serious cost overruns that averaged 41.5% (median 28.5%). Moreover on average railway projects took 25% longer to complete than estimated. Although most of the focus of OBOR commentator has been on railways, there are good arguments for increasing our attention on the less glamorous alternative of road improvements. The same Oxford survey suggests that road project managers were more successful in estimating costs. Only 70% of the 74 highway projects surveyed ran over budget, the shortfall (average 27.5%, median 16.1%) was less and they tended to be finished on schedule. On the other hand, most projects seriously overestimated the volume of traffic, although a few (mostly between and around large cities) erred in the other direction and became over congested almost as soon as they had been completed. The survey suggested that only 28% of transport projects delivered benefits in excess of 40-50% of their costs, the 40% threshold usually chosen by international development banks when assessing project viability. A further 17% delivered benefits, but below this standard. The survey suggests that benefits from half the projects did not cover their construction costs.[23] However, this assessment depend crucially on the inferred earnings of the capital assuming that it had been invested elsewhere and the length of time allowed. If these assumptions were relaxed, the conclusions need not have been so pessimistic.[24]

All transport improvements stimulate economic development by reducing costs, and thereby shifting the supply curve to the right. However there is a difference between roads and rail. Since rail freight requires a minimum scale of operation, the locational advantages tend to lie in larger cities where the marshalling yards and delivery terminals are located, and from which trucks and containers leave for their final destination. Rail termini, which are the only points of access to the network, tend to reinforce the locational advantages of urban conurbations. By contrast, highways can be accessed at almost any point along their route and improvements in local roads tend to have a demonstrable welfare effect up to two-three kms distance along the entire

[23] A. Ansar, B. Flyvbjerg, A. Budzier and D. Lunn, 'Does infrastructure investment lead to economic growth or economic fragility? Evidence from China', *Oxford Review of Economic Policy*, 32/3, 2016, 360-390.

[24] *The Economist*, 14.1.2017 (Hunting White Elephants)

route, though studies are silent over whether this represents new growth, or whether the observed impact is at the costs of producers located further away. There have not been many studies on the impact of roads on development, but those that have been conducted suggest that incomes are raised along a broad corridor on either side of the highway. Although the effects on incomes might be slight, the calculation of the benefits is enhanced if access to health facilities and education is included.[25] Noting that it tended to be the richer among the poor that tended to utilise the improved infrastructure, at least for the purposes of travelling longer distances, one commentator added that some attention should be focused on the means of transport (e.g. cars, motorcycles or donkey carts) and not simply on transport infrastructure.[26]

Figure 3.2 Effect of Railways and Roads on Economic Development

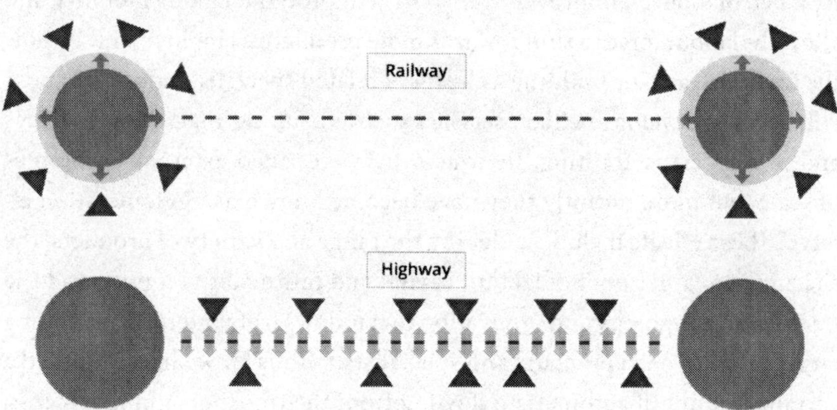

25 D. M. Brown *Highway Investment and Rural Economic Development An Annotated Bibliography*, USDA, Washington, 1999; E. Ghani, A.G. Goswami and W.R. Kerr, 'Highways to Success: The Impact of the Golden Quadrangle Project for the Location and Performance if Indian manufacturing', *The Economic Journal*, 126/591, 2016, 317-357; P. Lombard and L. Coetzer, *The Estimation Of The Impact Of Rural Road Investments On Socio-Economic Development*, 2006; World Bank *Rural Roads. A lifeline for villages in India*, Washington; D. van de Walle, 'Choosing Rural Road Investments to Help Reduce Poverty', *World Development*, 30/4, 2002, 575–89.

26 D.F. Bryceson, A. Bradbury, and T. Bradbury (2008) 'Roads to Poverty Reduction? Exploring Rural Roads' Impact on Mobility in Africa and Asia', *Development Policy Review*, 26/4, 459–82.

The forward linkages that occur depend on the conditions at the point of delivery – the size of the population, its concentration and level of development, local incomes and business productivity, and so forth. Let us work from the supposition that the local conditions are receptive to the reduced price of final goods and manufacturing inputs that transport improvement provides. Consumers will benefit by access to cheaper goods and reducing their costs of living. Of course, inefficient local producers of those same goods see their sales and profits reduced. On the other hand, local producers of goods that are competitive will find an increased demand at other points along the line, and their sales and profits will rise. This rise in profits would allow them to attract more investment funds and expand their production. If this enables them to increase the scale of operation, it may permit benefits of internal 'economies of scale' and allow a further leap forward in productivity. At a personal level, improved transport will promote labour mobility and allow the labour force to shift towards more productive employment. By now the town will also be building a cluster of related specialist industries and it will begin to develop ancillary services such as banking, marketing, logistics and even specialist training. These are what were called 'external' economies of scale, but more recently they have become known as 'agglomeration effects'. These effects include widening the range and variety of products, the sharing of a larger pool of labour, capital and raw material inputs, and the transfer of technology and innovation that follows from interactions among larger range of entrepreneurs and specialists.[27] Thus far we have assumed a certain amount of automatism flowing from the transport improvements, but this effect can all be enhanced by a sympathetic government strategy that acts as a catalyst and stimulates companies to take up their opportunities. Policies could be aimed at stimulating early demand for key products, reinforcing natural advantages, encouraging local competition (or at least by breaking up comfortable cabals and collusion) and facilitating the creation of clusters of activity and their support services.[28] Finally, if a region/country is to move beyond the phase of imitative technology (where they reap the

[27] P. Krugman, P., M. Fuijta and A. Venables, *The Spatial Economy – Cities, Regions and International Trade*, Cambridge, MA, 1999; T.R. Lakshmanan, 'The Broader Economic Consequences of Transport Infrastructure Investments', *Journal of Transport Geography*, 19/1, 2011, 1–12.

[28] M.E. Porter, *The Competitive Advantage of Nations* (2nd edition), New York, 1998.

rewards to cost savings while applying and adapting existing technologies) to the sphere of developing innovative technologies, they need to attract creative and entrepreneurial people. This can be done by creating a pleasant lifestyle, encouraging a diverse and welcoming community and creating the emergence of a vibrant environment full of exciting possibilities.[29]

The agglomeration effects associated with urban areas at the end of transport routes, or as nodes along them, also lie at the core of China's experiments with SEZs. They have also been part of its development model in Africa, and we will see them re-emerging at various points along the revived overland and maritime Silk Roads. China's experience in state-led development and the policy coherence afforded by the pervasive role of the CPC in all sectors of economy and society (even if tinged by corruption) is simply not present in many of the societies along the 'belt and road'. It is true that many of the SEZs envisaged will be run by Chinese enterprises, but one experienced observer questions whether private firms can succeed without the state/party framework to support them.[30] Most of the literature on SEZs emphasises the need for clear strategic planning that takes account of local conditions and comparative advantage, and that can cope with the evolution of both the SEZ's and the country's development.[31]

The potential forward linkage effects of energy provision are obvious. They depend on the reliability of supplies, without periodic outages or seasonal shortfalls, and upon the reduced price. There are, however, three points that require attention. The first is the possibility that several of the coal-fired power stations will reuse equipment from retired Chinese power plants. The dangers inherent in this strategy were revealed during Indonesia's

[29] R. Florida, *The Rise of the Creative Class: And How it is Transforming Work, Leisure, Community and Everyday Life*, New York, 2002.

[30] D. Bräutigam and X. Tang, 'Going Global in Groups': Structural Transformation and China's Special Economic Zones Overseas', *World Development*, 63, 2014, 78–91.

[31] D. Bräutigam and T. Xiaoyang, 'Economic Statecraft in China's New Overseas Special Economic Zones: Soft Power, Business or Resource Security?' *International Affairs*, 88/4, 2012, 799–816; V. Bricout, *Industrial Park Governance*, Singapore, 2014; A. Rodriguez-Pose and D. Hardy, *Technology and Industrial Parks in Emerging Countries. Panacea or Pipedream?*, Cham Heidelberg, 2014; UNDP, 2015. *If Africa Builds Nests, Will the Birds Come? Comparative Study on Special Economic Zones in Africa and China*, UNDP Working Paper 6-2015.

10,000MW crash power programme announced in 2004 with a total budget of $8.5 billion. The project was repeatedly delayed by difficulties in funding and by irregularities in the award of contracts. Eventually China stepped in with some of the extra funding[32] and Chinese-led consortiums built all but one of the largest coal plants using lo-tech boilers and second-hand equipment. The result was that many of the power stations did not live up to specifications and even after engineers had arrived to remedy the situation, only 70% of the capacity was operating efficiently.[33] The result is similar to running a transport network below capacity – the fixed costs have to be earned from a smaller revenue stream. A similar problem of aligning costs with possible revenues occurs in the case of hydro-electricity which holds the allure of cheap, clean energy. On the other hand they are extremely expensive to build and have large environmental impacts, often far beyond the borders of the initial project. They are also notoriously prone to the optimistic planning scenarios. A survey of 245 of the largest 300 dams in the world (184 generating hydroelectricity) suggested that 75% ran over their construction budget by an average of 96% (median 27%). 30% of the dams cost more than double the original budget. More than half the dams failed to meet the 1:1.4 cost benefit ratio employed in assessing their viability. No less than 80% of dams also failed to meet their construction schedules, with completion times averaging 8.6 years rather than the 5.9 years originally estimated. This meant that sums of money were tied up for far longer before any revenue flow materialised and once the flow commenced, the weight of fixed costs would be heavier than was budgeted.[34] The final problem comes with the target of all the energy sales. If the energy supplied were directed at the domestic population, and if there were indications that the facilities would not be loss-making, the forward linkages would still be positive. On the other had if there was little spin-off for the local population and if the

---

[32] The government secured a $650 million loan from China's Export Credit Agency for two of the plants and the China Development Bank later added a further $468 million and $293 from China's EXIM Bank. *The Jakarta Post*, 31.1.2008; 5.5.2009

[33] *South China Morning Post*, 11.12.2016 (Why does Indonesia cling to its plagued Chinese infrastructure projects?)

[34] A. Ansar, B. Flyvbjerg, A. Budzier and D. Lunn, 'Should we build more large dams? The actual costs of hydropower megaproject development', *Energy Policy*, 69, 2014, 43-56.

financial future were uncertain, such large-scale energy projects could well attract local and national opposition.

Chinese interest in constructing pipelines stems from two considerations. Inland sources of oil and gas need a means of conveyance to markets if exploitation is to be commercially viable. The cheapest means of transport is overseas by tanker overland, depending on volumes and distance, the best option is through pipelines. Thus, if China wanted to satisfy its burgeoning demand for primary energy and to diversify its sources of supply, pipelines would be the only solution. However, there is a security incentive to sourcing oil and gas from neighbouring inland countries. As long as the US naval power dominates the oceans' transit corridors it makes sense for China to reduce its reliance on ocean transport, especially at so-called 'choke points' as the Red Sea and the Straits of Malacca. This would explain China's interest in transhipping oil and gas from foreign ports and then by pipeline long before reaching Chinese waters. This would offer the additional advantage of servicing China's inland provinces directly and over a shorter total distance. The fact that pipelines can help resolve China's supply security problems need not imply that states in which oil and gas supplies are located will not benefit. Under the Soviet Union, pipelines in Asia were designed to satisfy Russia's spatial planning – pipelines were directed at specific markets rather than being merged into a single network. After the dissolution of the Soviet Union, the pipelines remained under the ownership of Transnept, which exercised its monopoly towards oil and gas producers – refusing rationalisation of the network and keeping a stranglehold over orders and pricing. Both the Western energy companies and the producer companies sought either to break the monopoly or to make Russian policy more complaint with mixed success. China, with its large demand and financial resources would offer Central Asian producers more options in resolving these issues.[35]

Risk Analysis

All major investment initiatives, such as those involved in OBOR, are bound to involve some degree of risk. One obvious risk is whether all this Chinese

---

[35] E.C. Chow and L.E. Hendrix, 'Central Asia's Pipelines: Field of Dreams and Reality', *National Bureau of Asian Research Special Report*, 23, 2010, 29-40.

foreign investment will ever be recovered. The OBOR investments are supposed to be run on market-based principles. Although (hidden) subsidies means that this will not be taken literally, they are supposed to at least break-even. In this chapter we have already seen the tendency of large infrastructural projects to overrun construction costs and to undershoot performance estimates. This 'soft' planning will only be further encouraged by the implicit government approval for helping to meet the country's foreign policy goals, and the pressures of local officials looking to enhance their standings by encouraging headline-grabbing projects undertaken by local industries. However the risk to profits is only part of a wider range of risk categories. One of the factors of foreign investment, as opposed to domestic investment, is that it is made in countries with different legal regimes, different financial systems and different types of governments. In addition the money is spent, and profits earned, in different currencies from that used in China. Thus one element of risk lies in whether Chinese investors are likely to be able to repatriate sums equivalent to the Rinminbi values invested. The Economist Intelligence Unit regularly makes a risk assessment for foreign investment for its subscribers and it has highlighted this particular aspect of the OBOR initiative in two separate publications. Central to its analysis is a composite index that combines economic data and expert opinion into ten sub-indices that it then weights equally to produce an overall risk assessment. The measures include factors influencing political stability as well as financial and macroeconomic risk and the final index claims to provide foreign banks and governments an indicator of the risk to their foreign portfolios.[36]

A second risk with which OBOR is likely to be confronted is corruption. In most developing countries the sectors of transport and energy are likely to be in the public domain and in such cases the projects envisaged by OBOR will have to be implemented in cooperation with national and local government departments. Even when relations at the top seem satisfactory, the fact remains that Chinese companies will be dealing with levels of administration that are completely unfamiliar to them and where standards of

---

[36] Economist Intelligence Unit *Prospects and Challenges on China's One Belt One road: A risk assessment report*, London, 2015; *'One Belt, One Road': An Economic Roadmap*, London, 2016. Recently the Fitch Ratings Agency suggested that most of the countries targeted by OBOR were debt rated in the 'B' to 'BBB' categories, *Reuters*, 26.1.2017 (China's One Belt, One Road Initiative Brings Risks).

public service are not as developed as at home or as in countries where they have traditionally had business dealings. There are several indicators that provide a measure of the degree of corruption in various countries. One of the oldest is the 'control of corruption indicator' constructed by the World Bank Institute.[37] This is based on various expert reports and it also incorporates Transparency International's corruption index. The indicator is not without its critics[38] but nevertheless it will serve in subsequent chapters as a rough guide to the difficulties foreign businesses face when operating in officialdom in different countries.

Finally we have to consider the risk of whether all the infrastructural investment envisaged by the OBOR initiative will actually trigger economic development in the recipient countries. Part of the answer to this question is hidden in the first two indicators already discussed. Infrastructure and labour market risk are two of the ten elements included in the Economist Intelligence Unit's index and, of course, domestic producers also have to confront corrupt officials. However the World Bank has also constructed an Ease of Doing Business Index which tracks process of doing business in ten steps from obtaining an the initial permit to dealing with insolvency (hopefully not one's own). The 190 countries are individually ranked for each of the steps and an overall ranking is also calculated.[39] Obviously if it is almost impossible to obtain a starting permit, or having access to credit or being able to enforce contracts, then new businesses are unlikely to flourish. On the other hand, if 'growing economies' were easy, the problems of stagnation and poverty would have been solved long ago. Enumerating the difficulties is not to intended to mock the intention, but to underscore the effort and ambition inherent in China's initiative.

Trade Facilitation

With the OBOR dream of new and upgraded transport routes crossing the Eurasian continent from East to West, it is not surprising that the scheme

[37] The Indicators are available from this website: http://info.worldbank.org/governance/wgi/index.aspx#home

[38] R.T. Griffiths, *Configuring the World. A critical political Economy approach,* Leiden, 2016, 213-222, 239-244.

[39] http://www.doingbusiness.org/rankings

also calls for improvements in trade facilitation. The first barrier to trade that we will consider is tariffs. These are taxes levied on imports either as a fixed charge or as a percentage on a sliding scale. In 2006–10 average applied tariffs in the OECD were 3.7% with 10.8% for agricultural goods and 2.8% for industry. For 'middle income countries' such as China the average is somewhat higher at 9.2% with 13.7% for agriculture and 8.8% for industrial products; and for 'low income countries' it is even higher still.[40] (Note that these are simple averages.) Evidently lowering or removing such barriers would reduce costs to consumers and so promote an increase in trade across borders. However, since the 1960s tariff rates have been progressively reduced and a far more pernicious form of government interference in trade has been formed by so-called non-tariff barriers, whose use has been increasing since the 1990s.[41] These are usually in the form of regulations and include instruments such as minimum safety standards or hygiene regulations against imports of (possibly) infected food products. These may have a legitimate function, but they do have a negative impact on imports – often deliberately so. They also include quantitative restrictions, technical product regulations, anti-dumping and countervailing measures, and any measures such as discretionary licensing that artificially create monopoly conditions. Among developing countries in Europe and Central Asia and in East Asia (this is not a happy clustering, but the authors do not disaggregate their data), the combined protectionist impact of non-tariff barriers is twice that of official tariffs. The situation in South Asia is even worse.[42]

It is not only government action that restricts trade, but there are also other cost penalties, known as 'transaction costs'. The first costs of these involve the transport of goods from one country to another, which obviously differs according to the nature of the product, the distance travelled and the means of transport. Matters do not end, however, when goods arrive at a port. They have to be unloaded, recorded and released for further

[40] World Bank database, Data on Trade and Import Barriers, Dec. 2011 http://econ.worldbank.org/WBSITE/EXTERNAL/EXTDEC/EXTRESEARCH/0,,contentMDK:21051044~pagePK:64214825~piPK:64214943~theSitePK:469382,00.html

[41] J. Gourdon, *CEPII NTM-MAP: A Tool for Assessing the Economic Impact of Non-Tariff Measures*, CEPII Working Paper 2014-24, 2014.

[42] B. Hoekman and A. Nicita, 'Trade Policy, Trade Costs, and Developing Country Trade', *Journal of World Development*, 39/12, 2011, 2071.

transhipment to its final destination. One well-known study estimated that, for developed countries, total border costs were twice as high as international transport costs and that only a small part of that (less than a fifth) was due to traditional measures such as tariffs.[43] The World Bank has calculated a border compliance indicator showing the administrative costs (documents, administration fees, handing charges) and the time lost in importing a 20 foot container containing car parts from a ship or airport in 2014 and the export of a typical export product to its largest (i.e. typical) market. The time lost in compiling the documents and waiting at the border to import a container of car parts averaged almost six and a half days.[44] Recently, however, China became the seventieth country to ratify the UN's TIR Convention (TIR stands for Transports Internationaux Routiers or International Road Transports). This allows goods to be sealed in containers and issued with a certificate that obviates the need to inspect the contents at each border crossing point, shaving hours off the entire operation.[45] Once across the borders there is still the domestic transport and logistics system to cope with. This is examined in the World Bank Logistics Performance Index, which surveys the opinions of logistics managers about the quality of services in the countries in which they operate.[46] These data will be examined in more detail in the individual chapters.

Reflections

The OBOR initiative reminds me very much of the early Western foreign development aid effort in the period from the second world war to the early 1980s. Then too there was a preference for large projects with strong powerful linkage effects that would stimulate industrial development further upstream. Big projects tend to be favoured by big money – there is an illusion that they are easier to monitor and control, and they confer a greater prestige on both donor and recipient. Infrastructure and large import-substituting

---

[43] J.E. Anderson and E. van Wincoop, 'Trade Costs', *Journal of Economic Literature*, 42/3, 2004, 691–751.

[44] World Bank database, Trading Across Borders. http://www.doingbusiness.org/data/exploretopics/trading-across-borders

[45] *China Daily*, 26.7.2016.

[46] World Bank database, Logistics Performance Index. http://lpi.worldbank.org/

industries were preferred but there was a confidence that the benefits would eventually 'trickle-down' to help the poorer elements of society. There was an almost technocratic belief that by filling the 'investment gap' such foreign assistance would trigger a process of 'self-sustained' growth. After years of waiting in vain for these efforts to bear fruit, and years of watching local elites enrich themselves, this approach was abandoned. Rural and grass-roots development became more popular and increased attention was paid to questions of governance at both local and national levels. The record of this new approach is mixed. Outside China, most of the poor are lifted from poverty when process for primary products (and especially agricultural goods) are relatively high compared to industrial goods. Within China, which has made the greatest contribution to the diminution of world poverty, it has been the outcome of the Chinese 'development model'.

China's OBOR policy differs from this Western effort in several important respects. One major difference is that OBOR is in the form of loans, rather than grants. A second is that China hopes to create the space for development by moving to higher value-added industries and allowing lower-value added enterprises to flourish anew where labour costs are lower. In theory, the provision of loans rather than grants should make the recipient more conscientious in selecting projects, knowing that the sums will need to be repaid. In practice, however, corrupt elites hope to be long gone before repayments are due or else they are hopeful that the degree of commitment shown from the donor will tie them into giving further loans (a form of 'donor capture'). In respecting country's sovereignty and following a policy of non-interference, China has side-stepped the governance issue but it cannot remain immune from its effects. Poor governance and corruption do not just deflect resources away from productive investment, they also suck the life-blood from the local entrepreneurship necessary if OBOR investment is ever to spark large-scale economic development.

Perhaps connectivity and trade facilitation are the answer. Western aid in the past has generally not placed a high priority on infrastructure, though the Asian Development Bank (ADB) has performed better than most in this respect. Perhaps roads and railways, ports and power stations will provide the charge to unlock the potential latent in less developed countries and allow their populations to break out of vicious cycles of poverty. If not then all the underutilised investment will become the cause of a debt bondage that will crush the remaining sparks of development potential.

Neither development assistance nor the transfer of development models has a good track record of success. It is too early to judge whether OBOR will succeed. If it does succeed it will reopen the land routes to commerce between the development nodes of Europe and the Far East, and will rekindle prosperity in the lands of Central, South and South-East Asia. If it fails, well, we have Western precedents aplenty to deal with that situation as well.

CHAPTER FOUR

The Northern Routes

Since 1916 there has been a continuous Eurasian railway that has linked Moscow in the West to the Vladivostok on the Pacific Ocean. The 10555km Trans-Siberian Railway requires no changes in railway gauge on its route nor stops for customs duties and other border formalities. The passenger train runs on alternate days and it takes seven days to reach its destination. In 2008 the railway also carried 600,000 containers (or TEUs, twenty foot equivalents), mostly for domestic transport and for direct trade. Transit trade in that year was only 29,000 TEU[1]. China's industrial heartlands, however, lie much further south from the Trans-Siberian railroad and the already congested domestic network means it may not always make sense to look for the shortest connection. Nevertheless, at some stage on a journey to Europe it makes sound economic sense to connect with the Trans-Siberian railway. This, in turn, requires maintaining good relations with Russia which sees itself still as a superpower in the region, and which is a competitor for influence in Central Asian states such as Kazakhstan.

---

[1] D. Macheret, Development of the transit potential of the Trans-Siberian Railway. Powerpoint Presentation, Geneva, 18-20 November 2009.

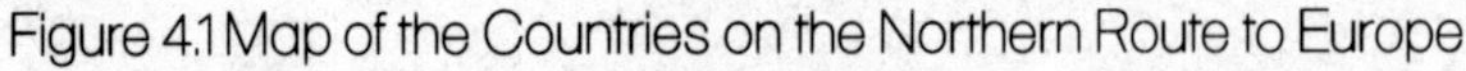

Figure 4.1 Map of the Countries on the Northern Route to Europe

In this chapter we will examine the two northern rail routes from China to Europe. The first runs through Western China, Kazakhstan and Russia before arriving in Germany via Belarus and Poland. The second route links cities and ports in Eastern China to the existing Trans-Siberian Railway either directly through Russia or through Mongolia. The chapter first describes some of the basic demographic and economic data of the countries involved before looking at the more important institutional frameworks fostering cooperation between them. The position of both Russia and Mongolia are particularly interesting since neither country was mentioned in the original OBOR plans. The more detailed study of relations with Kazakhstan will be reserved for Chapter 5 on Central Asia.

The basic details of the countries along the Northern routes are shown in Table 4.1. In physical terms the countries we are dealing with are huge. The Russian Federation is the largest country in the world and even though its landmass is only half that of Russia, China is the world's third largest country. Kazakhstan is the world's ninth largest and Mongolia eighteenth. By way of comparison, the largest country in the EU is France, which has an area of 640,000 km^2 and ranks forty-first. Belarus is by far the smallest in the group. It lies eighty-fourth, but is still significantly larger in size than England and Wales combined.

Table 4.1 Basic details of the Countries involved in the Northern Routes

	Area	Population	Per capita GDP
	Km2	Thousands	Current US$
China	9,596,961	1,376,049	7,617
Belarus	207,600	9,496	8,014
Kazakhstan	2,724,900	17,625	12,436
Mongolia	1,564,116	2,959	4,147
Russia	17,098,242	143,457	12,898

Sources: Area http://unstats.un.org/unsd/environment/totalarea.htm;
Population https://esa.un.org/unpd/wpp/Download/Standard/Population/
pc GDP http://data.un.org/Search.aspx?q=GDP+per+capita

The contrast between these countries is even greater when the comparison is made in terms of population. China is the world's most populous country whilst the Russian Federation is ninth in the rankings. Kazakhstan, with a population slightly more than that of the Netherlands, lies sixty-third in world rankings. Belarus and Mongolia trail far behind. Turning to income, despite three decades of stupendous growth, China is not a rich country. The Russian Federation and Kazakhstan are both richer while Mongolia is by far the poorest of the group. By way of contrast, the per capita income of Germany, the end destination for that original shipment of rail freight, is $47,822.

Before December 1991, both Kazakhstan and Belarus had been part of the Soviet Union, and they obtained their independence after its collapse. Mongolia owes its independence from China in 1921 to the military intervention of the Soviet army, and for much of its subsequent existence it has been one of the Soviet Union's satellite states. In the 1990s China rapidly supplanted the Russian Federation as Mongolia's major trading partner, but more recently, through the supply of energy, Russia has regained some of its economic and political influence.

Even after gaining independence, the physical and commercial infrastructure of Kazakhstan and Belarus, like many of the other former republics, still bore the imprint of a long history of relations with Russia. Russian leaders still see the whole region of the former Soviet Union as part of their 'sphere of interest' (or their 'near abroad' if we adopt Kremlin terminology) and tried to hold the area together in a Commonwealth of Independent States (CIS). As the CIS began to fragment, in March 1996 Russia, Kazakhstan and Belarus formed the nucleus of a Eurasian Economic Community (EAEC) together with Tajikistan and, for a while, Uzbekistan (2005–8). In 2009 Russia, Kazakhstan and Belarus agreed to form a Eurasian Customs Union (EACU) among themselves, which came into effect a year later.[2] Like all customs unions, this has the effect of eliminating all import tariffs and quantitative restrictions among the member states and erecting a common barrier to trade with the rest of the world. Depending on the complementarity and competitiveness of the production structures in the member countries, the effect should be to promote intra-regional trade, possibly at the expense of trade with non-member countries. Recent research has indeed suggested has been the case with the EACU, and especially towards China.[3] Tariff barriers, however, are not a major impediment to trade in the region.

Table 4.2 Trade Cost Indicators of China and the Countries on the Northern Routes

	MFN Applied Tariffs		Border Compliance (Imports)		Logistics Performance Index
	Non-Agriculture	Agriculture			
	Simple Average %		Time (hours)	Cost (US$)	Rank n/160
China	9.0	15.6	158	360	27
Belarus	7.3	10.7	327	1664	120
Kazakhstan	7.3	10.7	344	709	77
Mongolia	4.9	5.1	280	667	108
Russia	7.3	10.8	276	1743	99

Sources: MFN Tariffs: WTO, ITC, UNCTAD, *World Tariff Profiles*,Geneva, 2016; Border Compliance: Wold Bank, Doing Business, http://www.doingbusiness.org/data/exploretopics/trading-across-borders; LPI: World Bank, LPI Global Ranking (2016) http://lpi.worldbank.org/international/global

2 R. Dragneva and K. Wolczuk, *Russia, the Eurasian Customs Union and the EU: Cooperation, Stagnation or Rivalry?*, Chatham House Briefing Paper, August 2012; I. Dreyer and N. Popescu, *The Eurasian Customs Union: The Economics and the Politics*, ISS Brief, November 2014; H-M. Wolffgang, G. Brovka and I. Belozerov, 'The Eurasian Customs Union in Transition', *World Customs Journal*, 7/2, 2013, 93–103.

3 A. Khitakhunov, B. Mukhamediyev and R. Pomfret, 'Eurasian Economic Union: Present and Future Perspectives', *Economic Change and Restructuring*, 2016.

The details of some of the trade impediments are shown in Table 4.2. Average applied tariff levels were not high but one must always remember that these are averages, and that they can conceal some high peaks of protection for certain products. Using this indicator, China is more protectionist than the rest of the group and Mongolia the most open. On the other hand, Russia, China and to a lesser extent Kazakhstan rely heavily on quantitative restrictions (QRs) on their trade, the effect of which can be much more restrictive than tariffs.[4]

The World Bank's Doing Business Survey includes a category for trading across borders. It measures the time and cost of border compliance and time and cost of assembling the necessary documentation. All the calculations are for a small to medium-sized enterprise importing and exporting one container of goods. Since imports are standardised in that they are all one container of car parts from a major supplier, its calculation is best suited for comparison. China is by far the most efficient in both time and costs in processing its container of car parts, whereas Russia and Belarus are time-consuming and tearfully expensive. However, the ease in engaging in international trade is not simply a question of what happens at a border, but of organising the entire shipment from its point of origin to its final destination. To this end the World Bank has constructed a Logistics Performance Index based on a survey conducted among logistics managers, supplemented with quantitative data on the performance of key components of the logistics chain in the country in each of 160 countries.[5] China ranks best in the index with twenty-seventh place, far ahead of Kazakhstan and Russia. The worst country is Belarus with a ranking of 120th.

---

[4] CEPII NTM-MAP database. http://www.cepii.fr/cepii/en/bdd_modele/presentation.asp?id=28 The range of such restrictions is measured by the number of items covered and the proportion of total imports that they represent (the latter having already been affected by the imposition of QRs). Russia is the worst offender with 28.2% of items covered by QRs representing 34.9% of its imports. China performs marginally better with QRs on 19.7% items in their trade classification, covering 27.5% of total imports. Kazakhstan has QRs on only 11.2% of items but that still covers 24.6% of its imports.

[5] It includes an assessment of customs, but it also incorporates the quality of trade and transport services, the ease of arranging international shipments, the quality of logistics services (trucking, forwarding and customs brokerage), the ability to track and trace consignments and the likelihood that goods arrive within the scheduled delivery times.

The Yuxinou Railway

Every week an express train will leave from a special loading yard in Chongqing on the start of its 11,179 km journey to Duisburg. This will happen three times a week; five in the peak season. The service is run by Trans Eurasia Logistics, a joint venture between Germany's national rail company Deutsche Bahn and Russian Railways. Chongqing itself is an industrial city of some 29 million inhabitants situated at the point where the Jialing River flows into the giant Yangtze. Its population has almost doubled in the last twenty years and its economic base has diversified into chemicals, electronics and motor vehicles for domestic consumption and export. However, the city is 1800 km from the seaport of Shanghai, so transport to Europe by sea would first entail a long haul in the wrong direction.

Ten years ago, virtually all the trade between China and Europe went by sea – slightly over 4% by train. Road and air transport scarcely figured at all. Air transport was prohibitively expensive, and rail was not only more expensive than by container ship, but took much longer as well. By 2014 the direct railway connection had been changed the situation dramatically. The data that we have is shown in Figure 4.2. The first thing to note is that the two routes are not comparable. In 2004, the train had to cover the entire coast-to-coast distance, whereas in 2014 it started 2000 km further inland, which may explain much of the difference. However rail was still more expensive. In 2014, trains are much faster, though now it is the goods carried by ship that had to undertake the 2000 km overland journey (which also contributed one third to the final price). The picture presented today suggests that air freight is only profitable for high value goods where speed of delivery is essential. Rail, too, might offer advantages for high value goods by allowing firms to hold smaller inventories but would be uncompetitive for low value bulk traffic for which there is no premium for faster delivery.[6]

[6] C. Rastogi and J-F. Arvis, *The Eurasian Connection. Supply-Chain Efficiency along the Modern Silk Route through Central Asia,* Washington DC. 2014, 40–9.

Figure 4.2 Cost Time Comparison of Europe–China Trade by different means 2004 and 2014

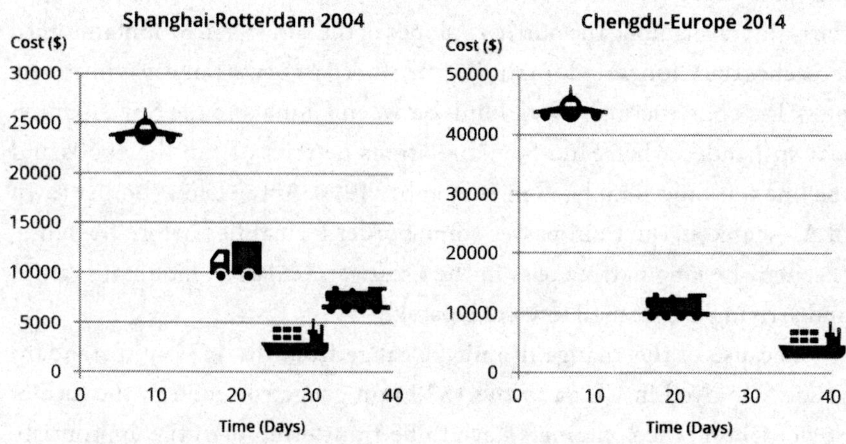

Sources 2004: US Chamber of Commerce, *Land Transport Options between Europe and Asia*, Washington DC, 2006. 2014: CAREC, *Corridor Performance Measurement and Monitoring. Annual Report, 2014*, 2015, 41.

One of the reasons behind the improved performance of rail is that trains like the Yuxinou express are 'block trains'. This means that it will travel as one unit from start to finish. This obviates the need for any stops for decoupling and coupling of wagons and it also makes possible a single set of documents for the whole journey. Each train from Chongqing will transport 41 FUE containers (forty foot unit equivalent containers) filled with a cargo notebooks, display instruments, flat screen TVs, hard disks, LED lightings, automobile spare parts and portable remote controls for games. The loading in Chongqing is practised and smooth, with special loading bays and bonded warehouses, cutting the 'dwell time' for cargo at the start of the journey. The customs controls and loading can be completed in less than a day.[7] The train soon leaves the more urbanised parts of China and travels through a vast territory with few inhabitants and with towns and cities few and far between. It is in fact skirting the Taklimakan Desert, shadowing the former northern route of the Silk Road. The journey times have been reduced by the opening in December 2014 of a 1176 km high-speed passenger line from Lanzhou to

[7] CAREC, *Corridor Performance Measurement and Monitoring. Annual Report, 2014*, 2015

Urumqi, the capital of Xinjiang province.[8] The advantage of the high-speed line is that it clears the conventional line for freight traffic – at least that is the rationale. Having passed the city of Urumqi with its 3 million inhabitants, the train travels along the northern slopes of the Tina Shan Mountains until it reaches the Chinese side of the border. This part of the railway is relatively new. The construction of a rail link between China and the Soviet Union was suspended when Sino-Soviet relations deteriorated in the 1960s and the line was only completed in September 1990. At the China border town of Alashankou, the train passes some border formalities before travelling through the long narrow pass in the Dzungaria/Ala-Tau mountain range, and arriving at the small town of Dostyk.

Because of the change in railway gauge from the 1435 mm standard gauge employed in China to the 1520 mm gauge common in the former Soviet Union, the containers have to be transferred onto the appropriate rolling stock. This operation is always performed at the incoming border crossing point (BCP) and the capacity at Dostyk in Kazakhstan is cramped (and its location unsuitable for enlargement)[9] Customs clearance is quick: because of the special documentation carried by the express train, the whole operation should only take a few hours. However, delays are common and so it often takes a day or two (at most). Once the train leaves Dostyk there are no further customs controls or gauge changes until arriving at the Polish border. The train travels northwards past the new Kazakh capital of Astana, crosses the border at Kairak/Troitsk and then links with the Trans-Siberian Railway at Yekaterinburg. When the train reaches the BCP at Małaszewicze in Poland, it requires another gauge change, back to standard gauge and from there it progresses to its final destination in Duisburg.

It is worth examining this journey in a little more detail because, if you are like me, you may be thinking that the time of the journey depends primarily on the speed of the train and that shortening that time hinges on increasing the speed of the train. In this line of thinking, your solutions

[8] The 403 km extension from Lanzhou eastward to Baoij is scheduled to become operational in 2017.

[9] This was recognised over ten years ago, and there were plans to move the facilities to a larger site at Aktogai 310 km away and construct a double track corridor, including one with standard gauge. See K.K. Zhangaskin, 'Trans-Kazakhstan Link will Complete Standard-Gauge Transcontinental Artery', *Railway Gazette*, 1.8.2004.

will drift towards more powerful locomotives and improved track, and at the pinnacle of your expectation will be the high-speed rail – gleaming stream-lined trains travelling at speeds of 300-350 km/hr. Of course, all of these improvements will eventually cut the journey time between China and Europe. However much of the problem lies not in the speed of train when it is moving, but in the time it stands still.

The Yuxinou express is privileged. It carries special documentation and it is afforded priority treatment. Counting loading times at the beginning and end of the journeys, the whole journey in 2014 averaged 447 hours, or eighteen and a half days. Of this time, only 343 hours were spent moving forward. The remaining 104 were spent waiting. This included loading and unloading at each end of the journey as well as the two transfers of cargo necessitated by the gauge changes. In addition, time was lost on changes of crew, changes of engine and safety inspections. Another source of lost time, from which the express is spared, is frequent diversion onto loops or sidings in order for faster passenger trains to pass. In this respect, spending much of the time travelling through the middle of nowhere was an advantage. Nevertheless, when discounting all the delays the average speed of the Yuxinou express was only 33 km/hr. This was far slower than the 50-60 km/hr achieved by conventional freight on other routes.[10] The reason for the discrepancy lay in the fact that Chinese and Central Asian wagons are subjected to slack actions that can send strong shocks to wagons near the end of the train. As a result drivers need deliberately to reduce speeds to prevent damage to sensitive cargo. The advantage of being an express train comes when the overall speed is considered. The express averaged a total journey speed of 25 km/hr whereas the other two routes averaged speeds of 10 and 7 km/hr respectively. All trains crossed the border at the same Alashankou and Dostyk BCP, but whereas the express had no lost time at the Chinese side of the border, other trains often had to wait until there was room to receive them in Dostyk and, once they had arrived in Dostyk, there were further delays while waiting their turn to change gauge, or waiting for wagons to become available, or changing composition in the marshalling yards. A second reason for delay was inside the Chinese railway terminals at

[10] Trains on the 4619 km of the Chongqing–Almaty route averaged 60 kmh and those on the 1281 km Urumqi–Almaty route managed 50 kmh.

Xi'an, Lanzhou and Urumqi. At each of these stations, waiting for 'priority trains' to pass averaged twenty to thirty hours. Combine the two and it is easy to see how conventional freight trains could spend slightly over 80% of their journey time simply waiting.[11]

Russia

With a regular freight service from China to Europe already running through Russia[12], the authorities could not be blamed for being perplexed by their country's total omission from China's announcement of the overland Silk Road initiative in September 2013. Moreover, the semi-official map, issued by the Chinese news bureau in May 2014 showed an overland route that seemed deliberately to skirt south of Russian territory. There were also other good reasons for Kremlin officials to feel piqued, In the first place, China's proposals seemed to be encouraging the creation of an alternative framework for the existing institutional arrangements that Russia had helped create. Second, the speech was made in the capital of Kazakhstan, and Kazakhstan was a member of the Russian-conceived and Russian-led EACU and its successor initiative, agreed in January 2012, for complementing the already existing customs union with a single market for goods, services, capital and labour, and the coordination of industrial, transport, energy and agricultural policies. China's initiatives seemed to cut across all these achievements. Some Russian officials saw this as a demonstration of their country's diminishing status as a regional superpower and argued that they should pressure the Central Asian states into not participating in the Chinese project.[13] The fact that nothing of the kind happened was due to the growing crisis in the Ukraine.

In November 2013 the pro-Russian Ukrainian President Yanukovych

---

[11] CAREC, *Corridor Performance*, 39-45.

[12] Robert H. Donaldson and Joseph L Nogee, *The Foreign Policy of Russia: Changing Systems, Enduring Interests*, London, New York, 2014; B. Lo, *Russia and the New World Disorder*, London, 2015; N. Robinson (ed.), *The Political Economy of Russia*, Lanham, MA, 2013; P. Sutela, *The Political Economy of Putin's Russia*, Abingdon, 2012; A.P. Tsygankov, *Russia's Foreign Policy: Change and Continuity*, Lanham, MA, 2016.

[13] A. Gabuev, 'Post-Soviet States Jostle For Role in One Belt One Road Initiative', *HKTDC Research*, 6.8.2015.

announced the suspension of talks with the European Union in favour of closer ties with the Russian Federation. This decision prompted protests and disturbances in Kiev that culminated in the president fleeing the country in February 2014. So began the Ukrainian crisis that has led to the Russian annexation of the Crimea and the civil war in the east of the country. The West responded with an escalating series of economic sanctions that included the freezing of financial assets and bans on the export of strategic products.[14] Faced with increasing isolation in the West, Russia (in almost a caricature of the two-headed eagle on its emblem) turned its attention to the East.

The Chinese reaction to the Crimea/Ukraine crisis was sympathetic to the Russian position. Relations between the two countries became warmer and more collaborative, involving currency swaps, energy projects and several declarations of good neighbourliness and friendship. It also involved an assurance by Russia that it was preparing an agreement that would associate the OBOR project with its own plans for a Eurasian Economic Union.[15] Relations took a step further during a State visit to Beijing in May 2014, Presidents Putin and Xi finalised a gas and pipeline deal between Gazprom and China National Petroleum Corporation (CNPC) that had been under negotiation for almost a decade. The deal involved an undertaking over a thirty-year period to supply China with gas worth $400 billion. Deliveries of 38 billion cubic metres (bcm) would start in 2020, by which time China (through pre-payment) would have funded $80 billion worth of new production and pipeline infrastructure.[16] It was Gazprom's largest contract ever and the Russians committed themselves to $55 billion in pipeline construction costs while China would pay $22 billion.[17] Gazprom, which accounts for more than 10% of Russia's export revenues, was hoping that the project to

[14] H.B.L. Larsen, *Great Power Politics and the Ukrainian Crisis: NATO, EU and Russia after 2014*, Report 2014:18, Copenhagen: DIIS, Danish Institute for International Studies; R. Sakwa, *Frontline Ukraine: Crisis in the Borderlands*, London, 2015; D. Trenin, *The Ukraine Crisis and the Resumption of Great-Power Rivalry*, Moscow, 2014.

[15] A. Gabuev, *A 'Soft Alliance'? Russia China Relations after the Ukraine Crisis*, European Council on Foreign Relations, Policy Brief, 2015.

[16] J. Koch-Weser and C. Murray, *The China–Russia Gas Deal: Background and Implications for the Broader Relationship*, U.S.–China Economic and Security Review Commission Staff Research Backgrounder, 9.6.2014.

[17] *Russian Times*, 21.5.2014.

supply gas to China would reduce its dependence on exports to Europe.[18] There were to be two routes – a 3200 km eastern route linking the Chayanda oil and gas field to the Pacific coast, and to China and a 3000 km western route from the fields in the Altai region to Xinjiang, known as the Power of Siberia-1 and -2 respectively. China consented to the Russians issuing an open tender for the project with the intention of winning it themselves. However such hopes were dashed when a Gazprom director reportedly stated, 'we do not need Chinese men and equipment here, we never did and never will'.[19]

Almost a year later China officially started work on the construction of its side of the Power of Siberia-1, which would stretch from the border town of Heihi to Shanghai. On the Russian side, 455 kms of pipeline had been laid by the end of 2016, and a further 663 kms were planned for 2017. Gazprom's investment in the pipeline was estimated at $2.7 billion.[20] However work on the Power of Siberia-2 pipeline link to China was suspended indefinitely in July 2015 because of low energy prices and the slow-down in the Chinese economy.[21] Gazprom was suffering serious liquidity problems since it had been denied access to Western capital markets by sanctions imposed in the wake of the Ukrainian crisis. China agreed in late 2015 to increase its stake in a $27 billion liquefied natural gas project in the Arctic that was blocked from dollar financing. In March 2016 the Bank of China granted Gazprom a five-year $2.17 billion loan. Chinese prepayments for supplies from Russian state oil firm OAO Rosneft have provided an alternative form of financing. Russia's second largest gas producer, OAO Novatek (on the US sanctions list), was also looking to conclude a deal with China for financing its Arctic LNG plant, which would start deliveries to Asia in 2017.[22]

---

[18] J. Marson and A. Ostroukh, 'Gazprom Secures $2.17 Billion Loan From Bank of China', *Wall Street Journal*, 3.3.2016.

[19] Economist Intelligence Unit (2016)*'One Belt, One Road': An Economic Roadmap*, London, 61-62; S. Su, 'Risky Business: Financing "One Belt, One Road"', *Foreign Brief*, 23.8.2016.

[20] *TASS*, 28.2.2017; 10.3.2017.

[21] *Russian Times*, 22.7.2015.

[22] Marson and Ostroukh, 'Gazprom'. See also J. Henderson and T. Mitrova, *Energy Relations betweenRussia and China: Playing Chess with the Dragon*, Oxford Institute for Energy Studies, Working Paper 67, 2016.

Meanwhile, it was to take twelve months before China officially recognised the EAEU and indicated its willingness in principle to deal with it as a body rather than to talk directly with individual states. This occurred on President Xi's visit to Moscow commemorate the seventieth anniversary of Russia's victory in the 'Great Patriotic War'. It remains to be seen what this is worth in practice. While Moscow is busy writing up rules, the reality is that China has no overall timetable for OBOR projects and has little patience or practice with multilateral dealing. At best, Russia will hope to obtain some benefits from the investments involved (most of which will come from China) while maintaining some influence on the region as the dominant hard security provider.[23]

The first project announced as part of the agreement was for the construction of a high-speed passenger service between Moscow and Kazan which, when completed, would cut the time on the 770 km line from fourteen hours to three and a half. China agreed to invest $5.2 billion in the project ($4.3 billion as a twenty-year loan and the remainder as equity).[24] In October the German firm Siemens opened the prospect of funding $2 billion, which would be intended to provide equipment and rolling stock.[25] Siemens had already provided the high-speed trains, called *Sapsan* ('peregrine falcon' in Russian) for the Moscow–St Petersburg line which had started operation in December 2009.[26] By early 2017 the sums quoted as required for the whole project had risen to $22.4 billion, including rail and locomotives. The latter would be produced in Russia, possibly as part of a joint venture between Siemens and the China Railway Rolling Stock Corporation (CRRC).[27]

While all the talk was about building a Russian HSR to Kazan, and expressing the intention of eventually extending the route all the way to Beijing, everyone seems to have forgotten about the Trans-Siberian Railway. This already carries the Yuxinou express trains westwards to Europe, but

---

[23] Gabuev, 'Post-Soviet States'.

[24] *Russian Times*, 30.3.2015.

[25] *TASS*, 14.10.2015. By November 2016 the sum had risen to $3 billion, with the prospect of a further $0.8 billion later, *TASS*, 15.11.2016.

[26] S. Fischer, *Sapsan: A Parable of Russian Modernisation*, ISS Analysis, December 2010

[27] *TASS*, 28.2.2017.

it also connects Moscow to Vladivostok. It is worth looking at again, because it shows how it is possible to cut journey times without recourse to expensive infrastructural investment. Today the passenger train takes six and a half days to complete the journey but because they are longer and heavier, the freight trains used to take almost twice as long, completing the journey in twelve days. In 2009 the Russian railway authorities adopted an audacious plan to cut that time to seven days,[28] and finally, in May 2013, they succeeded. A seventy-one-wagon express train completed the journey from the port of Nakhoda to Moscow in exactly seven days. Nakhoda is a Pacific commercial port that serves container traffic from Japan. There is now a twice-weekly 'express train' service between the two stations. The conventional freight service still takes eleven to fourteen days.[29]

So how was this impressive achievement attained? The first improvement involved enhancing the logistics at the port itself so that the goods were loaded expeditiously. The second was that the train made no stops at intervening stations. Finally, the number of routine stops en route was also reduced – technical inspections of the freight were cut from seven to three, the change of crews cut from thirty-three to twenty-seven and the time-consuming changes in locomotive were reduced to seven. Further savings could still be squeezed by streamlining the processing of documentation, improving the coordination with other traffic on the line, cutting unnecessary speed restrictions and trimming the time taken at the remaining routine stops. Combined with further improvements on the lines themselves and new rolling stock, the average speed could be raised to 100 km/hr for much of the track, allowing 1500 kms to be covered in a day and shaving almost another twenty-four hours from the time.[30]

While much of the attention in Europe at least has been focussed on the direct connections between Chinese and European cities, it is often forgotten that the plans for OBOR issued in March 2015 had specifically called for improvement in the railway links connecting the provinces in the north of China with Russia's Far East region with the aim opening the

---

[28] *Railway Gazette*, 5.5.2009.

[29] *Railway Gazette*, 23.5.2013.

[30] P. Kaderaveh, 'China-Europe Link: How Russia Succeeds?', *RAIL Turkey*, 14.1.2015.

economic potential of the North.[31] This is a highly sensitive area. In the mid-19th century, when the Chinese empire had been embroiled by war and rebellion, Tsarist Russia annexed huge swathes of territory along the Amur and Ussuri rivers. In the late 1960s a territorial dispute occurred along the Amur River that almost pitched the two countries into a full-scale war.[32] Running parallel to a stretch of the river was a canal, and between them lay an 'island' known as Bear Island. Russian maps claimed both banks of the river as its border, including the canal as part of the river. Various Chinese governments had been in no position to contest the claims and the dispute had remained latent for decades. The area was sparsely populated, the border lightly defended and the local population had gone about its daily business without much interference. However, the issue regained salience in the 1960s with the deterioration in Sino-Soviet relations and the emergence of a more strident Chinese government during the 'cultural revolution'. The Soviet Union, realising the unfavourable demographic balance in the region, stepped up the intensity of its border patrols whilst the Chinese government backed the local economic rights enjoyed by the (largely Chinese) population. In late 1968/early 1969 the confrontations between the border patrols of the two sides spilled over into military clashes, leading in March 1969 to a Soviet attempt, backed by tanks and artillery, to occupy one of the contested islands. When this was successfully repulsed by the Chinese, the situation was delicately poised between de-escalation and outright war. Both sides agreed to pull back their troops. The border dispute remained frozen until 1986 when the Soviet leadership, exhausted by the Afghan war and the burden of maintaining high troop levels in the Far East, accepted the Chinese principle that when rivers marked borders the demarcation line should lie in the middle as the basis for a settlement. That still left the issue of the disputed islands. In 2005 Russia finally relinquished its claims in the area and resolved the dispute, thus removing one obstacle to improved relations between the two sides.

31 PRC, National Development and Reform Commission, *Vision and Actions*.

32 N. Maxwell, 'How the Sino-Russian Boundary Conflict was Finally Settled: From Nerchinsk 1689 to Vladivostok 2005 via Zhenbao Island 1969', *Slavic-Eurasian Studies*, 16/2, 2006, 47–72; K. Yang, 'The Sino-Soviet Border Clash of 1969: From Zhenbao Island to Sino-American Rapprochement', *Cold War History*, 1/1, 2000, 21–52.

The city of Harbin is one of the designated OBOR hubs within China. It is the largest city in the North-West with 5 million inhabitants and it boasts a wide range of light industry. A high-speed passenger line connecting Harbin to Beijing has been operating since December 2013. It is from here that the new network in the North-East will radiate. One route follows the twice-weekly passenger service running south-east from Harbin to Suifenhe, on the border with Russia. The 480 km journey takes a shade under nine hours. At the BCP there is a time-consuming change in locomotives before the train continues at an excruciating slow pace to cover the remaining 93 km to Ussuriysk in four hours; and there is still another 98 km before reaching Vladivostok. Little wonder, therefore, that the Provincial authorities preferred to look westward. A second route from Harbin north-west to the BCP at Manzhouli/Zabykutsk in the Inner Mongolia Autonomous Region where it would cross into Russia and connect with the trans-Siberian railway at Chita.[33] In June 2013 the first regular weekly freight service to Europe started on this route, taking trains straight through to Hamburg.[34] There are also plans for a more direct northern connection from Harbin to the town of Heihi. This would require the building of a railway bridge across the Amur River between Heihi and the Russian town of Blagoveshchensk, which would be the first rail bridge between the two countries. The two towns are only 700 metres apart, but to travel between them by car would involve a journey of 3500km. The two cities belong to a common free trade zone, but without a bridge there is little trade, and the lack of trade is used as an excuse to justify not constructing an expensive bridge. But the Chinese side has a heavy industrial region and the Russian side already connects with the Trans-Siberian Railway.[35] The plans were agreed in 2008 but nothing happened. A new agreement was signed in 2013, with China undertaking the construction of 2.2 km of the bridge and Russia the remaining 0.3 km and the station and logistics on the other side (remember the gauge change). However, wrangles over funding and specifications, mostly on the Russian side, have delayed the project.[36] In total it is estimated to cost $425 million,

[33] *Global Times*, 2.4.2015.

[34] *Russia Beyond the Headlines*, 22.5.2015.

[35] Greater Tumin Initiative, *Integrated Transport Infrastructure*, 14.

[36] M. Lyotova, 'Российско-Китайский мост пока строит только Китай' *газетный бизнес Ведомости*, 20.4.2015 (Only China is Building the Russia–China Bridge).

and although the Chinese end is scheduled to be completed on time, work only started on the Russian side in December 2016.[37]

For trains travelling from further south and trying to connect with the Trans-Siberian Railway, there is a route through Mongolia crossing the border at Erenhot/Zamyn Uud.

Mongolia

As was the case with Russia, Mongolia[38] was also beginning to worry about its place in the new Chinese order. Unlike Russia, which had not been central to the history of the Silk Road, the intervals of peace during Mongol rule in China and military dominance over much of Central Asia in the long centuries between 1200 and 1400 coincided with some of its most prosperous periods.[39] Mongolia, with a vast area and a small population, is one of the least densely populated countries on the planet; it lies uncomfortably sandwiched between Russia and China. Relations with China were traditionally cool but they softened in the 1990s with the opening of new border crossings that greatly boosted bilateral trade.[40] By 2012, China had become Mongolia's main trading partner, taking 93% of its exports. On the back of the boom in mineral processing and China's almost insatiable demand for minerals and raw materials, the Mongolian economy grew rapidly, but as the Chinese economy slowed and raw material prices fell, the Mongolian economy slumped. By 2016, it was in deep financial trouble. However, while the boom lasted, the dependence on China was a source of festering resentment, and a kind of 'resource nationalism' entered Mongolian politics.

[37] *Russian Times*, 24.12.2016. The plans are to construct a road bridge first and then build the rail bridge alongside it. Hwoever, in February 2017 the China Investment Corporation released $110 million to allow the Russians to make a start on their side of the rail bridge. *Yibada*, 9.2.2017.

[38] O. Bruun and O. Odgaard (eds.), *Mongolia in Transition. Old Patterns, New Challenges*, Abingdon, 1996; C. Kaplonski, Creating National Identity in Socialist Mongolia, *Central Asian Survey*, 17/1, 1998, 35–49; D. Sneath and C. Kaplonski, *The History of Mongolia, Volume Three*, Biggleswade, Bedfordshire, 2010.

[39] A.J. Campi, 'Mongolia's Place in China's "One Belt, One Road"', Jamestown Foundation, *China Brief*, 15/16, 18.8.2015.

[40] A.J. Campi, 'Sino-Mongolian Relations from Beijing's Viewpoint', Jamestown Foundation, *China Brief*, 5/10, 5.5.2005.

In May 2012 the parliament amended its Foreign Investment Law so as to require approval of all foreign investment in the mining, finance, media and telecommunications sectors by a state-owned foreign investor or organization regardless of level of ownership. This was immediately used to block the efforts of the state-controlled Aluminum Corporation of China from taking a controlling stake in the Ovoot Tolgoi coal-mine.[41] China's response was remarkably restrained, limited only to pressing for a stable legal environment for bilateral trade and investment. At the same time the Mongolian authorities tried to diversify the market for their mineral exports by exploring the possibility of raising $250 million to improve rail connections to the North, and onwards to Japan and Korea.[42] South Korean companies won a $483 million contract for building contract to build the 267 km railway from the Tavan Tolgoi coal field to the Chinese border (using Russian gauge) and for constructing a 365 km highway between the capital Ulaanbaatar and the northern border town Altanbulag, the site of a Mongolian–Russian free trade zone.[43]

While Mongolia was trying to reduce reliance on China as a market, it was also concerned to reduce its reliance on Russia as a supplier. Mongolia imports 100% of its refined oil and diesel, 90% of it from Russia. The impact of this dependence was brought home when in May 2011, in response to petrol shortages in Russia, the Russian authorities temporarily suspended exports. Ironically, Mongolia's domestic oil production was entirely in the hands of the Chinese. This had not been the original intention. When, after the fall of communism, the government allowed foreign bidding for contracts, China had been deliberately excluded, but all the early entrants (American, Canadian and Japanese) had later sold out to Chinese firms. Thus, the government had no alternative but to cooperate with China in expanding domestic output. The oil is exported to China for refining and a guaranteed proportion is returned as refined oil. At the same time, the

[41] A.J. Campi, 'Mongolia's Coal Development Policies Tied to Goal of Reducing Proportion of Chinese Investment', Jamestown Foundation, *Eurasia Daily Monitor*, 9/159, 4.9.2012.

[42] A.J. Campi, 'The Bumpy Path to Sino-Mongolian Cooperation in the Mining Sector', Jamestown Foundation, *China Brief*, 13, 3, 1.2.2013.

[43] A.J. Campi, 'Sino-Mongolian Coal Relationship Continues Downward Spiral in 2013' Jamestown Foundation, *China Brief*, 13/17, 23.8.2013.

government wanted a state oil refinery, with a capacity for 2 million tons (and constructed with the help of Japanese technology), to be functional by 2015.[44]

In September 2014 the heads of state of Mongolia, China and Russia met for the first time in Dushanbe. At that meeting President Tsahiagiin Elbegdorzj unveiled his 'Steppe Road' (Taliin Zam) plan for Mongolia's economic future that built on his country's central location between Europe and Asia. The $50 billion Steppe Road project combines highway construction, electricity distribution, an extension of the Trans-Mongolia Railway and new natural gas and petroleum pipelines.[45] Chinese support for Mongolia took the form of a 'three-in-one' cooperation model, embracing mineral resources, infrastructure construction and financial cooperation.[46] Over the following three years China agreed to provide Mongolia $260 million in aid for major economic projects and to grant a soft loan worth a further $162.7 million (but with conditions attached that might make it impossible to use much of the money). Six Chinese seaports, including Tianjin and Dalian, were designated to facilitate Mongolian exports to Asian shipping routes and overseas markets and Mongolia was promised easier access to Chinese railways (and a 40% reduction in the price they paid).[47] The three leaders pledged themselves to forging the China–Mongolia–Russia Economic Corridor.[48]

When the Chinese revealed their Vision and Action Plan in March 2015, it mentioned Harbin as a hub for the new Economic Corridor, but said little else.[49] The following month the Mongolian authorities authorised survey work to start on improving the 550 km road from Maanit to Zamyn-Uud, which was intended to facilitate the transport of copper from a Rio Tinto-operated mine at Oyu Tolgoi. At a trilateral foreign ministers' meet-

[44] Campi, 'The Bumpy Path'; A.J. Campi, 'New Sino-Mongolian Oil Deal Undercuts Russia's Old Role', Jamestown Foundation, *China Brief*, 13/10, 9.5.2013.

[45] *Voice of Mongolia*, 24.9.2014.

[46] *China Daily*, 22.8.2014.

[47] A.J. Campi, 'Xi and Putin in Ulaanbaatar: Mongolia's Balancing Act', Jamestown Foundation, *China Brief*, 14/18, 25.9.2014.

[48] A. Panda, 'Russia, China and Mongolia are boosting Trilateral Ties', *The Diplomat*, 13.9.2014

[49] PRC, National Development and Reform Commission, *Vision and Actions*.

ing later in April, agreement was reached to pave the 990 km north–south Altanbulag–Ulaanbaatar–Zamiin–Uud highway. When the project was officially started in May, the Chinese contractor agreed to employ Mongolian companies and labour in the project, creating an estimated 20–30,000 temporary jobs during the construction phase and possibly as many as 50,000 in the new residential zones.[50]

The three leaders held a second meeting in the Russian city of Ufa in July 2015. This saw the official adoption of the Mid-Term Roadmap for Development of Trilateral Co-operation between China, Russia and Mongolia. The joint declaration now explicitly mentioned the incorporation of Mongolia's 'Steppe Road' Programme..[51] On the side-lines, it was agreed to work on building electrical power-lines between Russia and China and improving the Ulan Bator railway.[52] The following month work began on improving the rail links between the Mongolian town of Erenhot on the border with Russia and the Chinese border town of Manzhouli and upgrading the cargo clearance facilities in Erenhot.[53]

In June 2016 the three leaders met again and agreed a thirty-two project package for the Economic Corridor. Among these projects, 13 are focused on transportation infrastructure. However the precise funding arrangements were left open, leaving Mongolia room to find extra backers. The main project involved double-tracking and electrifying the main North-South railway from UlaanUde on the Trans-Siberian Railway to Zamiin Uud/Erenhot and through to the Chinese port of Tianjin. In addition, feasibility studies would be undertaken to build new lines connecting the coal and mineral mines in the North West and in the South to the main-line. Further studies would also be undertaken to link Mongolia to the main road highways and, finally, the countries all agreed to improve the facilities at their respective BCPs.[54]

For those who argue that China's policy represents a skilful use of

---

[50] Campi, 'Mongolia's Place'.

[51] CCTV English, 15.7.2015. (Strategic significance of second meeting by presidents of China, Russia and Mongolia).

[52] TASS, 9.7.2015.

[53] Campi, 'Mongolia's Place'.

[54] *UB Post*, 29.6.2016. Speeches released by the Office of the President of Mongolia, http://www.president.mn/eng/newsCenter/viewNews.php?newsId=1890)

economic diplomacy, the story we have told of its dealings with Mongolia show a remarkable record of sensitivity. All this came to a stop when the Dalai Lama arrived in town in November 2016 for a private, religious visit. It is almost automatic for China to react in incidents as this when a country seems to fail to acknowledge its stance on Tibet. It did so again.[55] China's response began by suspending all bilateral talks, including those on a much needed $4.2 billion emergency loan agreement to stave off financial collapse.[56] By sheer coincidence, this was followed by a decision of Chinese local government to levy transit fees on trucks crossing the border. The sums were not extortionate, but the re-routing of traffic to collect the new levies contributed to such congestion and tailbacks of trucks that Rio Tinto suspended deliveries.[57]

Mongolia responded to the difficulties trying to find an alternative source of support. The usual tactic of turning to Russia was ruled out because of the closeness of Sino-Russian links. The government turned to India by announcing that it would accept the offer of a $1 billion credit line that had been extended by the Indian Prime Minister on a visit eighteen months earlier.[58] The loan was intended to construct an oil refinery, and the necessary pipelines, that would have the capacity to produce all the petroleum and diesel that the country requires.[59] This would reduce its need to use China's to refine its crude oil and reduce its dependence on Russia for refined oil products. India failed to respond in time[60] leaving the authorities with little alternative than to offer the apology demanded by China and to agree that the Dalai Lama would not visit the country again under the current government. The financial talks with China soon resumed and in

---

[55] S. Holcomb, 'A Crisis in Two Parts: Mongolia's Buddhism Question and its Economic Failings' The *McGill International Review*, 16.1.2017.

[56] *South China Morning Post*, 26.11.2016. See also Chinese Ministry of Foreign Affairs, *Foreign Ministry Spokesperson Geng Shuang's Regular Press Conference on November 23, 2016.*

[57] *Reuters*, 1.12.2016; *Financial Times*, 2.12.2016.

[58] *Times of India*, 9.12.2016; *The Diplomat*, 10.12.2016.

[59] *Oxford Business Group*, 7.3.2017 (Mongolia looks to develop its downstream oil industry).

[60] *Sputnik International*, 19.12.2016; S. Ramachandran, 'India Drives Mongolia Into China's Submission', *The Citizen*, 26.12.2016.

February 2017 an IMF rescue package for Mongolia was agreed. China has pledged a currency swap of $2.18 billion while the World Bank, the ADB, Korea and Japan together have agreed to $3 billion in financial aid.[61]

Belarus

Despite the fact that Belarus[62] is the third party to the EACU and has been on the Chongqing–Duisburg route since its inception, it was only on 1 April 2015, during a visit from the foreign minister, Wang Yi, that its government officially endorsed the OBOR project and established formal bilateral co-operation.[63] However, cooperation between the two sides stretches back a little further. When still vice-president, Xi Jinping on a visit to Belarus in March 2010 mooted the creation of a joint industrial park, and an agreement was signed later that year.

The 80 km² site of the so-called Great Stone Industrial Park lies 25 km outside Minsk, close to the international airport, and it was officially opened in June 2014. Companies establishing themselves there enjoy exemption from corporation tax and customs preferences (Belarus government website). Yet despite all the hype afforded to official visits, the sad fact is that Belarus has little to offer China diplomatically or economically. Its technology is far behind that of China and Chinese companies are put off by the Soviet-style management culture and lack of efficiency. Many of the much-vaunted 'investments' that Belarus websites announce are in fact credits awarded to Chinese firms for the sale of Chinese goods. Chinese FDI in the country is pitifully low, and likely to remain so. The only export in which China is interested is potash for fertiliser for use in its agriculture. Development of the park itself has been delayed because of red tape and poor management.[64] In his annual address to the National Assembly in

61 *ECNS.cn*, 21.2.2017.

62 B.M. Bennett, *The Last Dictatorship in Europe: Belarus under Lukashenko*, New York, 2011; V. Smok, *Belarusian Identity: The Impact of Lukashenka's Rule*, Belarus Digest Analytical Paper no. 3, 2013; A. Wilson, *Belarus. The Last European Dictatorship*, New Haven, CT, 2011.

63 *Russian Insider*, 10.4.2015.

64 V. Smok, 'Belarus-China Relations: More Hype Than Substance?' *Belarus Digest*, 22.5.2015.

April 2016, President Alexander Lukashenko deplored the fact that work on the scheme was going from bad to worse, and he threatened that the most severe measures would be taken. The park, he declared, was a place for 'the enterprises for the day after tomorrow' and that there was 'no place for businesses of yesterday and today'.[65] Nevertheless work has pressed ahead, and in May the first consignments of pre-cast metal structures arrived by rail from China.[66] This has been followed up with the appointment of a new management team with closer ties with Chinese technical experts. By September 2016 the authorities were boasting that the Park's infrastructure was almost complete, far ahead of schedule.[67] However, of the target of one hundred participating companies, only eight had finalised agreements, and only two had started construction.[68]

Meanwhile, almost as symmetry to events in Mongolia, Belarus has entered an increasing querulous dispute with Russia. Belarus has long been a typical client state, heavily reliant on largess from its larger neighbour in a deal commonly called 'oil for kisses'. The country regularly fails to pay for its energy imports and then begs, and receives, more lenient terms. On this occasion, however, Russia cut back the supplies of subsidised oil exports. Lukashenko replied by recalling the country's representatives from the EACU and, as part of a move to relax relations with the West, it freed visa entry for visitors from the US and Europe. This provoked a counter response from Russia which then re-established passport controls (also for citizens from Belarus) on their mutual borders. Lukashenko then launched a seven and a half hour tirade against Russia's treatment of his country before assuring his fellow countrymen that the forthcoming military exercises on Belarus territory were not a prelude to war[69]... but after the Ukraine crisis, neighbours have reason to be nervous.

---

[65] A. Lukashenko, Обращение с ежегодным Посланием к белорусскому народу и Национальному собранию, 21.3.2016.

[66] BeATA, 16.5.2016.

[67] BeATA, 15.9.2016.

[68] *Belarus Digest*, 30.8.2016 (Trade Policy: Low-Ball from the Great Wall). In January 2017 the numbers had remained unchanged. *Charter 97*, 26.1.2017.

[69] A. Shraibman, 'The Far-Reaching Consequences of Belarus's Conflict with Russia', *Carnegie Moscow Centre*, 8.2.2017.

Reflections

Last year 1700 freight trains left Chinese cities for European destinations carrying 40,000 containers; double the number of the previous year. Most of the trains were loaded with high value-added cargo and the extra costs were probably justified by the capital saved by the reduced time that manufacturers were holding stocks. However romantic the story and however dramatic growth, this is still all marginal in terms of development. Remember, the trains are still largely travelling on rails that have already been laid and along routes that already exist. Moreover the figures cited in the literature are usually for containers travelling from China to Europe. This conceals the fact that in the opposite direction as many as one half and two-thirds return empty, reflecting the trade imbalance between the two partners. At the moment the subsidies to keep the traffic moving are paid by the Chinese cities, but how long this can continue remains a question. Finally, just as in the days of the ancient Silk Road, most of the trade is conducted over the oceans. The container traffic by train still represents less than one per cent of the traffic carried by sea.[70]

If we look at the development of OBOR along the Northern routes, with the notable exception of Mongolia, there is so far very little Chinese penetration of the economies. Cooperation with Russia has seen an acceptance of Chinese money but a limitation on China's involvement in construction. The oil pipelines on Russian territory are built with Russian labour and Russian technology, and the nature of the connectivity is from source to market, without touching the rest of the economy. As far as the Moscow-Kazan HSR is concerned, the authorities are avoiding tying themselves too exclusively to China and still holding the open for more foreign participation. Similarly in Belarus, despite China undertaking the construction of the SEZ, there is little evidence of Chinese firms (or many others) establishing themselves there. Mongolia is different to the extent that Chinese firms are already well-established in mining industries and many of the infrastructure plans will be implemented by Chinese firms.

---

[70] In 2014 China shipped 5,750,000 containers to Europe by sea

Table 4.3 Risk Indicators for China and countries on the Northern Routes

	EIU Risk Assessment	Control of Corruption	Ease of Doing Business
	Score 0-100	Score 0-100	Rank 1/190
China	45	50	78/190
Belarus	63	53,33	37/190
Mongolia	57	62.02	64/190
Russia	56	80.07	40/190

Source: EIU Overall Risk Assessement: http://viewswire.eiu.com/index.asp?layout=RKAllCountryVW3; World Bank Control of Corruption Indicator: http://data.worldbank.org/data-catalog/worldwide-governance-indicators (the original scores have been deducted from 100 to make them consistent with the EIU results). World Bank Ease of doing Business Index: http://www.doingbusiness.org/rankings

Do these activities pose a risk to China and what are the chances that they will stimulate further growth? Table 4.3 displays some of the risk indicators that were discussed at the end of the previous chapter. The EIU risk indicator shows that all three countries pose a greater risk for foreign investment that for foreigners investing in China (and an even greater risk that for Chinese investing in China). They also all show higher levels of business corruption than in China, and especially so in the case of Russia. On the other hand, it is easier to conduct a business in any of these countries than it is in China. All of this suggests that there are opportunities for any businesses stimulated by the increased connectivity to establish themselves and to flourish, whether they be domestic or Chinese or that of any other entrant into the new markets.

The Chinese authorities are happy with their relations with Russia and Mongolia (which they rate as first and ninth respectively in their cooperation index.[71] The closeness of cooperation with Russia is slightly illusory given the arms-length attitude in Russia to accepting Chinese infrastructural investment. Moreover, the single largest project, the pipelines, reinforce the Russian economy's reliance on energy exports. Back in 2014 China signed a deal that promised it a cheap supply of energy and helped Russia at

[71] Country Cooperation Index: PRC, National Development and Reform Commission, 一带一路大数据报告, Beijing, 2016 (One belt One Road. Big Data Report)

times of financial difficulties and diplomatic isolation. When prices recover, however, watch out for Russia's attempt to claw back its bargaining position. Turning briefly to Belarus (20/64 in the cooperation index), we have a less developed economy whose main interest for China is as a supplier of potash for fertiliser. It was poetic of President Xi to describe the Great Stone Park as 'a pearl on the Great Silk Road' but nothing can disguise its marginal importance in the greater scheme of things.

Mongolia is more of a puzzle. It is a small economy with a lop-sided dependence on larger neighbours and desperate to diversify its levers of influence. As a compliant neighbour, it can expect generous treatment from China. For Mongolia, OBOR investment will have greater implications for the country's development than most of the other countries under consideration in this volume. In return the state is expected to maintain at least some deference to sensitivities of its larger neighbour. This is really the logic behind what is called 'geo-economics'. However, in Mongolia's case (and also in the case of Belarus) we had a flash of what happened when geo-economics met geo-politics and it was a disturbing sight. It helps to lend credibility to those who argue that behind the OBOR rhetoric lurks the intention of establishing Chinese hegemonic power in the Eurasian continent.

CHAPTER FIVE

Xinjiang and Central Asia

Central Asia is literally at the heart of the entire OBOR initiative. After all, it was in Kazakhstan that President Xi Jinping first launched the idea in September 2013 and it was there that the first investments of $60 billion were announced. Moreover, the main overland routes to Europe but also to the Caucuses, Iran and Turkey lie through Central Asia. It is also an area rich in oil and minerals that are needed to fuel the Chinese economy and the construction of new pipeline could reduce China's dependence on Middle East supplies. In addition the overland route through Central Asia would be less vulnerable to sanctions or blockades in the event of any international disputes. Finally, and it is hardly worth saying, the entire silk road metaphor would be redundant were Central Asia not involved.

However, China does not have a free hand in its dealings with Central Asia. All the states of Central Asia states had been part of the Soviet Union and they are still considered by Russia to form part of its sphere of influence. The trading pattern of these states still reflects a dependence on Russia which had provided the main market for their energy and mineral output and was the source of most of their consumer and investment goods. Although since then the pattern of trade has become more diverse, Russia remains the first or second largest source of imports for all these countries.[1] Kazakhstan is also home to a sizeable ethnic Russian minority, the remains of Khrushchev's 'virgin lands scheme' in the late 1950s, which attempted

[1] World Integrated Trade Solutions, http://wits.worldbank.org/countrystats.aspx. The import dependence ranges from 33% in Kazakhstan to 15.6% in Turkmenistan.

to boost Soviet agricultural output by ploughing and planting vast acres of Kazakh steppe.[2] In order not to have this sizeable migrant population in the north of the country too isolated (and detachable) in 1997 the government moved the country's capital from Almaty 1200 km to the north to Astana. Although all the countries in the region flirted for a time with the idea of joining Russia in a Eurasian Economic Community, it was only Kazakhstan in 2009 that took the final step of agreeing to create the Eurasian Customs Union, together with Russia and Belarus.[3]

Figure 5.1 Map of Xinjiang and the Countries of Central Asia

For other countries the explanation for Russia's continuing importance to the region lies in the security problems formed by Afghanistan. Except for Kazakhstan and Kyrgyzstan, the other Central Asian countries all share

---

[2] A.M. Khazanov, 'The Ethnic Problems of Contemporary Kazakhstan', *Central Asian Survey*, 14./2, 1995, 243–64; R, Krämer, A. Prishchepov, D. Müller and M. Fruehauf, 'Long-Term Agricultural Land-Cover Change and Potential for Cropland Expansion in the Former Virgin Lands Area of Kazakhstan', *Environmental Research Letters*, 10/5, 2015, 054012; R.M. Mills, 'The Formation of the Virgin Lands Policy.' *Slavic Review*, 29/1, 1970, 58–69.

[3] D. Satpaev, 'Kazakhstan and the Eurasian Economic Union: The View from Astana', *ECFR Wider Europe Forum*, 12.1.2015.

a border with Afghanistan and are vulnerable to the spill-over of violence from there. Even before the US-led intervention in Afghanistan in 2002, the Islamic Movement of Uzbekistan had led incursions into Tajikistan (1999) and Kyrgyzstan (2000). The appearance of the USA in the Afghan wars was generally welcomed in the region since it offered a chance to balance Russian influence, and, of course, it provided a new source of revenue. Kyrgyzstan offered the use of the Manas airbase, just outside Bishkent. Uzbekistan provided the USA with the Karshi-Khanabad airbase, as well as a base for German troops in Termez. Tajikistan provided refuelling facilities at the international airport at Dushanbe. All countries allowed overflights. Relations were always tense, and when the US authorities had been less than approving after the killing of demonstrators by Uzbek troops in Andijan in May 2005, the government ordered the closure of the base (though it did later allow US troops to transit through the Termez base). In July 2014, the USA also lost the use of the Manas airbase in Kyrgyzstan, though by then it had been running down military commitments in Afghanistan for some time. The gradual withdrawal of the USA from Central Asia reopened the security dilemma. None of the states, singularly or collectively, were capable of maintaining their own border security, whether against terrorist infiltration, drug-running or other criminal activities. Very soon, the Russians were back. In 2012 they signed an agreement with Kyrgyzstan for the use of the airbase at Kant and an agreement with Tajikistan to increase their troop presence in the country.[4]

Relations among the Central Asian states are not particularly warm. Many have been continuously ruled by the same leader since the collapse of communism. Each leader has always been re-elected by overwhelming majorities by the thankful citizenry, but the autocratic styles of government exacerbate personality differences and make collaboration difficult. This undermines the resolution of resource disputes. Three of the countries (Kazakhstan, Uzbekistan and Turkmenistan) are energy rich whilst the remaining two (Tajikistan and Kyrgyzstan) are water rich. In any regional arrangement, the former should supply the latter with energy in return for water access. However, when energy prices are high it has proved more

[4] N. Kassenova, *Relations between Afghanistan and Central Asian States after 2014 Incentives, Constraints and Prospects*, SIPRI, Stockholm, 2014.

profitable to export electricity to foreign countries rather than to poor neighbours thereby exacerbating their energy problems and reinforcing their resolve to use their upstream water reserves to provide hydro-electricity that would their own self-sufficiency and possibly allow for some energy exports. For example Uzbekistan has a long-running dispute with Tajikistan over the latter's resumption of plans to build the world's tallest dam, the Rogun dam, on the Vakhsh river which would negatively affect the flow of water necessary to irrigate the cotton crop in neighbouring Uzbekistan. The dispute had lain dormant for years since Tajikistan lacked the funding to advance the project, but Uzbekistan has in the past retaliated by selective border closures and by blocking Tajik access to energy supplies.[5] In addition all the states contain sizeable minorities of neighbouring ethnicities. This is because the former Soviet republics were somewhat artificial creations and there had never been any real consensus where the borders should be. This border issue came to a head at the end of the millennium for two reasons. First, armed guerrillas were crossing from Tajikistan through Kyrgyzstan with the aim of overthrowing the regime in Uzbekistan. The Uzbeks responded unilaterally to the threat by mining their borders and restricting free movement across their frontiers. At the same time, concerned by the flow of drugs, contraband, illegal immigrants and terrorists, Russia withdrew from the agreement among the CIS states for visa-free travel and reimposed stringent border controls, which had a ripple effect throughout the region.[6]

The OBOR initiative not only places China in a situation in which it will increase its influence in a region that Russia has long considered to be its own back-yard, but it also plunges Beijing into the middle of the overlapping disputes among the Central Asian countries themselves. On the other hand, the intrusion of China into the region had the side-effect of affording the Central Asian states some room for policy manoeuvre by playing one great(er) power off against the other.

Ironically, the one regional power with no territorial disputes in the

---

[5] N. Chugh, 'Will Central Asia's Water Wars Derail China's Silk Road', *The Diplomat*, 24.3.2017; C. Michel, 'Tajikistan's Rogun Dam Rankles Uzbekistan', *The Diplomat*, 21.7.2016; C. Putz, 'What Can Be Done About Central Asia's Water and Electricity Woes?', *The Diplomat*, 27.10.2016.

[6] F. Tolipov, 'Uzbekistan and Kazakhstan: Competitors, Strategic Partners or Eternal Friends?' *Central Asia-Caucus Analyst*, 9.8.2013.

region is China, which shares 2800 km of its border with three of the five Central Asian republics (Kazakhstan, Tajikistan and Kyrgyzstan). With the dissolution of the Soviet Union, the newly independent states inherited the territorial claims that had lain dormant from the time of Tsarist Russia and the Qing Empire, the last of the Chinese dynasties. The disputes were finally closed in 2011, leaving Beijing in control of only a fraction of the lands claimed.[7] These concessions were probably in return for support from local governments in managing the Uyghur threat. The Uyghurs are a Muslim group living in Xinjiang and Central Asia that speak a Turkic language and with their aspiration for independence have been a major source of concern for Beijing.[8]

Despite all the regional tensions, one important framework for regional cooperation is the Central Asian Regional Economic Cooperation Programme (CAREC), which was originally established in 1998 under the umbrella of the Asian Development Bank (ADB). CAREC's membership embraces ten Central Asian countries, including China. In addition to the countries upon which this chapter concentrates its attention, the membership also includes Afghanistan, Azerbaijan, Mongolia and Pakistan. CAREC is a development assistance programme focused on infrastructural investment and trade facilitation, which dovetails nicely with the aims of OBOR. Between the start of operations in 2001 and 2014, it had helped fund projects worth $24.6 billion, with the ADB providing 38% of the funding.[9] Almost 80% of the funds has been devoted to improving and upgrading road and rail links identified along one of the six CAREC transport corridors. By 2014 no less than 4970 km of highway and 3190 km of railways had been constructed or improved. By 2020 the programme envisaged upgrading a further 3000 km of highways, upgrading 2000 km of railway track and building 1800 km of new track. Most of the rest of the funding was devoted to energy improvement in the form of increased power generation

---

7 China held 3.5%, 22% and 32% of what was initially asked from Tajikistan, Kazakhstan and Kyrgyzstan respectively.

8 M.T. Fravel, 'Regime Insecurity and International Cooperation: Explaining China's Compromises in Territorial Disputes', *International Security*, 30/2, 2005, 46–83.

9 37% comes from the other partner institutions, 20% from the member governments themselves and 5% from other co-financiers.

and expansion of the electricity network. The programme is also active in attempting to improve logistics at BCPs[10] and, incidentally, is a useful source of data for the day-to-day difficulties experienced by truck and railway drivers along different routes in the region.

Let us now turn to examine in more detail the individual characteristics of these Central Asian countries. Some of the basic statistics are shown in Table 5.1. In terms of land area, after China Kazakhstan is the largest country in Central Asia and it is the tenth largest country in the world. It dwarfs all the others under discussion here. Even combined, the total area of their territories is less than half that of Kazakhstan. Looking at population size, it is Uzbekistan that is the largest country in the region. The population of the whole region is about the same as that of France, but spread over seven times the land area and with a GDP of only 10% that of France. Kazakhstan is the richest country in the group, by some considerable margin. However, while both Kazakhstan and Turkmenistan are more prosperous than China, the rest are desperately poor.

Table 5.1 Basic details of China and the Countries of China and Central Asia

	Area	Population	Per capita GDP
	Km2	Thousand(2015)	Current US$
China	9,596,961	1,376,049	7,617
Kazakhstan	2,724,900	17,625	12,436
Kyrgyzstan	199,900	5,940	1,267
Tajikistan	143,100	8,482	1,114
Turkmenistan	488,100	5,374	9,032
Uzbekistan	447,400	29,893	2,139

Sources: Area http://unstats.un.org/unsd/environment/totalarea.htm;
Population https://esa.un.org/unpd/wpp/Download/Standard/Population/
pc GDP http://data.un.org/Search.aspx?q=GDP+per+capita

[10] Central Asian Regional Economic Cooperation Programme (CAREC), *Development Effectiveness Review 2014*, 2015; *From Landlocked to Linked In*, Mandaluyong City, 2014, 3rd edition.

If we turn now to Table 5.2 and look at traditional forms of protection, we can see that the tariffs levied by Uzbekistan were the highest in the region. Elsewhere they were not particularly high and Kazakhstan, Kyrgyzstan and Tajikistan all had agricultural and industrial tariffs substantially below those levied by China. There are no data for Turkmenistan. Until 2013, the country did not levy tariffs in the legal sense of the word. Instead it employed a system of specific customs duties and discriminatory excise rates that also had a protectionist effect.[11] As mentioned earlier, the World Bank's Doing Business Survey includes a category for trading across borders which provides the cost in terms of time and money for a small to medium-sized enterprise to import a container of car parts. In Chapter 4 we saw that China took almost seven days to compile the documentation and to get its container out of the port, at a total document cost of $948. We also saw how joining the EACU had slashed the cost and time of importing car parts into Kazakhstan from fellow-member Russia. All the other countries took more time than China to compile the documentation, but the total charges for documents was less. Once again there is no data for Turkmenistan.

Table 5.2 Basic Trade Cost Indicators of China and the Countries of Central Asia

	Tariffs		Border Compliance		Logistics Performance Index
	Non-Agricultural	Agricultural	Time	Cost	Rank n/160
China	9.0	15.6	158	948	27
Kazakhstan	7.3	10.7	8	0	77
Kyrgyzstan	7.1	9.3	63	712	146
Tajikistan	7.2	10.5	234	483	153
Turkmenistan	n/a	n/a	n/a	n/a	140
Uzbekistan	14.1	19.0	285	570	118

Sources: Sources: MFN Tariffs: WTO, ITC, UNCTAD, *World Tariff Profiles*, Geneva, 2016; Border Compliance: Wold Bank, Doing Business, http://www.doingbusiness.org/data/exploretopics/trading-across-borders; LPI: World Bank, LPI Global Ranking (2016) http://lpi.worldbank.org/international/global

[11] World Bank databases, Tariffs. http://data.worldbank.org/indicator/TM.TAX.MRCH.WM.AR.ZS

To help widen our focus from the border and to examine the entire task of organising the entire shipment from its point of origin to its final destination, the World Bank has constructed a Logistics Performance Index. China's overall ranking was a respectable twenty-eighth in the world. Kazakhstan was the best-performing Central Asia country while Turkmenistan and Kyrgyzstan, which were considered among the worst in the world.

Central Asia lies literally at the cross-roads of the Eurasian landmass and three of the eight highways of international importance identified as part of UNESCAP Asian Highway Network, amounting to nearly 7,000 kms, pass through its territory. Besides these major international routes, the region hosts 15,000 km of Asian highways of more local regional importance. Over the past decade there has been a concerted attempt to improve the condition and capacity of these roads, although there is still some way to go. Many of the road systems were allowed to deteriorate for lack of funds. Table 5.3 gives some indication of their current condition.

Table 5.3 Length and Condition of the Asian Highway in China and the countries of Central Asia

	Length	Class (per cent)				
	Kms	Primary	I	II	III	<III
China	10847.28	77.8	2.1	17.1	3.0	Neg.
Kazakhstan	12828,00	-	4.4	42.1	49.8	3.7
Kyrgyzstan	1763,00	-	-	17.2	75.1	7.7
Tajikistan	1912,00	-	1.0	51.1	-	47.8
Turkmanistan	2204,00	-	2.7	-	96.2	1.1
Uzbekistan	2966,00	-	40.3	37.1	22.6	-

Primary: Access controlled motorway; Class I: Three or four lane asphalt or concrete highway; Class II: Two lane asphalt or concrete highway; Class III: Two lane bituminous highway
Source: http://www.unescap.org/resources/status-asian-highway-member-countries

In 2015 slightly only 8.5% of the AH roads in Central Asia were four-lane highways A further 36% were well-surfaced Class II two-lane roads, but over half fell below that standard. Turkmenistan had the worst road surfaces followed closely by Kyrgyzstan. In Kyrgyzstan, for example, 20%

of the roads have deteriorated to the point where repair is impossible and they will need to be constructed anew.[12] The best performing country was Uzbekistan, with only 22.5% of its network constructed to these lowest classifications.[13]

The total length of railways in the five central Asian countries is approximately 22,000 kms most of which was built during the Soviet period. Most of it, therefore, was designed to serve Russia rather than local regional interests and the lines in Central Asia represented the outer reaches of a system radiating from Moscow. With the collapse of the Soviet Union, the network was cut off from its main markets, finance and expertise. Kazakhstan inherited the greatest share of the network and the best equipped. 37% of the network was double-tracked and 28.5% was electrified but the system is ageing fast and is relatively inefficient. This has helped hamper its efforts to secure a larger market for the transit trade as too has the fact that the entire network of the region shares the broad gauge (1520mm) used in the Soviet Union rather than the standard gauge (1400mm) employed by both China and Europe.[14]

Xinjiang

Xinjiang[15] is one of five autonomous regions in China. Situated in the northwest of the country it covers 1.6 million km^2 of territory. Much of it is desert,

[12] International Crisis Group, *Central Asia Decay and Decline*, Asia Report 201, 3.2.2011, 16.

[13] UNESCAP Asia Highway database. http://www.unescap.org/our-work/transport/asian-highway/database

[14] The length of the network was Kazakhstan (14184km), Uzbekistan (3645 km) Turkmenistan (2980km) Tajikistan (680 km) and Kyrgyzstan (470km). Statistics from *CIA World Factbook*. See also International Crisis Group, *Central Asia Decay and Decline*, Asia Report 201, 3.2.2011.

[15] R. Guo, *China's Spatial (Dis)integration: Political Economy of the Interethnic Unrest in Xinjiang*, Waltham, MA, 2015; N. Holdstock, *China's Forgotten People: Xinjiang, Terror and the Chinese State*, London, New York, 2015; A. Howell and C. Fan, 'Migration and Inequality in Xinjiang: A Survey of Han and Uyghur Migrants in Urumqi', *Eurasian Geography and Economics*, 52/1, 2011, 119–39; J. Millward, *Eurasian Crossroads: A History of Xinjiang*, New York, 2007; B. Singh, *Separatism in Xinjiang Between Local Problems and International Jihad?*, New Delhi, 2012.

so it is not surprising that it only has a population of about 23 million people, most of whom are clustered in the west where the mountains provide a source of water. At its furthest western reach, beyond the capital of Urumqi, the region is flanked by the Dzungarian Alatau Mountains, with a natural crossing through a pass known as the Dzungarian Gate ('Alashankou Pass' in Chinese). This was one of the entry points of Silk Road travellers into ancient China, but it was not a favoured route. The sparse population and harsh climate made the journey perilous, and caravans were vulnerable to attack by bands of steppe nomads. Further South there was a more popular crossing point, at the oasis town of Kashgar. This led travellers into a more settled farming area, populated by a Muslim Turkic-speaking people now known as Uyghurs, which was considered less dangerous and also offered better prospects for trade.

After its conquest in 1759, the entire area was incorporated into the Qing Empire. However the North and South were governed separately until 1884 when they were merged into a single Xinjiang region. When the Qing dynasty collapsed in 1912, Xinjiang remained within the new Chinese Republic, but in the early 1930s a separatist Muslim/Turkik rebellion in the south-west of the province briefly established the First East Turkistan Republic before it was crushed by Kuomintang forces. A second rebellion in 1937 prompted the intervention of Soviet troops, who held the region for the next decade. When the Second World War ended, the Soviet Union supported the creation of a Second East Turkistan Republic, but when Communist forces wrested control of the area from the Kuomintang, the East Turkik Republic was re-assimilated into the restored province of Xinjiang.

The Xinjiang region is rich in minerals and hydrocarbons. Once the chaos of the interwar and immediate post-revolutionary years had subsided, these resources were increasingly exploited. Although they contributed to the economic growth of the country, little of this wealth filtered beyond the towns in the north-west; the rest of Xinjiang remains among the poorer areas of China. The region's economic development and urbanisation also brought in waves of government officials and workers, which started to alter its ethnic composition. Back in the 1950s, Han Chinese constituted about 6% of the region's population, but these developments contributed to an increase in their proportion in the region until they approached parity with the Uyghurs. However, this concentration is very much in the North, which is not 'traditional' Uyghur territory; in the South the largely Muslim Uyghur population still predominates. The change in ethnic balance, an inequality of income that reflected the ethnic balance and a rediscovery/invention of historical and cultural 'roots' all helped fuel a culture of resentment that increasingly erupted into ethnic violence. In 2009 these spilled over into street demonstrations and riots in the capital, which led to a large-scale clamp-down in the area. The veneer of calm is periodically punctuated by random acts of terror. In such circumstances the development prescriptions contained the 'belt and road' initiative may equally apply to China's North-West.

Currently, 83% of Xinjiang's total trade is focused on Central Asian states, and 80% of China's total trade with Central Asia transits through the territory. In addition to the colossal push to the 'Go West Strategy,' right after the 2009 Urumqi riots the autonomous region was granted 'extraordinarily important strategic status' in the nation's development programme. A complex of measures resulted in the establishment of the new SEZ in Kashgar and the granting of the status of special trade zones to the land-ports of Alatau and Khorgas, making the region China's most important gateway to Central Asia.[16] In the year 2016 the government spent $145 billion on infrastructure in the region and plans a total of $218 billion in 2017, including $29 billion on highways and $5 billion on expanding the railway network.[17]

The main crossing point for rail traffic is the BCP at the small town of Alashankou located at the Chinese end of the pass through the mountains, and which is battered by gale-force winds for 100 days a year. We discussed the town briefly in Chapter 4. Because of the change in gauge the containers have to be transferred between trains before continuing on their journey, which contributes to long delays for local traffic (other than the block trains that receive priority treatment). Nevertheless, it still is the major conduit for trade with or through Central Asia. In order to boost its potential the town

[16] A. Colarizi, 'China and Kyrgyzstan: So Near, Yet So Far', *The Diplomat,* 11.8.2015.

[17] *China Daily,* 20.1.2017 (Xinjiang to spur growth via heavy infrastructure investment). The highway expenditure is a fivefold increase over 2016 and will see a start made on the construction 6096kms of highway, *China.org.cn,* 18.1.2017.

was granted free trade zone status in 2014. Already, eighty firms have plans to settle there. Even so, the take-off is slow. The few locations are scattered through the industrial zone, and the duty-free shopping centre is almost deserted.[18] In the course of 2015, the average handling times for rail freight at Alashankou fell by almost 40% to a little over twenty hours, but the trains then pass through to the cramped facilities in Dostyk, where hardly any time-saving has taken place and where the average delay remains above forty hours. In autumn 2014, CAREC timed and costed a run from Urumqi to Almaty, the former capital of Kazakhstan and still its largest city, by road and by rail. The results are shown in Table 5.4

Table 5.4 Comparison of Journey Urumqi-Almaty by Road and by Rail

	Road	Rail
Distance	1046km (via Khorgos)	1277kms (via Alashankou)
Total Time	40.8 hours	155.9 hours
Time Moving	*19.1 hours*	*25.7 hours*
Time Stationary	*21.7 hours*	*130.2 hours*
Total Cost	$2728	$5505
Operating Cost	*$1617*	*$4576*
Documentation and Border fees	*$1057*	*$930*

Source: Central Asian Regional Economic Cooperation Programme, *Corridor Performance and Measurement and Monitoring, Quarterly Report 2015 Q3*, 2015, 6.

The truck was almost four times faster and cost half as much. The only compensation was that a rail freight container could carry twice the weight of a truck, but given the flexibility afforded by a truck at the point of delivery, it is not clear that there will never be any advantage in rail as long as delays are allowed to pile up.

Possibly exasperated by the inability to force an upgrade of facilities on the Kazak side of the border, the Chinese authorities have developed a new BCP and 'dry port' further south at Khorgos, the site of an old Silk Road town. The location is not far from the Eurasian pole of inaccessibility – the point on the Eurasian landmass that is furthest from the sea (46°17′N

18 *The West Australian*, 19.6.2016.

86°40′E). On the other hand, looked at from another angle, one could say that it is at the centre of the Eurasian landmass. In 2009 trial runs were started on the Jinghe–Yining–Khorgos Railway, a 286 km fork off the main Northern Xinjiang line. The rail crossing into Kazakhstan was opened in December 2012. The Chinese town of Khorgos is being developed from scratch with a $3.25 billion grant from the government and with a population planned of 200,000. It is currently home to 85,000 inhabitants. Eventually it will share a cross-border free trade zone with its twin town on the other side of the border.[19] Already Khorgos is a sprawling grid of broad avenues with the feel of a Californian town. Tree-lined streets have wide, pristine pavements. Looking from a distance there is a nascent line of skyscrapers. A recent visitor could barely contain his excitement. 'A shop selling Georgian wine on a commercial side-street has signs in five different scripts: Chinese, Cyrillic, Roman, Georgian and Arabic — used for Uighur… The place is buzzing, and the feeling mirrors that in the town: Everyone is too busy making a fortune to care about following the rules too strictly. China's youngest city brims with ambition. This is the new Wild West — quite literally, for the many young people flocking to Khorgos from big Chinese mega-cities to the East.' He was less enthusiastic about the other side of the border.[20]

In 2014 the freight trains arriving at the Khorgos BCP took on average 32.6 hours to proceed. Much of the delay was caused by trains having to wait to enter the facilities because the rate of processing them is too slow. The responsibility for this state of affairs lies not in Khorgos but on the other side of the border, making it impossible for trains to proceed and clear the facilities. But Khorgos is also a road BCP and the delays for road users are also alarmingly long. In mid-2014 (after changing the calculation base) it took on average almost twenty-four hours to clear the border facilities. What happened was that trucks arriving in Khorgos unloaded their cargo into a warehouse, where the goods would await the arrival of trucks from Kazakhstan before being reloaded and then escorted to the BCP on that side of the border. This procedure relied heavily on good logistical planning

[19] W. Shepard, 'Khorgos: Where East meets West', *The Diplomat*, 1.4.2016.

[20] B. Maçães, 'New Western Frontier, Conquered by China', *Politico*, 20.6.2016; See also W. Shepherd, 'Horgos: The First New City Of The New Silk Road Emerges As A Robot Manufacturing Hub', *Forbes Magazine*, 7.1.2017.

and on the availability of sufficient forklifts and personnel to complete the operation effectively. It also depended on the prompt arrival of Kazak trucks and drivers, and the coincidence of operational times on both sides of the border. Already, new warehouses, wholesale centres and separate vehicle inspection zones were under construction and steps were being undertaken to help simplify border crossing procedures. By autumn 2015 the time had been slashed to seven hours.[21]

Kazakhstan

The plan to upgrade the BCP at Khorgos was already taken by presidential decree in Kazakhstan[22] in November 2010, long before China's new Silk Road initiative had been taken. The scheme would include new transport facilities and an industrial and commercial centre. Participants would benefit from tax exemptions, and other privileges and goods traded there would be free of all customs duties. The object was to promote trade and to integrate the country better into the global trading system.[23] It was also a year before the formation of the customs union with Russia, which would make Khorgos the frontier with China not only for Kazakhstan but for the whole EACU. The problem was that corruption in the area was endemic. In April 2011 the Kazak authorities arrested the head of customs at Khorgos and forty-five accomplices, including many high-placed local officials, for involvement in a lucrative car smuggling ring, and sentenced them to swingeing gaol terms, some as high as sixteen to seventeen years.[24] Clearly some action was needed to tackle corruption.

On the Kazak side of the border, road operations took a fairly constant seven hours to complete border formalities. The problems lay in the train

[21] CAREC, *Corridor Performance Measurement and Monitoring. Annual Report, 2014; Quarterly Report 2015 Q3.*

[22] J. Aitken, *Kazakhstan: Surprises and Stereotypes After 20 Years of Independence*, London, New York, 2012; R. Weitz, *Kazakhstan and the New International Politics of Eurasia*, Silk Road Paper, July 2008, Washington; R. Wright, *Vanished Khans And Empty Steppes. A History of Kazakhstan: From Pre-History to Post-Independence*, Hemel Hempstead, 2015.

[23] http://www.mcps-khorgos.kz/en/sez_ptez.

[24] *Eurasianet*, 5.5.2011; *Interfax.kz*, 14.4.2014.

delays, which were substantial. Passenger trains from China started arriving in September 2011 and the freight crossing became operational several months later. From the start the passage of rail freight through the BCP was held up by inadequate facilities reloading (note that gauge changes occur at the importing side!), compounded by a lack of space in the marshalling yards. Delays here could mount to close on fifty hours.[25] In 2012 the World Bank agreed a $1 billion loan to upgrade the 305 km Almaty–Khorgos section of the main highway (it had already contributed $2.125 billion to improve the 1065 km stretch from south Kazakhstan to Kyzylorda Oblasts in the centre of the country).[26] Construction work started in spring 2014 and was scheduled to be completed in 2016.

The new trade zone was planned eventually to accommodate some 50,000 workers and their families. Central to the entire operation was the construction of a dry-port called Khorgos East Gate with four parallel railway tracks for transferring containers on through trains. Trials were finally started in May 2015, and when fully operational the port will have a capacity of 540,000 TEU (Twenty Foot-Equivalent Units) a year. The logistics of the Khorgos East Gate are operated by the Dubai-based terminal operator DPWorld, a choice presumably made with the hope of injecting some of the seaport handling experience into the more lethargic world of Central Asian railway yards. It is also involved in advising the Kazak government on the development of the Port of Aktau, Kazakhstan's main cargo and bulk terminal on the Caspian Sea.[27] In September 2015 China's eastern Jiangsu province agreed to invest $600 million over five years in the Khorgos–Eastern Gate SEZ.[28] Six months later Nanjing became a 49% partner in the Khorgos East Gate Dry-Port.[29] In February 2016, China launched a freight train service linking Kazakhstan's business capital, Almaty, to the Pacific port city of Lianyungang in Jiangsu province, which is probably why it agreed to invest.

The actual development of the town and shopping facilities has lagged some way behind its Chinese counterpart. It was only in February 2013

---

[25] CAREC, *Corridor Performance Measurement Annual Report, 2014*; *Quarterly Report 2015 Q3*.

[26] World Bank Projects database. http://projects.worldbank.org/

[27] *Journal of Commerce*, 21.6.2016.

[28] *Kazinform*, 1.9.2015.

[29] Shepard, 'Khorgos: Where East meets West'.

that the management cooperation agreement was signed, but no sooner had the project started than the vice-president of the whole Khorgos operation was charged with corruption in the allocation for the contract for providing electrical distribution.[30] In September 2016 the head of the free trade zone was arrested for accepting a $1 million bribe for allocating a hotel project in the zone.[31] There are various reasons for the delays besides deficiencies in local management. The past few years have not been kind to the Kazak economy. It has been battered by a downturn in foreign investment following the banking crisis of 2008/9, squeezed by the slowdown in the economies of both China and Russia, its largest trading partners, and it has seen foreign earnings shrink with the collapse of prices for energy and raw materials that formed the bulk of its exports. In November 2014, President Nazarbayev agreed to invest $730 million in Khorgos and the National Industrial Petrochemical Technological Park in Atyrau and Taaz.[32]

The town had been described as 'a couple of dozen old houses congregated around a pretty mosque'. Arriving at the station, a recent traveller found himself left alone, 'sand dunes on one side and a pasturing herd of sheep on the other. The imposing train station and modern two-lane highway stand in sharp contrast to the unshakable feeling that I am — quite literally this time — in the middle of nowhere.'[33] All that there was for anxious shoppers (in the autumn of 2015) was a large yurt, which sold German sweets and Russian beer. Outside, for the tourists to photograph, stood a line of plastic camels.[34] This has now changed radically. The loading yards are fully operational, though still handling only an average two large container trains a day and new housing provides homes for 2000 people and a large shopping centre.[35]

Kazakhstan is the leading oil producer in the region, with an output

---

[30] *Kazinform*, 20.6.2013.

[31] Organised Crime and Corruption Reporting Project, 9.9.2016.

[32] N. Nazarbajev, *Nurly Zhol - The Path To The Future*, speech 11.11.2014.

[33] Maçães, 'New Western Frontier'.

[34] M. Rudolf, 'China's "Silk Road" Initiative Is at Risk of Failure', *The Diplomat*, 24.9.2015.

[35] W. Shepard, 'Absurd. China's And Kazakhstan's Remote Cross-Border FTZ May Finally Be Set To Boom', Forbes Magazine, 9.2.2017; W. Shepard, 'Khorgos: The New Silk Road's Central Station Comes To Life', *Forbes Magazine*, 20.2.2017.

of 1.6 million barrels per day (bbl/day),. Approximately 90% is exported. China's interest in Kazakh oil started in 1997 when China National Petroleum Corporation spent $9 billion acquiring controlling shares in two Kazak oil concerns that controlled estimated reserves of 2.5 billion barrels. At the same time, it started a feasibility study to link the fields via a 2230 km pipeline directly to Western China, at an estimated cost of $3.5 billion, which would also remove the necessity of transporting the oil through Russian territory. A lull in oil prices helped delay the start of the pipeline's construction, but in 2004 the two governments agreed to revive the project, which was eventually completed in 2009.[36] Today, China produces 25% of the oil extracted in Kazakhstan but owing to the delays in exploiting the oil fields, the pipeline operates at 50% of its capacity, sometimes less.[37] We will discuss the gas pipeline later in this chapter.

It is always useful when the plans and policies of two countries converge, and this is the case with Kazakhstan and China. The global connectivity ideas inherent in the OBOR were reflected from the start in the logic behind developing Khorgos and an important hub in the overall pattern. In November 2014 President Nazarbayev set out his vision of a 'bright path', *Nurly Zhol*.[38] The intention was to use $9 billion of the sovereign wealth fund to support the economy and to ensure that it emerged from the recession better equipped to resume growth. Central to this vision was the improvement of road and rail infrastructure. In addition the country's Strategy2050 plans envisage a diversification of the country's economic base in its ambition to become one of the world's richest thirty nations.[39] In July 2015 the president launched 'one hundred steps' of institutional reform towards creating a 'modern state'.[40] Little wonder that when Foreign Minister Wang Li

---

[36] M. Meidan, *The Structure of China's Oil Industry: Past Trends and Future Prospects*, OIES Working Paper 66, 2016: 24–5, 42.

[37] L. Parkhomchik, 'Energy Relations between China and the Caspian Littoral States', *Eurasian Research Institute Weekly e-Bulletin*, 48, 29.12.2015–4.1.2016.

[38] Nazarbajev, *Nurly Zhol*.

[39] http://kazakhstan2050.com/.

[40] E. Idrissov, 'Kazakhstan: 100 Steps Toward a New Nation', *The Diplomat*, 25.7.2015.. They were grouped under five headings: formation of a professional state apparatus; the rule of law; industrialisation and economic growth; identity and unity; formation of accountable government.

visited the country in May 2016, there were mutual congratulations on the warmth of their bilateral relations.[41] In the memorandum of understanding signed in 2015, the two countries identified forty-eight investment projects totalling $30 billion.[42] A year later, the Chinese Embassy to Kazakhstan reported that in the three years since OBOR's launch the two countries had reached fifty-one agreements, with the total investment amounting to an impressive (but lower!!) $26.5 billion. However the twelve projects already launched or to be launched by mid-2016 amounted to only $4 billion.[43] The figure is not that large once investments in Khorgos and in the energy sector are discounted.

At present, China's economic offensive in Kazakhstan has raised few problems with its relations with Russia, which is presenting the issue as a win-win cooperation. Russia's present economic situation, hit by low commodity prices and by sanctions, is hardly in a position to compete with China's financial resources. However, there are Russian concerns that the development of transit routes through Kazakhstan must diminish any hopes of promoting the advantages of the Trans-Siberian Railway and that 'tied-purchasing' clauses in most of the OBOR deals will cut Russian firms out of lucrative contracts. Officially Moscow still hopes that it can link the OBOR initiative to the EAEU project, but it is difficult to see how this can occur. The Russian foreign ministry is drafting a centralised set of 'rules' that will govern the new relationship, but OBOR has no central counterpart and this does not even confront China's reluctance to engage in multilateral

---

[41] C. Putz, 'China Pushes One Belt, One Road in Central Asia', *The Diplomat*, 24.5.2016. Although the official media is positive towards developments in China and the country's bilateral relations, private newspapers continue to peddle negative stereotypes about the Chinese, stoking fears that Chinese migrants are taking jobs and Chinese imports are damaging local production (A. Burkhanov and Y-W. Chen, 'Kazakh Perspective on China, the Chinese, and Chinese Migration', *Ethnic and Racial Studies*, 2016, 1–20). In May 2015 the prospect of land reforms provoked widespread protests in cities throughout the country over fears that it would lead to large numbers of Chinese buying land and settling in the country (S. Snow, 'Central Asia's Lukewarm Pivot to China', *The Diplomat*, 16.8.2016).

[42] *Kazinform*, 21.9.2015.

[43] *Xinhuanet* press release, 16.8.2016.

discourse.[44] Moreover, the Kazak leadership's warmth towards Russia has recently cooled and the pace of closer integration is being increasingly resisted. In addition there is particular concern over Russia's claims in the wake of the Georgian and Ukrainian crises to protect its (former) citizens. Although 23.7% of Kazakhstan's population is Russian and the idea of a multi-ethnic state has helped shape the country's post-Soviet identity, there are signs on this front, too, that Kazakh nationalism is on the rise.[45]

Kyrgyzstan

If we travel along the Chinese border to the south we come to the mountainous country of Kyrgyzstan[46] with which it shares an 858 km border. It includes two BCPs, one in Torugart and the other at Erkeshtam, 165 km further south. One travel firm described Torugart as 'the sorriest, most problematic and adventurous border crossing in the world, complete with a howling wind, chilly temperatures, excruciatingly long waits, patrol dogs and the meanest and most difficult border guards you are ever going to meet' (if you are still interested, they are the Kashgar New Land International Travel Service). Despite its bad reputation among tourists, freight traffic passes through the border with few problems.[47]

Erkeshtam is the name of the village on the Kyrgyz side of the border that nestles in the deep gorge of the Irkeshtam Pass, which had been a main southern thoroughfare on the ancient Silk Road, leading on the Chinese side to the famous oasis city of Kashgar. The border crossing was officially opened in 1998, but it is the lesser used of the two BCPs because of the difficult nature of the narrow, winding road. The road itself is in good condition,

---

[44] A. Gabuev, 'Post-Soviet States Jostle For Role in One Belt One Road Initiative', *HKTDC Research*, 6.8.2015.

[45] International Crisis Group, *Stress Test for Kazakhstan*, Crisis Group Europe and Central Asia Briefing No. 74, Bishkek, Brussels, 13.5.2015.

[46] Asian Development Bank, *The Kyrgyz Republic Strategic Assessment Of The Economy. Promoting Inclusive Growth*, Metro Manila, 2014; J. Anderson, Kyrgyzstan: *Central Asia's Island of Democracy?*, London, New York, 2013; M. Laruelle and J. Engvall, *Kyrgyzstan beyond 'Democracy Island' and 'Failing State': Social and Political Changes in a Post-Soviet Society*, Lanham, MA, 2015.

[47] CAREC, *Corridor Performance Measurement Annual Report, 2014*.

having been resurfaced in 2013 at the cost of $600 million. The highway is intended to be part of an upgraded road reaching down into Pakistan.[48] The crossing is open for six hours on weekdays and is closed at weekends, and the waits are horrendous. In the late summer of 2015, a truck passing from China spent an average of nineteen hours on the Chinese side of the border and a further five hours passing through Kyrgyz formalities.[49] Nevertheless, there are plans for expansion. On the Chinese side of the border 'there is an impressive modern structure resembling an airport terminal. But inside, nobody is there to welcome you. No trace of officers either: only their photos, names and ethnicity posted at the entrance.'[50]

Further inland in China, the hopes are pinned on developing Kashgar, which was designated as an SEZ in May 2010. Kashgar is China's most Western city, closer to Baghdad than to Beijing, with a population of 350,000. Visiting the city three years later, a reporter was shown impressive architects' models of the SEZ with 280 metre skyscrapers and luxury shopping malls. As for the site itself, 'Contrary to what I was expecting, I found myself in the middle of the countryside. I first followed an old, narrow road, flanked by two lines of poplar trees and a water channel. Such roads are a quite common sight in Xinjiang's numerous oases, but in this case I was expecting a busy construction site. After a while, I found what I was looking for in the form of a road of another kind: a modern six-lane highway, cutting straight through the fields. Han Chinese workers were asphalting it, while Uyghur kids rode their bikes and played on the unpaved sections.'[51] Two years later, in 2015, and the towers have still not been built and the SEZ 'is little more than a white elephant project on the outskirts of the city that only few people know how to reach. Just next to a forest of cranes, a billboard covered with dust unconvincingly reads: "Chinese Dream, Kashgar Dream".'[52]

China has also been active in the provision of electrical power. Under the Soviet system, the country had been completely dependent on power

---

[48] M. Alymbekov, 'Kyrgyzstan and the Great Silk Road: Compatibility of Concepts', *Kabar*, 6.10.2013.

[49] CAREC, *Corridor Performance Measurement Annual Report, 2014*; *Quarterly Report 2015 Q3*.

[50] A. Colarizi, 'China and Kyrgyzstan: So Near, Yet So Far', *The Diplomat*, 11.8.2015.

[51] A. Rippa, 'Kashgar on the Move', *The Diplomat*, 14.10.2013.

[52] Colarizi, 'China and Kyrgyzstan'.

supplies from Uzbekistan and since then it has desperate to harness its own potential for hydro-power. In 2015 the Datka–Kemin 405 km power-line project was completed with a $390 million loan from China's EXIM bank. China is also upgrading the Bishkek heating and power plant with a loan of $386 million. Both projects were being completed by the Chinese Tebian Electric Apparatus Company. Russia is also involved in the country, but lacks the financial resources to do much. For example Russia's state-owned RusHydro has the contract to build Upper Naryn Cascade of four hydro-power dams with a capacity of 240 megawatts. Work started in 2013 and the project was supposed to be finished by 2019.[53] However, in December 2015 the Kyrgyz government grew tired of the delays and cancelled the contract. The Russian offer to resume work, but to change the terms of the lean agreement so that the interest rate reflected commercial rates was rejected. So far the search for new partners has proved fruitless [54]

In 2016 Kyrgyzstan and China started negotiations on relocating forty Chinese factories and plants to the country. This idea had first been mooted during a prime ministerial visit to Beijing in May 2015, and it was intended to help stave off bankruptcy in many firms and to help industrialise the country. Among the conditions attached were an 80% local labour clause and an undertaking to minimize environmental damage. Nonetheless parliamentary reaction has been cautious about the value of the environmental guarantees, sceptical about the cash that will be creamed off by domestic corruption and fearful of illegal Chinese migration. As in Kazakhstan, illegal Chinese migration has become an increasingly visible public concern. Although the official figure for temporary labour migrants is 13,500 (85% from China), unofficial estimates can climb as high as 300,000.[55]

Russia may have lacked the financial clout of the Chinese but it has never been far from the scene, and Kyrgyzstan also agreed to join the EACU in January 2015. Part of the deal was aid of $300 million to enhance border security.[56] The effect of accession to the EACU would be to increase tariffs

[53] *Eurasianet.org*, 31.8.2015.

[54] M. Levina, 'The Upper Naryn hydropower plants cascade: a hopeless project in Kyrgyzstan?', *The Times of Central Asia*, 19.12.2016.

[55] C. Orozobekova, 'China Relocating Heavy Enterprises to Kyrgyzstan', *Eurasia Daily Monitor*, 13/114, 24.6.2016.

[56] *World Bulletin*, 24.12.2014.

and technical requirements on imports from China at the borders. This would damage Kyrgyzstan position as a re-exporter of Chinese goods. On the other hand the country's industry would benefit from its continued export advantage in textiles and in re-export of goods that are otherwise difficult to obtain in neighbouring Kazakhstan and in Russia. Both countries are already far larger export markets than China. In addition Russia has also pledged $500 million to assist the country's integration into the EACU, much of which would go to the private sector.[57] The decision to join the EACU, the increasing antipathy towards Chinese workers, the parliamentary bickering over land rights legislation and various bureaucratic problems have all helped reduce the attraction of Kyrgyzstan as an investment prospect. For example, at the Taldy-Bulak Levoberezhny gold project, where the Chinese Zijin Mining Group holds a 60% interest, the company had to evacuate 250 employees after clashes with the local population, and the project has faced delays in operation because of electricity shortages.[58]

The Junda China Petrol Company has also been struggling. In 2014 the new $430 million oil refinery near Kara-Balta was forced to close for a time after local protests over pollution. Moreover failure to secure access to sufficient crude condemned it to operating for long periods at only one third capacity, with neither Russian nor Kazak suppliers keen to resolve the problem. A year later it was hit by strikes by local workers demanding equal wages with Chinese employees. More recently the plant was closed after it became enveloped in a tax evasion scandal.[59]

Tajikistan

Tajikistan[60] shares a 414 km border with China. The only crossing point is on the Kulma Pass, with the Tajik BCP at the top of the pass and the

[57] G. Bowring, 'Kyrgyzstan's Dilemma over Joining Russian-Led Customs Union', *Financial Times* blog, 21.11.2014.

[58] C. Rickleton, 'Are Chinese Investors Ditching Kyrgyzstan for Tajikistan?', *Eurasianet.org*, 30.1.2015.

[59] *Eurasianet.org*, 19.2.2014, 27.1.2015, 22.6.2016; *24 Hour Press Club Agency*, 26.1.2016, 10.1.2017.

[60] K. Nourzhanov and C. Bleuer, *Tajikistan: A Political and Social History*, Canberra, 2013; M.B. Olcott, *Tajikistan's Difficult Development Path*, Washington DC, 2012; K.

Chinese BCP 14 km away, next to the Karakorum Highway running south to link China with Pakistan. It is open from 11.00 to 17.00, with an hour's break for lunch, and it is closed at weekends. When the weather is bad it is closed altogether. Believe it or not, this is an improvement on the previous situation, when it was open for only fifteen days a month. The BCP is not on any of the internationally recognised highways. When it is open, the crossing takes about five hours.[61]

Tajikistan's need for Chinese investment has increased since the decline in Russia's involvement in the economy and the sharp decline in remittances (which may have contributed as much as 50% of GDP) sent back to the country from the thousands of migrants working abroad.[62] It also coincides with the increasing disenchantment of Chinese investors with the prospects in Kyrgyzstan.

Chinese investment in construction has grown apace. Since Huaxin Cement signed an agreement to build a cement plant with a capacity of 1.2 million tonnes per annum near the capital Dushanbe in 2011, the country's cement output has quintupled. The company opened a second plant of similar size in the north of the country in March 2016. It has been argued that this is part of an effort to shift a highly polluting industry away from Chinese cities, but markets such as that of Tajikistan scarcely scratch the surface of the problem.[63] All this cement is useful in road building and construction. For example, in 2015, Chinese companies were invited to be part of a consortium building an entirely new city at Saikhun, at present 14,000 hectares of desert near Khujand in the north of the country. The city will eventually be the home for 250,000 people.[64]

The plans to improve connectivity with neighbouring Uzbekistan rest on shakier foundations. Relations between the two states have always been troubled. Uzbek intervention, with Russian support, played a decisive role

---

Warikoo, *Tajikistan in the 21st Century: Society, Politics and Economy*, Oxford, 2015.

[61] CAREC, *Corridor Performance Measurement and Monitoring. Annual Report, 2014.*

[62] World Bank Group, *Tajikistan: Slowing Growth, Rising Uncertainties*, Washington DC, 2015, 12–13.

[63] D. van der Kley, 'China shifts Polluting Cement to Tajikistan', *The Diplomat*, 8.8.2016.

[64] A. Colarizi, 'A "China Town" in Northern Tajikistan', *The Diplomat*, 20.10.2015.

in determining the outcome of the Tajik civil war in the 1990s.[65] In 2000, ostensibly to prevent Islamic militants' infiltration into the country from Tajikistan, a claim which it denied, Uzbekistan mined part of the border and introduced new visa requirements. The most recent escalation in tension started with the 'rail war' in 2011 when Uzbekistan stopped rail cars entering Tajikistan following an explosion that closed part of the Termez–Kurgan Tyube line, cutting off supplies to the south of the country. A year later, the Uzbek government seemed to be dismantling the line rather than repairing it. Coincidentally, at the same time Uzbekistan also suspended natural gas supplies, citing contractual obligations to prioritise supplies to China. Behind all these incidents, the root cause of the problems has been water. The vast proportion of the water needs of Uzbekistan are met by resources located in Tajikistan, and it has started damming some of the rivers to produce hydro-electricity and so end its acute power shortages.[66]

Uzbekistan and Turkmenistan

Uzebkistan[67] and Turkmenistan[68] have no borders with China, but they do have something else that fits the OBOR's win-win strategy and that is energy. Uzbekistan has large oil and natural gas reserves, but currently lacks the investment to exploit them and the pipeline capacity to transport it. Turkmenistan contains most of the proven reserves of natural gas.

Since independence Uzbekistan has, more than the other central Asian states, attempted to steer a neutral course among its diplomatic partners,

[65] S. Horsman, 'Uzbekistan's Involvement in the Tajik Civil War 1992–97: Domestic considerations', *Central Asian Survey*, 18/1, 1999, 37–48; D. Lynch, 'The Tajik Civil War and Peace Process.' *Civil Wars* 4/4 2001, 49–72.

[66] S. Juraev, *Central Asia's Cold War? Water and Politics in Uzbek-Tajik Relations*, PONARS Eurasia Policy Memo No. 217, 2012.

[67] V. Popov, *An Economic Miracle in the Post-Soviet Space. How Uzbekistan Managed to Achieve what No Other Post-Soviet State Has*, PONARS Eurasia working paper, 2013; M.C. Spechler, *The Political Economy of Reform in Central Asia: Uzbekistan under Authoritarianism*, Abingdon, 2008.

[68] A.C. Kuchins, J. Mankoff and O. Backes, *Central Asia in a Reconnecting Eurasia: Turkmenistan's Evolving Foreign Economic and Security Interests*, Boulder, CO, New York, London, 2015; S. Peyrouse, *Turkmenistan: Strategies of Power, Dilemmas of Development*, Abingdon, New York, 2011.

but the stagnation of exports to Russia and the fall in remittances have tilted the balance decidedly in China's favour. In June 2016 President Xi Jinping became the first ever foreign leader to address the Uzbek parliament, where he urged the county to 'unlock new opportunities for cooperation'. President Islam Karimov replied by referring to a proverb: 'You know a friend in times of hardship'. China, he said, was such a friend. Both leaders went to the opening of the 19.2 km tunnel on the 124 km Angren–Pap line, linking the populous Ferghana Valley and the remainder of Uzbekistan, including Tashkent. China's $350 million help had been part of the assistance package agreed in November 2013 under the OBOR banner. In this regard it is ironic that the line is designed not to increase international connectivity in the region but to allow Uzbekistan to dispense with the existing rail link that cuts through neighbouring Tajikistan.[69] The major part of China's OBOR initiative, however, is a $15 billion deal for the exploitation of the oil, gas and uranium resources in the country agreed in September 2013.[70] The following year the two countries agreed a five-year development partnership, backed by a further $5.2 billion in Chinese financial assistance. Once again, energy was to the forefront of the arrangements as well as improving rail connections to Kazakhstan and Kyrgyzstan.[71] We will discuss energy later in this chapter.

Relations between Uzbekistan and Turkmenistan had always been tense but they plumbed new depths when in November 2002 Turkmenistan implicated the Uzbek ambassador of involvement in an assassination attempt on its President. However, in 2007 his successor started a concerted attempt to rebuild relations between the two countries, and in 2012 there was a tangible breakthrough in personal relations between the two heads of state. Economic cooperation, trade and transportation were named as priority spheres. One factor behind the breakthrough was Uzbekistan's need for support in the water conflict with Tajikistan, but more important was their mutual interest in diversifying energy markets. Turkmenistan's gas exports had to cross Uzbek territory, while Turkmenistan controlled Uzbek access to the Caspian Sea.[72]

---

[69] *Eurasianet.org*, 23.6.2016; *Sputniknews*, 29.11.2013.

[70] *South China Morning Post*, 10.9.2013.

[71] *GBTimes*, 20.8.2014.

[72] A. Kim, 'Uzbekistan and Turkmenistan: Can Common Interests Push Old Quarrels Aside?', *Eurasia Daily Monitor*, 10/18, 23.10.2013; D. Asilbekov, 'A Cautious

Until 2009, Turkmenistan sold most of its natural gas to Gazprom under a twenty-five-year contract. However exports were disrupted in April 2009 ostensibly because of an explosion in the Davletbat–Daryalik pipeline near the border with Uzbekistan. What was actually happening was a little more interesting. Since Gazprom had been the main customer and the only pipelines had run to Russia, Gazprom was buying gas cheap and selling through, with high oil-indexed margins, to customers in the CIS and later to Western markets. When the global economic downturn began in 2009, Gazprom had no need for supplies from Turkmenistan and so the timing of the 'accident' (and the duration of the repairs) was extremely fortunate. When deliveries were resumed in 2010 they were on a 'take or pay' basis, but only at 25% of the previous level. Then, in 2014, when energy prices were sagging, Gazprom unilaterally broke the contract, but eventually agreed to take an even lower volume (down to 4 billion bcm from a pre-2009 level of 40 bcm) and at a more disadvantageous base for calculating prices. Against this background the government now considered the option of switching exports to China, fully utilising the exiting gas pipelines (A, B and C), which were only operating at 50% capacity and expanding operations even further[73] by taking out huge loans from the Chinese Development Bank. When pipeline C came on line it brought the total capacity of the three pipelines to 55 bcm. In 2013 the CNPC agreed to develop the second phase of the Galkynysh field and expand its capacity to 30 bcm per year, with China taking 25 bcm.[74].

At the same time China signed a contract with the governments of Uzbekistan, Krygystan and Tajikistan to construct a fourth gas pipeline (Line D) through their territories to connect with the existing pipeline in Turkmenistan and to carry the gas through to the terminal at Khorgos. The pipeline would be 1000 km long, with 840 km outside China, and it would have a capacity of 30 bcm. Joint companies were formed between CNPC and Uzbekniftegaz and Tajiktransgaz to undertake the work.[75] At the beginning of 2016, however, the Uzbek government unilaterally suspended work on its

Embrace between Turkmenistan and Uzbekistan', *Silk Road Reporters*, 26.6.2015.

[73] M. Vladimirov, 'Gazprom, Turkmenistan Locked in a Gas Dispute', *Russia Insider*, 29.7.2015.

[74] *Eurasianet.org*, 24.6.2016.

[75] Aid data: http://china.aiddata.org/projects/39955?iframe=y.

section of the project for 'technical reasons'.[76] This was followed in May by an announcement by the Kyrgyzstan economics minister of the indefinite postponement of its part of the project, citing the escalation of the cost projections owing to the mountainous terrain and uncertainties over the conditions attached to Chinese finance.[77] These incidents are unlikely to have much immediate impact on China, where energy demand has dropped, but it will rob Kyrgyzstan and Tajikistan of their share of transit fees. It will also stymie Turkmenistan's intentions of further increasing gas sales in the future, leaving it to service the large loans from China but without the underlying income to support this. On the other hand, should conditions change, the construction work could easily resume.[78]

Connecting the Rest of World

Long before the launch of OBOR, the idea of constructing an 'iron Silk Road' originated in Turkey. It was used to describe the Baku–Tbilisi–Kars Railway, designed to connect the oil-rich Caspian Sea region to Turkey. An older rail link running through Armenia had lain abandoned since 1993 when Turkey had sided with Azerbaijan during the Nagorno-Karabakh War.[79] Discussions for an alternative route started almost immediately, but it was not until 2002 that the three countries (Turkey, Georgia and Azerbaijan) signed a protocol for the construction of a new line. It was in a statement after a meeting of the leaders of the three countries in February 2007 that the Turkish prime minister Recep Tayyip Erdogan referred to the rail project as the 'iron Silk Road'. He went on to proclaim that the railway, as well as new oil and gas pipelines, would send a signal of solidarity in what was seen as a troubled region. 'However, this solidarity is not limited to the

[76] C. Michel 'Can China Really Save Central Asian Economies?', *The Diplomat*, 13.2.2016.

[77] Press Club New Agency, 25.5.2016.

[78] C. Michel 'Line D of the Central Asia-China Gas Pipeline Delayed', *The Diplomat*, 31.5.2016; C. Michel, 'The Central-Asia China Gas Pipeline Network: Line D(ead)', *The Diplomat*, 21.3.2017. At the time of writing the project was still stalled. M.Lelyveld, 'China shelves Central Asia Gas Plan', *Radio Free Asia*, 20.3.2017.

[79] B. Forrest, 'Eurasian Silk Road: The New Silk Road', *National Geographic*, August 2010.

regional cooperation. At the same time, each station of this railway, becoming as the station of peace, a station of friendship and solidarity and sends its message to the world.'[80]

The 826 km rail line was projected to carry 3 million passengers and 17 million tonnes of freight annually. Completion of the work was originally envisaged for 2010. But it was not until January 2015 that the first test trains could run on the upgraded 721 km section from Baku to Akhalkalaki (financed by the Azerbaijani government at a cost of $775 million). On the Turkish side of the line the groundwork had been completed, but no start had been made in laying the tracks and the $400 million budget was virtually exhausted. A further $250 million would be required to complete the project. The cause of both the cost overrun and the delay had been unexpected difficulties in tunnel construction owing to the harder rock encountered and the cessation of work by the contractor until payment had been made. The release of funds had then been delayed by political difficulties.[81] In January 2017 it was announced that the entire line should be completed within months.[82]

On the other side of the Caspian Sea, in 1993 plans were conceived for a Trans-Caspian Railway linking China and Europe through Kazakhstan, Azerbaijan, Georgia and Turkey. The route runs 4256 km by rail and 508 km by sea (the Black Sea and the Caspian Sea). Although the European Union had initially pushed hard for the scheme, good intentions had not been matched by subsequent action. Nonetheless, in August 2015 the 'Nomad Express' became the first container train to complete a journey leg of over 4000 km along the Trans-Caspian International Transport Route (TITR). Loaded with eighty-two containers of caustic soda, the train departed from Shihezi in Northern China and arrived six days later at the Baku International Sea Trade Port in Alyat, Azerbaijan. Previously, goods from China to Baku had travelled by sea through the Iranian port of Bandar Abbas and the journey had taken anything from twenty-five to forty days. The final part of the route is still incomplete.[83] In December 2015 a trial

---

[80] Azerbaijan Railways site, http://railway.gov.az/index/en/2nd-column-3/baku-tbilisi-kars

[81] O. Uysal, 'Why Baku-Tbilisi-Kars Project Stagnated?' *Rail Turkey*, 16.10.2015.

[82] *Daily Sahab*, 22.1.2017.

[83] E. Grey, 'Can the Trans-Caspian Route Deliver the Next Freight Revolution?', *Railway-Technology.com*, 4.11.2015.

run reached Tblisi. This also served to open up the route to traffic from the Ukraine which, since the civil war, had been unable any longer to use its traditional route through Russia. The journey of a container train from Kiev to the port of Aktau in Kazakhstan would usually take about nine days.[84]

In November 2015 the China Railway Corporation proposed building a high-speed line from Urumqi through to Iran, via Kazakhstan, Kyrgyzstan, Uzbekistan and Turkmenistan. The first advantage was that it would have the high-speed standard gauge of 1435 mm throughout, and so would overcome the problem of changing gauges and the delays that this causes.[85] A new container train service from Yiwu (in East China) to Iran was launched in February 2016. This first journey had taken a total of fourteen days as opposed to the twenty-five to thirty days by sea.[86]

Reflections

OBOR's entry into Central Asia disturbs a complex pattern of cross-dependence. This has already China's interrupted plans for increased energy security and it carries the seed for further delays. All the countries in the region had a political and economic dependence on the former Soviet Union and it was clearly easier to claim formal political independence than it would be to achieve economic emancipation. Trade with Russia and remittances from workers in Russia remained important sources of prosperity, and that trade often ran along channels of connectivity that were determined by the planners in the Soviet Union rather than by market considerations. Roads, rail and pipeline connections were directed towards Russia while energy flowed through networks designed on a regional basis that were not designed to coincide with later national borders. By altering the nature and direction of regional connectivity, China is economically emancipating these countries but only by creating an alternative source of dependence, namely itself. This process, of course, has been developing over a couple of decades but more recently China's predominance has coincided with a decline in Russia's

[84] Z. Dyussembekova, 'Silk Road Renewed With Launch of New Commercial Transit Route', *Astana Times*, 21.1.2016.

[85] Y. Zheng, 'New Rail Route Proposed from Urumqi to Iran', *China Daily*, 21.11.2015.

[86] *Think Railways*, 1.2.2016.

financial muscle as a result of falling energy prices and, later, of Western economic sanctions. What is curious is that in parallel with these developments, Russia has managed to recover some of its position. Both Kazakhstan and Kyrgyzstan have joined the EACU and signed up for the EAEU which involved eliminating border barriers to trade with each other and with Russia, while maintaining them with China. This has the effect of increasing the degree of preference within the bloc against China. In this instance it is evident that, for the present at least, China's goal of trade facilitation in the region has a lower priority than the promotion of infrastructural investment. Put another way, the benefits of improved transit through the area, coupled with the market for capital goods captured by OBOR outweigh concerns of increasing exports of consumer goods to what are, after all, small and underdeveloped markets. What is also interesting is that China seems to have been relatively successful in avoiding becoming embroiled in regional rivalries among the central Asian states themselves or (too much) popular protest against its increased visibility in the local economy.

Table 5.5 Risk Indicators of China and the Countries of Central Asia

	EIU Risk Assessment	Control of Corruption	Ease of Doing Business
	Score 0-100	Score 0-100	Rank 1/190
China	45	50	78/190
Kazakhstan	50	75.48	35/190
Kyrgyzstan	60	88.48	75/190
Tajikistan	78	86.06	128/190
Turkmenistan	77	91.83	n/a
Uzbekistan	73	89.42	87/190

Source: Country Cooperation Index: PRC, National Development and Reform Commission, 一带一路大数据报告, Beijing, 2016 (One belt One Road. Big Data Report); EIU Overall Risk Assessement: http://viewswire.eiu.com/index.asp?layout=RKAllCountryVW3 ; WBI Control of Corruption Indicator; http://data.worldbank.org/data-catalog/worldwide-governance-indicators; WB Ease of doing Business Index: http://www.doingbusiness.org/rankings

Looking at the experience in Central Asia it is not surprising to find that China's cooperation index has Kazakhstan in second place. I would consider the real degree of economic cooperation to be even higher than that of Russia. A look at the risk indicators in Table 5.5 would also suggest that Kazakhstan is the safest of the areas for investment with a good result for facilitating business activity (better than that of even of China). Corruption in the country is endemic, but then it is throughout the region, and it is the least bad of the group. It is the other two countries with which it has a border - Kyrgyzstan (19/64) and Tajikistan (22/64) – that China considers to have the next closest cooperation relations. Although the Chapter suggests a growing disenchantment with Kyrgyzstan and a growing warmth of Tajikistan, the ease of doing business ranking suggests that prospects of sparking grass roots development in Tajikistan are not promising. Uzbekistan (26/64) and Turkmenistan (36/64)[87] are part of OBOR for one overwhelming reason. They both wish to diversify their energy export markets, and China wants to diversify its sources of imports.

To date China has managed to expand its interest in the region without antagonising the interests of Russia. However, although the mechanism whereby this can occur is China's willingness to concede the position of security provider to Russia, their economic interests in the area do not coincide. This does not necessarily mean that they have to compete – it is a question of how each country prioritises its economic and political goals, and the opportunities for realising them. Nevertheless Russia will remain a factor conditioning China's relationships in the region. Having said that, it is remarkable how China has found a way to cooperate with all the other governments in Central Asia, despite their often latent antipathy towards each other. In the next chapter we will see how this was not always possible.

[87] Country Cooperation Index: PRC, National Development and Reform Commission, 一带一路大数据报告, Beijing, 2016 (One belt One Road. Big Data Report)

CHAPTER SIX

South Asia

In this chapter we will examine two separate corridors that are mentioned specifically in the Silk Road action plans. The first one is the China-Pakistan Economic Corridor (CPEC) that links the seaport of Gwadar in Pakistan (which will be discussed in more detail in Chapter 8) with South-West China. Since the start of the OBOR initiative, this has been the scene of a great deal of economic diplomacy. The second is the corridor that is envisaged to stretch from North-East India, starting near the port of Calcutta and running through Bangladesh and Myanmar before reaching the south of China, known as the Bangladesh-China-India-Myanmar (BCIM) corridor. Progress along this corridor is proving far slower, partly through administrative inertia but primarily because of the muted response to the entire initiative from the countries involved. In India's case this is in no small measure owing to China's close relations with Pakistan, its traditional enemy. On the other hand, India does have its own interest in developing part of the BCIM corridor in the direction of Bangladesh, whose territory almost separates the states of North-East India from the rest of the country. Increasing connectivity through Bangladesh not only gives opportunities to Bangladesh, but promotes the integration of India as well. Bangladesh, in its turn, is in the happy position of being courted by both China and India. The literature tends to portray this as competition between the two, but their priorities rarely overlap. Finally, the cautious attitude of Myanmar is largely a consequence of China having to recalibrate its relationship with the newly elected democratic government after years of enjoying a cosy relationship with the former military dictatorship.

The entire Indian subcontinent was once part of the British Empire. It was granted independence in August 1947 on the understanding that two states would be created on the basis of religious affiliation – there would be a largely Hindu state of India and a predominantly Muslim state of Pakistan, which itself would be divided between East and West.[1] The new arrangements were poorly prepared and, against a backdrop of death and destruction, the religious minorities in each country fled across the new borders. Similar violent clashes occurred in the Punjab, where the Sikhs were predominant and the territory was divided between India and Pakistan. Myanmar, or Burma as it was called, became a separate colony in 1937 and was granted independence in January 1948.[2]

The violence that accompanied the partition of India, and the existence of disputed borders, have poisoned relations between India and Pakistan ever since.[3] There was a short but bloody war between the two countries in 1965 over the sovereignty of Kashmir, which was ruled by India. But more damaging was the war in December 1971. The lead-up to the war was the repression of the Bengali population in East Pakistan following their declaration of independence in March 1971 and Indian support and shelter for the separatists. This irked the Pakistani government, which took an increasingly strident position against both India and the population of East Pakistan and, in December 1971, launched pre-emptive strikes against Indian airfields. India replied by moving troops into East Pakistan and blockading the sea routes to prevent reinforcements. In less than two weeks, Pakistani forces in the East were forced to surrender, and the new state of Bangladesh was born.[4]

---

[1] P. French, *Liberty or Death: India's Journey to Independence and Division*, London, 1997; Y. Khan *The Great Partition: The Making of India and Pakistan*, New Haven, CT, London, 2008; A. von Tunzelmann, *Indian Summer: The Secret History of the End of an Empire*, New York, 2008.

[2] H. Tinker, *The Union of Burma: A Study of the First Years of Independence*, London, New York, 1967.

[3] D. Hiro, *The Longest August: The Unflinching Rivalry Between India and Pakistan*, New York, 2015; M.A. Mir 'India –Pakistan; the History of Unsolved Conflicts', *IOSR Journal of Humanities and Social Science*, 19/4, 2014, 101–10; V. Schofield, *Kashmir in Conflict: India, Pakistan and the Unending War*, London, New York, 2003.

[4] B.Z. Khasru, *Myths and Facts Bangladesh Liberation War: How India, US, China, and the USSR Shaped the Outcome*, New Delhi, 2010; M.H. Khan, *Bangladesh: Partitions, Nationalisms and Legacies for State-Building*, London, 2010.

In 1962 China had its own war with India.[5] Tension between the two countries had been building since the uprising in Tibet in 1959, when India provided sanctuary for the Dalai Lama. However, the direct reason was the attempt by India to demarcate the border between the two countries in the Himalayas, with several of the border posts placed north of the agreed line. With the failure of bilateral negotiations to resolve the dispute, in October 1962 China launched a major offensive. Indian troops were overwhelmed and China was able to capture a couple of towns in the area before declaring a ceasefire and returning to the pre-war borders. Relations between the two countries remain cool and the border disputes have stayed unresolved. In May 2016, China was able to create some alarm by upgrading its border security command in neighbouring Tibet[6] and in December 2016, following a visit of the Dalai Lama to Arunachal Pradesh, China increased its troop activity in the border region.[7]

Against the backdrop of its antagonism with India, China's relationship with Pakistan grew closer.[8] China backed Pakistan in its war with India in 1965 and helped Pakistan in its development of nuclear weapons in the 1970s. The relationship has not been without its complications, however. China traces some of its problems with the Uighur militants to Pakistan's inability to control terrorists within its own frontier. It is also irked by the failure of the authorities to protect Chinese workers engaged in infrastructural projects. Even so, Pakistan is afforded a high priority among the OBOR countries, with predictably negative consequences for the approaches towards India.

---

[5] M. Brecher, 'Non-Alignment Under Stress: The West and the India–China Border War', *Pacific Affairs*, 52/4, 1979, 612–30; X. Liu, *The Sino-Indian Border Dispute and Sino-Indian Relations*. Lanham, MD, 1994; N. Maxwell, *India's China War*, New York, 2000.

[6] *The Economic Times*, 13.5.2016.

[7] *India Today*, 5.12.2016; *UPI*, 6.12.2016.

[8] A. Jamal, and J. Bajoria, *China–Pakistan Relations, Council on Foreign Relations* 6, Washington, 2010; Q. Siddique, *Deeper than the Indian Ocean? An Analysis of Pakistan-China Relations*, SISA Report 16, Oslo, 2014; A. Small, *The China-Pakistan Axis: Asia's New Geopolitics*, London, New York, 2015.

Figure 6.1 Map of the countries of South Asia

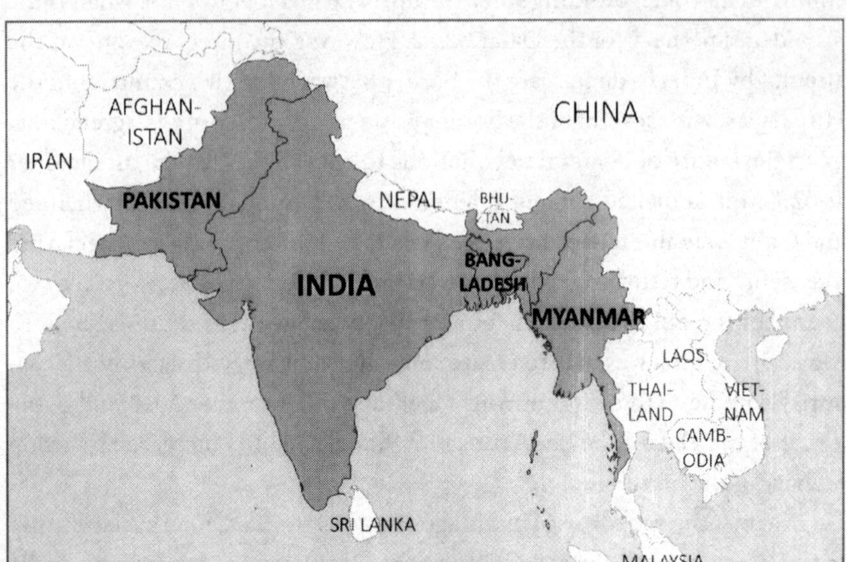

If we now turn to examine the countries more closely, there are vast discrepancies among them. The details are shown in Table 6.1. In terms of physical area, China is three times the size of India, which nevertheless is still 7th largest in the World. India, in its turn, is for to five times larger than Pakistan and Myanmar, but these two countries are still larger than any country in Europe. China and India are close in size in terms of population and they are the two most populous countries in the World. Although Pakistan and Bangladesh are sixth and eighth respectively, they still follow far behind. In terms of per capita income, China is far wealthier than any of the other countries in the group, all of which anchor the bottom end of the lower middle income classification of the World Bank. By contrast, China nestles comfortably in the upper middle income group.

Table 6.1 Basic details of China and the Countries of South Asia

	Area	Population	Per capita GDP
	Km2	Thousands	Current US$
China	9,596,961	1,376,049	7,617
Bangladesh	143,998	160,996	1,088
India	3,287,263	1,311,051	1,586
Myanmar	676,578	53,897	1,244
Pakistan	796,095	188,925	1,358

Sources: Area http://unstats.un.org/unsd/environment/totalarea.htm;
Population https://esa.un.org/unpd/wpp/Download/Standard/Population/
pc GDP http://data.un.org/Search.aspx?q=GDP+per+capita

Table 6.2 details some of the impediments to international trade. With the one exception of Myanmar, tariff levels in the Indian subcontinent were generally high but only in the case of India's tariffs on agricultural products could they be considered prohibitive. Possibly more restrictive is the performance in the border compliance indicator (the time and cost of assembling the necessary documentation for the import of a container of car parts from a typical supplier). In all cases the time involved in collecting and compiling the documentation are higher than in China and the costs involved in Bangladesh and Pakistan are the highest of all the countries studies in this volume. These differences are reflected in the Logistics Performance Index, although Myanmar's relative positon in the rankings is worse than one would expect from its border compliance performance.

Table 6.2 Trade Cost Indicators of China and the Countries of South Asia

	MFN Applied Tariffs		Border Compliance (Imports)		Logistics Performance Index
	Non-Agriculture	Agriculture			
	Simple Average %		Time (hours)	Cost (US$)	Rank
China	9.0	15.6	158	360	27
Bangladesh	13.4	16.9	327	1664	87
India	10.1	32.7	344	709	35
Myanmar	5.1	8.6	280	667	113
Pakistan	12.2	13.3	276	1743	68

Sources: Sources: MFN Tariffs: WTO, ITC, UNCTAD, *World Tariff Profiles*,Geneva, 2016; Border Compliance: Wold Bank, Doing Business, http://www.doingbusiness.org/data/exploretopics/trading-across-borders; LPI: World Bank, LPI Global Ranking (2016) http://lpi.worldbank.org/international/global

Turning to the land transport system, the Indian subcontinent contains sections of four highways of international importance, identified as part of UNESCAP Asian Highway Network.[9]. Taken together these international routes measure around 10,900 km. In addition the UNESCAP project has identified an additional 11,000 km of roads that are of sub-regional importance, 8000 km of them being located in India. Over the past decade there has been a concerted attempt to improve the condition and capacity of these roads, although there is still some way to go. In 2015 slightly over 40% of the roads were four-lane highways (Primary and Class I roads). A further 15% were well-surfaced two-/three-lane roads (Class II roads), but that still leaves 35% consisting of two-lane roads with only a bituminous treated surface (Class III roads) and 10% that did not even reach that standard.

[9] UN, ESCAP, *Intergovernmental Agreement on the Asian Highway Network*, s.l., 2003.

Table 6.3 Length and Condition of Asian Highway in China and the countries of South Asia

	Length	Class (per cent)				
	Kms	Primary	I	II	III	<III
China	10847.28	77.8	2.1	17.1	3.0	Neg.
Bangladesh	1760	-	17.7	79.5	2.5	0.3
India	11900.62	0.8	59.4	9.0	30.0	1.0
Myanmar	4524.99	-	7.1	12.7	37.6	42.6
Pakistan	5328,00	6.7	20.9	5.2	42.1	21.4

Source: http://www.unescap.org/resources/status-asian-highway-member-countries

Myanmar had the worst road surfaces, with 80% of its network classified as Class III or less, followed by Pakistan, with 67% of its roads in a poor condition. In India 31% of its network fell into this category, and the surprise was Bangladesh, with only 2.7% of its network in constructed to these lowest classifications.[10] However, this still marks a considerable improvement on the situation five years earlier. In 2008 no less than 75% of Bangladesh's network fell into the lowest two categories, and in India the figure had been an even more alarming 96%.[11] In Bangladesh much of the road improvement work on the international corridors had been helped by the ADB, and the Japan Debt Cancellation Fund has contributed to upgrading the local route between Chittagong and Dhaka.[12]

Of the envisaged Trans-Asian rail network no less than 15,848 km passes through the four countries of South Asia. At the turn of the last century, none of the track in Bangladesh and Myanmar and only 8.7% of the track in Pakistan was electrified. India stood out in stark contrast with 64.8% of its track electrified (this is in contrast with total domestic netwrok, where the figure drops to 30%). In both Bangladesh and Myanmar virtually 85% of the routes were single track only. The figure for Pakistan was 68%

---

[10] UNESCAP Asia Highway database.

[11] S. Madhur, G. Wignaraja and P. Darjes, *Roads for Asian Integration: Measuring ADB's Contribution to the Asian Highway Network*, ADB Working Paper Series on Regional Economic Integration, 37, 2009, 6–7.

[12] K.F. Begum, *Status Paper on Asian Highway. Bangladesh*, 2011.

and again India stood out, with only 26% single track. Two links were missing – one of 346 km (between India and Myanmar and another of 263 km between Myanmar and Thailand.[13] A further impediment to connectivity lies in the fact that India and Pakistan have 1676 mm gauge, Bangladesh has both 1676 gauge and 1000 mm gauge, while Myanmar has only 1000 mm.

Pakistan

China has had a close relationship with Pakistan[14] ever since its own war with India in 1962 and its support for Pakistan in its military conflicts with India, though possibly not always reaching the lyrical heights of 'sweeter than honey' or 'higher than Himalayas'.[15] Well aware of the fragility of Pakistan's standards of governance and of economic management, Chinese support has waxed and waned over the years. However the OBOR initiative seems to have injected a new dynamic into mutual relations. China has long been active in infrastructural projects in Pakistan. Back in 1979, it worked with the Pakistani government in constructing the Karakoram Highway linking Kashmir in Pakistan to Kashgar in China, and forming China's only overland route into Pakistan.[16] It also cooperated with the government in turning the small fishing village of Gwadar into a potential commercial deep-water port. Although China had loaned 75% of the $250 million initial construction costs, possibly under pressure from the USA, the government awarded the management of the port itself to the Port of Singapore Authority. This

---

[13] UN, ESCAP, *Development of the Trans Asian Railway. Trans Asian Railway in the Southern Corridor of Asia-Europe Routes*, New York, 1999. From Jiripam (India) toKale (Myanmar) and from Hanbyuzayat (Myanmar) to Nam Tok (Thailand).

[14] R.M. Hathaway and W. Lee (eds.), *Islamization and the Pakistani Economy*, Washington, 2004; A. Imam and E.A. Dar, *Democracy and Public Administration in Pakistan*, Boca Raton, FL, 2013; C. Jaffrelot, *The Pakistan Paradox: Instability and Resilience*, Oxford, New York, 2015; S. Khan, *The Military and Economic Development in Pakistan*, PERI Working Paper 291, Amherst, MA, 2012; A. Shah, *The Army and Democracy: Military Politics in Pakistan*, Boston, MA, 2014.

[15] I. Tharoor, 'What China's and Pakistan's Special Friendship Means', *Washington Post*, 21.4.2015.

[16] S.H. Sering, *Expansion of the Karakoram Corridor: Implications and Prospects*, IDSA Occasional Paper No. 27, New Delhi, 2012. It is now part of the Asian Highway Route Four.

setback, coupled with the political instability following the resignation of President Pervez Musharraf and an upsurge of Islamic militancy, somewhat dampened bilateral relations for a while. Meanwhile, because the port was cut off from the main road network, the project seemed to be heading for failure. As a result, in February 2013 the government reversed its decision and entrusted the management to China Overseas Ports Holding Company, which committed $750 million to the port's further development (more of this in Chapter 9). At the same time, the Pakistani government suggested the creation of an economic and energy corridor from the port linking it directly to the south of China, and it suggested recommencing work on improving the Karakoram Highway.[17] In May 2013, the two countries signed a memorandum of understanding for the long-term development of a China-Pakistan Economic Corridor (CPEC). The agreement envisaged pipelines and a rail link to China from the Gwadar, More immediately, the two countries agreed to accelerate work on the Attabad Lake. This had been formed by an earthquake in 2010 and was blocking the Karakorum Highway.[18] The 25 km Attabad Lake bypass with five tunnels, two long bridges and seventy-eight smaller ones was opened in September 2015.[19]

In May 2015, President Xi Jinping and Prime Minister Nawaz Sharif of Pakistan signed an agreement that committed $46 billion investment in the China–Pakistan Economic Corridor (CPEC) over the next ten years. Of this sum, $12 billion was targeted at transport improvements and the other $34 billion was earmarked for various energy projects. Taken together, the projects were expected to generate 700,000 jobs in Pakistan and, when completed, add 2–2.5% to the country's GDP.[20] We will look at the transport provisions first.

Immediately before the signature of the CPEC agreement, the Pakistani government announced a National Highways and Motorways Plan envisaging a network of 9,574 km. Although this comprised 3.65% of the total road network, it carried 80% of Pakistan's total traffic. The corridor itself would have three routes, many coinciding with the Asian Highway network.[21]

[17] *The Express Tribune*, 18.2.2013.

[18] *The Economic Times*, 21.5.2013; *The Nation*, 24.5.2013; *The Diplomat*, 30.7.2013.

[19] *The Express Tribune*, 14.9.2015.

[20] *The Wire*, 3.6.2016.

[21] *Dawn*, 15.5.2015.

Some of these improvement projects were incorporated into the CPEC agreement.[22] In December 2015 the EXIM Bank of China agreed to provide $2.89 billion to finance the 390 km highway improvement of the Karachi to Lahore highway and $1.3 billion for upgrading the 133 km stretch of highway north of Islamabad from Havelian to Thakot.[23]

There is a tendency in the OBOR literature to describe Chinese infrastructural investment as though there was nothing else happening before and that no one else had been interested. This is far from the truth. For example, the ADB has long been active in Pakistan, improving major corridors and building feeder roads to connect to them. Between 2010 and 2014 it had built and upgraded 1476 km of national highways and 2750 km of provincial and rural roads. Its 2015–19 programme envisaged the expenditure of $461 million for support of the National Highways plan and $970 billion for other road improvements. This would contribute to rehabilitating 1270 km of flood-damaged roads, improving 420 km of highway, building 360 km of new highways and motorways.[24]

The railways in Pakistan are in a parlous state, and starting afresh with a completely new high-speed line from the port of Gwadar to the Chinese city of Kashgar might not be a bad idea. Years of neglect have contributed to a significant decline in freight and passenger services. Over the last five years the number of daily passenger services has dropped from 230 to ninety-two, and the number of freight train services from ninety-six to one.[25] Notwithstanding the fact that the high-speed rail project is still in the survey stage, in April 2016 the Chinese authorities announced the start of a regular service from Linyi in Shandong province to Gwadar. Until the track was extended, the international freight train would take the goods to Kashgar where they would be loaded onto trucks for the rest of the journey.[26] Meanwhile, the only other agreement signed in the context of the CPEC was an undertaking to help upgrade the main western line from Karachi to Islamabad (ML1) and to establish a dry port at Havelain. In

---

22 *Dawn*, 20.4.2015.

23 H. Wu, 'Bankers Behind "Belt and Road" Business Surge', *Caixin Online*, 29.12.2015.

24 https://www.adb.org/projects/pakistan

25 https://www.adb.org/sites/default/files/linked-documents/cps-pak-2015-2019-ssa-05.pdf

26 *People's Daily*, 10.5.2016.

May 2016 the Pakistan government approved the $8.2 billion project 85% of which will be funded by a concessionary loan from China.[27]

Most of the Chinese investment envisaged for the CPEC was destined for power – the construction of pipelines to China but also the provision of electricity for Pakistan itself. In the former instance, in November 2015 the China National Petroleum Corporation decided to invest $1.47 billion in an oil refinery, petro-chemical plant and a land-based liquid natural gas receiving terminal at Gaddani, just north of Karachi.[28] Meanwhile, it is fair to say that Pakistan is indeed in the grip of a power crisis. The capacity is inadequate to satisfy peak demand and the tariffs charged to consumers are too low, leaving the industry mired in debt, unable either to raise sufficient public funding or to attract private investment.[29] The current crippling power shortages are estimated to cost the economy an annual loss of 2% of its GDP. The 'early harvest' power projects are expected to yield 10,400 MW of electricity by 2017–18.[30] The Chinese effort is impressive.[31] In January 2016 work started on the $1.65 billion Karot hydro-electric plant. This is the first project to be financed from China's Silk Road Fund.[32] In September 2016, the agreement was concluded for work to start on the Suki Kinari plant. The government would buy electricity from the plant for thirty years, after which it would take over the plant at no cost to itself.[33] Zonergy hooked up 300KW capacity to the national

27 *International Railway Journal*, 10.6.2016.

28 K. Mustafa, 'Chinese Company to set up Petrochemical, Refining Complexes at Gaddani', *The International News*, 5.11.2015.

29 M. Kugelman (ed.), *Pakistan's Interminable Energy Crisis*, Washington DC, 2015.

30 S. Tiezzi, 'China Powers up Pakistan: The Energy Component of the CPEC', *The Diplomat*, 13.1.2016.

31 The two sides signed agreements for building the 870 MW Hydro-Electric Suki Kinari Hydropower Project, the 720 MW Karot Hydropower Project, two 660 MW coal fire power plants at Port Qasim, the 1000 MW Zonergy solar project in Punjab, two wind power projects in Jhimpir and in Sindh, concessions for mining 3,8 million tons of coal annually in Sindh province and two 330 MW coal fired power stations linked to it, as well as several other smaller projects. *Dawn*, 20.4.2015.

32 Tiezzi, 'China Powers up Pakistan' . In March 2017 the World Bank's International Finance Corporation invetsed $100 million in the project, its first major collaboration with the China Export Import Bank, China Development Bank, and Silk Road Fund. *The International News*, 15.3.2017.

33 *The Express Tribune*, 25.8.2016.

grid in June 2016 but the project has since been delayed while the company is embroiled in a litigation against the government when it cut the rates it was willing to pay.[34] When everything is completed, the projects will add a further 21,000 MW to the national grid. But, as a parliamentary committee noted in summer 2016, a start had yet to be made in laying the underground transmission lines that would link the plants to the national grid.[35]

All this suggests two further possible problems. The first is that the crisis may not be primarily one of lack of primary capacity, but one of efficiency in its distribution and pricing, costing and funding. If indeed this is even partly correct, the Pakistani government may be saddling itself with overcapacity without resolving the root problem of sustainability (i.e. not to have it acting as a loss-making drain on the budget). The second problem lies in the chosen means of finance. China is offering concessionary loans. These bear interest (even if it is low) and the loans have to be repaid. The interest is probably front-ended, in that it has to be paid on the whole sum, even before the output is realised. Moreover, the interest, and whatever other terms have been guaranteed on the investment, are likely to be the first claimants against any revenues generated.[36] Both these problems are exacerbated if the loans are not actually so generous. Recent evidence suggests that interest rates are 4.5% higher than the Libor rates (1.3-1.7%) and that China Export and Credit Insurance Corporation (Sinosure) charges a one-off insurance fee of 7.5% on top of that. The loans cover 75-80% of the cost of the projects and in order to attract the balance., any investment promises a (local currency) return of 27-35% percent on coal-fired power stations which is double the usual rate. These returns have been justified as necessary to attract investment, but if projections are accurate, the total cost is considerable - involving annual foreign currency payments of $2.4 billion.[37] However if, as in the past, the energy prices do not even cover the costs of production, the prospect of a glittering future may quickly fade.

The CPEC faces problems in the south of the country which is the

---

[34] *SeeNews Renewables*, 20.6.2016, 20.9.2016.

[35] *Dawn*, 13.8.2016.

[36] S. Pal, 'The China-Pakistan Corridor is All About Power. Not Electricity, but the Real Thing', *The Wire*, 3.6.2016.

[37] S. Rana, 'Windfall for Chinese on coal fired projects', *Express Tribune*, 15.2.2017. For a wider critique see N. Jamal, 'The Cost of CPEC', *Dawn*, 12.3.2017.

home to the Baluch peoples and also one of the poorest areas of the country[38]. Having failed to obtain semi-autonomous status at the time of independence, the region has been the scene of recurrent periods of unrest, including the present insurgency that has simmered since 2003. This is the site of the Gwadar harbour development as well as the transport and pipelines reaching inland and northwards from the port. Moreover, the Iran–Pakistan pipeline (if Pakistan ever completes its section) also runs through the territory. All these facilities would be in danger if they become the target of separatist violence. It is interesting that Pakistan has regularly blamed India for interfering in the region, and has done so again – accusing India of trying thereby to destabilise the CPEC.[39] There have been shootouts between Afghan and Pakistani troops over Pakistani moves to define the Durand Line as an international border. In addition tensions have grown, with massive Pakistani military operations against Pashtun tribal forces in the Khyber and North Waziristan Agencies. Over 1.5 million inhabitants of Pashtun have been made homeless, with around 100,000 living as refugees in Afghanistan, 'vowing to return to their homes, and many ready to resort to the use of arms'.[40] The government envisaged that a force of 9000 soldiers and 5,000 paramilitary would be needed to protect all the CEPC projects.[41]

India

India[42] has not officially accepted an invitation to join the Chinese OBOR. In fact, until recently government ministers had said little on the subject at all. This has now started to change and, by implication, the government

---

[38] F. Grare, *Balochistan. The State Versus the Nation*, Carnegie Papers, 2013; M. Kupecz, 'Pakistan's Baloch Insurgency: History, Conflict Drivers, and Regional Implications', *International Affairs Review*, 20/3, 2012, 95–110.

[39] U. Shahid, 'Balochistan: The Troubled Heart of the CPEC', *The Diplomat*, 23.8.2016.

[40] G. Parthasarathy, 'India Right in Flagging Baluchistan' *The Hindu*, 24.8.2016.

[41] *Dawn*, 13.8.2016, 21.2.2017.

[42] S. Corbridge, J. Harriss and C. Jeffrey, *India Today: Economy, Politics and Society*, Cambridge, 2013; McKinsey & Company Inc., *Reimagining India: Unlocking the Potential of Asia's Next Superpower*, New York, 2013; A. Panagariya, *India: The Emerging Giant*, Oxford, New York, 2010.

has begun to criticise China's whole approach. The argument now is that whereas China seems to claim that connectivity can lead to cooperation and, therefore, overcome geopolitics, it has in fact been doing the opposite. It has been using its investments to create new geopolitical realities. In a way, it is suggested, the unilateral approach adopted has helped antagonise potential partners. Mutual confidence and trust are not outcomes of increased connectivity, but preconditions for it. Do not expect a ringing endorsement from New Delhi any time soon.[43]

The reasons are not hard to see. The strengthening relationship between Pakistan and China, especially when coupled with arms deals such as Pakistan's acquisition of eight Chinese 039-A submarines,[44] is bound to raise qualms in India. In addition, much of the road and rail building will take place in the disputed territory of Pakistani-occupied Kashmir and could therefore be construed as legitimising Pakistan's claim over the region. The railway through Kashmir would also assume strategic importance in the event of conflicts with India, and in such an event it would make it far easier for China to supply Pakistan with military equipment. Furthermore, the presence of Chinese workers in the area might itself lead to increased militarisation. In May 2016, a bomb attack that injured a Chinese worker and his driver prompted Chinese demands for greater military security.[45] The challenge is not only through Pakistan: China and India also have unsettled claims in the region. In this respect, it is interesting to reflect that nowhere in the entire initiative was any mention made of increasing the number of border connections between India and Pakistan,[46] or of opening a direct freight link (either improved road or rail) between China and India.

Indian authorities may also have initially been offended that the belt and road initiatives were both cloaked in a Chinese story: it was a Chinese envoy who discovered the overland route and a Chinese admiral who made the voyages all the way to Africa and Arabia. It may have rankled all the more

---

43 T. Madan, 'What India Thinks about China's One Belt, One Road Initiative (But Doesn't Explicitly Say)', *Brookings Briefings*, 14.3.2016; *The Wire*, 17.1.2017.

44 *Defence News*, 11.10.2015.

45 *Express Tribune*, 30.5.2016.

46 There is one rail crossing between Attari (India) and Wagah (Pakistan) and that is part of the Trans-Asian Railway network. In 2006 a passenger rail border point, which had been closed since the 1965 Indo-Pakistan War, was also reopened at Munsebao.

since only a few months before the OBOR announcement India launched Project Mausam: Maritime Routes and Cultural Landscapes with the aim of having it added to the World Heritage List.[47] Project Mausam refers to the seasons when sailors could sail safely. Their voyages made since the 4th century AD took them along the African and Arabian coasts and into the seas of South-East Asia, using the seasonal monsoons to carry them on their journeys. The routes established were used to trade spices, medicines, dyes, grain, wood, textiles, gems and ornaments. Although it had was trade that kept the network together, the voyages also made possible the exchange of cultures, religions and technologies.[48] Of course there is no reason why the MSR could not accommodate the Indian-led Mausam project as well,[49] and there were some who suggested that the government should use the opportunities offered;[50] but that is not quite the same as having its contribution recognised at the outset.

The only role left for India in the grand scheme of things is as part of the BCIM corridor which has been integrated into the OBOR initiative, with an estimated price tag of $22 billion. The BCIM concept, however, is not new. It was first mooted by Professor Che Zhimin[51] in November 1998. In August 1999, a meeting held in Kunming created the BCIM Forum for Regional Cooperation. While academics and civil society in India have generally been positive towards BCIM, for more than a decade after its announcement the government evinced little enthusiasm. This began to change, in 2013 particularly after the K2K Car Rally between Kolkata and Kunming. After the visit of Chinese Premier Li Keqiang to India in May 2013, the two countries agreed to establish a joint study group at governmental level to consider specific programmes that could contribute towards building the economic

---

[47] http://www.brics-info.org/project-mausam-mausam-mawsim-maritime-routes-and-cultural-landscapes/

[48] A. Pillalamarri, 'Project Mausam: India's Answer to China's "Maritime Silk Road"', *The Diplomat*, 18.9.2014.

[49] *Economic Times of India*, 20.10.2015.

[50] G. Nataraj and R. Sekhani, '"China's One Belt One Road Initiative": Analysis from an Indian Perspective', *Economic and Political Weekly*, 50/49, 5.12.2015.

[51] Then Deputy Director of the Economic and Technological Research Centre of the Yunnan Provincial People's Government.

corridor.[52] If the forum structure was supposed to foster genuine inter-state planning, it must be judged a sore disappointment. This was partly because of the shifting focus of the OBOR initiative and responsibility in both India and China. What had been propelled in the early stages as an inter-regional initiative (in Yunnan in China and in India's north-eastern provinces) became recentralised in China once the OBOR announcement had been made. The BCIM became a foreign and security policy matter rather than a regional development issue. Matters were not helped by China's reluctance for OBOR to be subsumed in regional structures, whether with Russia's EAEC or ASEAN or BCIM fora.[53]

The BCIM corridor has immense conventional and renewable energy resources, and the countries involved could benefit from collaboration in the power sector. They could exploit the hydrocarbons in Bangladesh, hydro-electric and mineral resources in North-East India, natural gas reserves in Myanmar, and coal reserves in East Indian as well as in China's Yunnan province. North-East India could export energy to Bangladesh and reduce its own reliance on Gulf oil by importing from Myanmar. This would also help to reduce the Myanmar's export dependence on China and Thailand. In terms of transport, an upgrade of the 312 km stretch of Stilwell Road, connecting North-East India with Yunnan through northern Myanmar, could lower transportation costs between India and China by 30% and further stimulate the growing Sino-Indian trade.[54] One recent radical proposal was for India to abandon plans for a $25 billion gas pipeline to Siberia and engage instead in a gas swap with China whereby China would increase its own purchases from Russia, and allow gas from Myanmar to be exported through a much shorter and cheaper pipeline to India.[55] However, it will require a massive build-up of trust on all sides before matters get that far.

To date the joint study group has held three meetings, the most recent

---

[52] A. Aneja, 'China, India Fast-Track BCIM Economic Corridor Project', *The Hindu*, 26.6.2015.

[53] P. Uberoi, *Moving Forward on Parallel Tracks? A New Perspective on the BCIM Initiatives?* ICS Working Paper, Delhi, September 2016.

[54] P. Sahoo and A. Bhunia, 'BCIM Corridor a Game Changer for South Asian Trade', *East Asia Forum*, 18.7.2014.

[55] *Indian Express*, 7.12.2016.

being in Kolkata in June 2015. All four countries agreed to prepare a combined country report on the seven thematic areas identified at the first joint study group.[56] The discussions mostly focused around the 2800 km long K-2-K route[57] which had also been part of the Southern Silk Route, and is considered possibly the best road route for the corridor.[58] All that was missing was a stretch of less than 200 km in Myanmar which required upgrading as an all-weather road.[59]

Meanwhile, the Indian government has also announced an ambitious $30 billion national railway improvement programme to be undertaken between 2015 and 2019. The previous decade's demand for both passenger and freight traffic had far exceeded the growth of capacity, though this had also contributed to the fortuitous situation that the railways had succeeded in generating a profit on their overall operations. The programme envisages the building of dedicated freight lines in the so-called 'golden quadrangle' connecting Delhi, Mumbai, Chennai and Kolkata, existing lines being estimated to be running at up to 150% of capacity. These lines represented only 16% of total length of the Indian network but carried 55% of the total traffic. The new tracks would run parallel to existing tracks, which would then be freed for passenger traffic. The advantage of building the new lines for freight rather than for passengers is that the freight lines would be cheaper to build and would enable trains to carry a higher axle load. In addition two new rail freight corridors would be built – a 1483 km western line from Dadri in Uttar Pradesh to Mumbai, to be built with a $20 billion loan from the Japan International Cooperation Agency, and a 1839 km eastern line from Dankuni in West Bengal to Ludhiana in the Punjab, built with the help of a $2.7 billion loan from the World Bank, and linked from there into the TAR network.[60]

---

[56] J.S. Pattnaik, 'BCIM Corridor: The Road Map for Northeast', *The Arunachal Times*, 2.12.2016.

[57] Kunming–Ruili–Bhamo–Lashio–Mandalay–Tamu–Imphal–Sylhet–Dhaka–Kolkata.

[58] M. Vaid and T.S. Maini, 'BCIM: Can India Be a Driving Force?', *The Diplomat*, 1.1.2015.

[59] Aneja, 'China, India Fast-Track'.

[60] A.K. Mishra, *Dedicated Freight Corridors of Indian Railways. Harbinger of Accelerated Infrastructural Growth*, Presentation at Project Management National Conference

To round off this section on India's domestic rail plans, it is worth mentioning that Japan will build India's first high-speed railway. When finished, this will run for 508 km up the west coast from Mumbai to Ahmedabad, completing the journey in about two hours. The entire project is estimated to cost $15 billion, of which 81% will be covered by a soft loan from Japan. The loan will run for fifty years and carry an annual interest of 0.1%.[61]

We have already seen that India's participation in the BCIM framework has been slow. In fact one commentator has suggested that India has been proceeding 'at less than glacial speed', but that does not mean that it has no interest in helping improve connectivity with its neighbours.[62] As far back as 1991 the government adopted a 'look east' policy, but at the time mainly directed towards South-East Asia rather than towards its immediate neighbours. In November 2014 the newly elected government led by Prime Minister Narendra Modi renamed and recalibrated the policy, now named 'Act East'. The new title did not just represent an increased dynamic and priority imparted to the policy, but a new focus on Bangladesh, Myanmar and China.[63] Bangladesh is of immediate interest since its landmass effectively separates mainland India from its north-eastern provinces. The two parts are linked by a 22 km wide stretch of hilly territory that is known as the 'chicken neck'. To travel from Kolkata to Agartala via this route involves a journey of 1650 km. The direct geographical distance between the two (through Bangladesh) is 350 km,[64] though the rail route would be somewhat longer.

India, Bengaluru, 10-12.9.2015.

61 *Indian Express*, 20.4.2016.

62 R. Bhoothalingam, 'One-Belt-One-Road – to Join or Not to Join?', *The Wire*, 14.6.2016.

63 A. Sajjanhar, '2 Years On, Has Modi's "Act East" Policy Made a Difference for India?', *The Diplomat*, 3.6.2016.

64 A.B.R. Chaudhury, and P. Basu, *Proximity To Connectivity: India And Its Eastern And Southeastern Neighbours PART 1 India-Bangladesh Connectivity: Possibilities and Challenges*, Kolkata, 2015, 16–17.

Bangladesh

The idea of constructing a link running through Bangladesh[65] that connects the two parts of India is not new. It is not as though there are no railways criss-crossing the country, but with India's railways using the broad gauge of 1676 mm and Bangladesh employing the 1000 mm gauge the systems simply did not connect. The idea was raised in 1974 and again in 1998, but nothing was done. This was partly because the Bangladeshi authorities suspected that India was only interested in a transit route for its own products and that Bangladeshi products would not be granted access to the Indian market. In January 2010 the idea emerged again, but this time with India willing to offer a $1 billion grant to help convert the line to broad gauge and to supply the carriages and locomotives. In addition a 15 km missing link had to be constructed on the eastern border of Bangladesh, between Akhaura to Agartala, on the Indian side of the border.[66]

India's second major project was to link India's north-eastern states with the Bangladeshi port of Chittagon, to the south. Ironically, this side of the country was also running on 1000 mm gauge, so 447 km of the track from Agartala northwards had also to be converted to 1676 mm .Work had started in December 1996 but progress was slow for several reasons – funding was not always available, the hilly terrain was extremely difficult, work was only possible for four months a year and a simmering insurgency saw the murder or kidnapping of sixty workers and executives between 2006 and 2009. Work resumed on the difficult 220 km Lumding–Silchar section in October 2014,[67] and it was completed six months later. The final 227 km section to Agartala was finished at the end of 2015.[68] Completing the new line from Agartala down to India's southernmost border town of Sabroom, 135 km away, is envisaged by 2020.[69] From there to the Chittagong international

---

[65] A.R. Khan, *The Economy of Bangladesh: A Quarter Century of Development*, Houndsmills, 2015; D. Lewis, *Bangladesh: Politics, Economy and Civil Society*, Cambridge, 2011; A. Riaz, *Bangladesh: A Political History since Independence*, London, New York, 2016.

[66] Chaudhury and Basu, *Proximity To Connectivity*, 22–3.

[67] *Hindustan Times*, 1.10.2014.

[68] *NDTV*, 22.2.2016.

[69] *Assam Tribune*, 13.9.2016.

seaport is only another 72 km. This final link would be made by road. To this end, in June 2015 work started to replace the ferry over the Feni River, which marked the border between the two countries, with a 150 metre two-lane bridge. The cost of building the bridge and the approach roads on both sides of the border will be met by the Indian authorities.[70]

Indian interest in Bangladesh also stretched to the power sector. In February 2016 Bharat Heavy Electricals Ltd beat Chinese competition to secure the $1.6 billion contract for building a 1320 MW thermal power station in Khulna in southern Bangladesh. India's EXIM Bank provided a soft loan (1% above Libor rates) to cover 70% of the costs of the project.[71] In July 2016 the Bangladesh–India Friendship Power Company (50:50 joint venture between the two countries) won the $1.49 billion contract to build two 660 MW power stations in Rampal Upazila in the Bagerhat district of Bangladesh. Once again, the project was financed by the EXIM Bank of India.[72]

An even more ambitious plan was (at the time of writing) still in the planning phase. This involves the construction of a network of oil and LPG pipelines through the territories of Bangladesh, Myanmar and India. One part would involve reviving the project for a 900 km pipeline linking the Shwe gas field in Myanmar through Bangladesh to India. The so-called BMI initiative dates as far back as 1997, but the idea was revived during Prime Minister Modi's visit to Dhaka in June 2015. A second part of the scheme would be to transport LPG from the huge Bangladeshi reserves in the Bay of Bengal via pipelines into India's north-eastern states. A third part of the scheme, which was agreed in April 2015, involves the building of a 130 km pipeline to transport diesel from India's refinery in Siliguri in North Bengal to Parbatipur in Bangladesh.[73] In August 2016, as part of its Hydrocarbon Vision 2030, the government proposed a 6900 km network of pipelines based on a main natural gas pipeline from Kolkata, through Bangladesh and Tripura (North-East India) and the port city of Sittwe in Myanmar,

---

70 *Hindustan Times*, 11.6.2016.

71 *Reuters*, 22.2.2016.

72 *BDNews24.com*, 13.7.2016; *Times of India*, 14.7.2016.

73 R. Bhattacharjee, 'Bangladesh Can Harness Its Vast Oil And Gas Potential With India's Assistance – Analysis', *South Asia Monitor*, 4.5.2016

including thirteen distribution routes. The scheme would also explore expansion of the exploitation of gas reserves in Tripura itself.[74]

China too has been active in the energy field. In March 2016, two Chinese firms and the Bangladesh-China Power Company, itself a joint venture) secured the $1.56 billion contract for building a 1320 MW coal-fired power station near the Payra Maritime Port.[75] In August the Bangladesh–China Power Company won a second contract to build another 1320 MW power plant next to the first. The funding was on the basis of a 30:70 equity:debt ratio.[76]

Turning our attention to transport infrastructure, in December 2015 the China Communications Construction Company was awarded the $705 million contract for the construction of a 2 km two-lane tunnel under the Karnaphuli River to relive the pressure on the two existing bridges and to improve connections to the Chittagong port. The EXIM Bank of China covered about two-thirds of the estimated costs of the project.[77] In September 2016 the China Harbour Engineering Company was appointed to build two road projects. One was a $1.6 billion project to expand the 226 km Dhaka–Sylhet road into a four-lane highway. The second was a $2.8 billion project to construct a marine drive and a 160 km four-lane expressway from Sitakunda to Cox's Bazar.[78]

In 2010 a consortium of aid donors agreed a loan package of $2.9 billion to build a bridge spanning the treacherous 5 km wide Padma River. The river could only be crossed by ferry, which impaired the links between Dhaka (on the northern side) and the south-west of the country. In 2012, however, the World Bank claimed to have discovered evidence of high-level corruption in selecting the consultants for the project, and made the release of its tranche of $1 billion conditional on the government taking appropriate action. When no action was forthcoming, the financial arrangements collapsed.[79] In May 2014 the contract for constructing the two-level bridge was

---

[74] *Energy Global*, 15.8.2016.

[75] *China Daily* 30.3.2016; *Dhaka Tribune*, 29.3.2016.

[76] *Dhaka Tribune*, 13.8.2016.

[77] *BDNews24*, 23.12.2015

[78] *Daily Star*, 22.9.2016.

[79] World Bank, *Final Report of the External Panel of Experts re; the Padma Multi-Purpose Bridge Project*, 20.2.2013.

awarded to China Major Bridge Engineering Company Ltd (which had built the famous 36 km Hangzhou Bay Bridge, the longest sea-crossing bridge in the world), after the company made a bid 12% below the original estimated costs and China offered $2 billion in investment on a BOT (build–operate–transfer) basis.[80] In July 2016 the $3.14 billion contract for the 215 km rail link from Dahka, over the bridge to Jessore was awarded to China Railway Group, chosen by the Chinese government.[81]

China had also been interested in the construction of a 129 km railway line from Dohazari in Chittagong to Gundum near the Myanmar border via Cox's Bazar but the government had had difficulties in closing the deal. As a result, at the end of September 2016, just weeks before President Xi's visit, the government announced that it had secured a $1.5 billion loan from the ADB for the first phase of the project (102 km from Dohazari to Cox's Bazar), the cost of which was estimated to be $2 billion. The loans would be for twenty-five years, with interest based on the Libor rates. The ADB expressed a willingness to fund the second phase, which would extend the line to Gundum, as well as connecting it to the new deep-water seaport in Matarbari.[82] In addition, a British firm, DP Rail, has proposed investing $7.5 billion in a 280 km rail link from Joydevpur, via Dhaka and the Padma Bridge and south to the new Payra port.[83]

In October 2016 President Xi's visit to Bangladesh marked the opportunity to unveil a five-year comprehensive cooperation plan, involving the extension of soft loans worth $23 billion for twenty separate projects to be undertaken before 2020. Some of the projects had already been agreed before the visit, such as the Payra power plant. Seven of the projects, worth $7.7 billion, are in the power and energy sector, including the Payra plant and a 350 MW coal-fired thermal power plant at Munshiganj, on the outskirts of Dhaka and on the Padma River. A further $6.65 billion was allocated to tunnel and road improvements.[84] Another $6.21 billion was earmarked for

[80] *BDNews24*, 14.5.2014; 22.5.2014.

[81] *Daily Star*, 21.7.2016.

[82] *Daily Star*, 29.9.2016.

[83] *Daily Star*, 19.9.2016.

[84] This included the construction of the Karpaphuli River tunnel, the Dhaka–Sylhet highway and the Sitakunda–Cox's Bazar Marine Drive Expressway. The new venture was the proposed Dhaka–Ashulia Elevated Expressway.

four rail ventures, which included the Padma rail link project.[85] Bangladesh also wants investment in its two economic zones. Chinese companies were expected to invest around $4.5 billion in the designated SEZs in each city, one in south Chittagong on 774 acres of land and another in south Dhaka. The latter, which is being built in collaboration with the Bangladesh Garment Manufacturers and Exporters Association (BGMEA) was expected to create 200,000–250,000 new jobs in the country.[86]

Myanmar

If the BCIM corridor is ever going to represent an integrated regional development scheme, rather than a series of disconnected projects, it is essential for China that Myanmar[87] is a willing and active partner. For many years this did not seem a problem. After a series of brutal government repressions, in 1988 many Western powers suspended aid, and later, when human rights abuses continued, they imposed various sanctions on the regime. This coincided with the start of the economic boom in neighbouring China, and resource-rich Myanmar became an attractive object for Chinese investment. It presented Beijing with two strategic interests. The first was energy procurement. This involved constructing a gas pipeline from China to the sea-bed Shwe gas field and, parallel to this, an oil pipeline to transport crude oil that could be off-loaded at the port of Kyaukpyu. Another energy source lay in tapping the opportunities for generating hydro-electricity through a series of dams on the rivers in the border regions. In 2012 the Shweli I Hydropower Plant (600 MW) had started transmission of energy, mostly destined for China, and there were plans to construct a further forty-eight power plants across the country: forty-five hydroelectric power plants, two coal-fired power plants, and one gas-fired power plant. Over thirty-five of

[85] The three other projects involve upgrading the rail links between Joydevpur to Mymensingh, Joydevpur to Ishwardi and Akhaura to Sylhet to dual gauge/double track. *Daily Star*, 26.9.2016; *Reuters*, 14.10.2016.

[86] *Bangladesh Today*, Oct. 2015.

[87] R. Cockett, *Blood, Dreams and Gold: The Changing Face of Burma*, New Haven, CT, 2015; N. Kipgen, *Myanmar: A Political History*, Oxford, 2016; M. Lall, *Understanding Reform in Myanmar: People and Society in the Wake of Military Rule*, London, 2016; K. Odaka, (ed.), *The Myanmar Economy: Its Past, Present and Prospects*, Berlin, 2015.

these planned power plants are confirmed to be implemented by Chinese corporations. If all these were to be completed the total installed capacity would be 36,635 MW, the equivalent of more than double the country's entire current consumption. A second strategic interest lay in securing for Yunnan access to the sea, to help save time and distance for both imports and exports. One option would be to build roads/railways to connect the Yunnan border town of Ruili (Muse, on the Myanmar side) through to the deep-water seaport near Kyaukpyu. On 27April 2011, the China Railway Engineering Corporation (CREC) and Myanmar Union Ministry of Rail Transportation signed a memorandum of understanding for the construction of a railway from Muse to Kyaukpyu. The total cost of $20 billion for the work in Myanmar would be borne by the CREC on a BOT basis, with the line reverting to Myanmar after fifty years.[88] All these plans began to unravel after 2011 when Myanmar began its reform process and its transition to democratic elections.

In September 2011, six months after the transitional government had come to power, it suspended work on the Myitsone Dam. The dam would have been built at the confluence of where the Malikha and Maykha Rivers converged to form the headwaters of the Irrawaddy River. The idea of a dam at the site has been conceived as long ago as 1952, but nothing happened until 2002 when the Japanese company KEPCO was invited to prepare a feasibility study. It decided not to move forward with the project for two reasons – it was worried about (armed) resistance to the project and it doubted whether there was a market in Myanmar for the electricity produced, especially as it had no means of selling the surplus to China. In October 2006 the government turned to the China Power Investment Corporation to take over the scheme. The scheme would have a total of seven upstream cascade hydropower projects with the final dam and power station at Myitsone. The scheme would have involved the flooding of 390 km^2 and the relocation of 14,000 villagers.[89] The dam, if completed, would be one of the largest in the world, with a capacity of 6000 MW. It is a joint venture with China

[88] T. Kudo, *China's Policy toward Myanmar: Challenges and Prospects,* IDE-JETRO Working paper, 2012; P. Scally, '20 Billion Sino-Burmese Railroad Abruptly Cancelled', *GoKunming,* 22.7.2016.

[89] R. Huang, 'The Truth behind Suspension of the Myitsone Hydropower Project', *Global Times,* 17.8.2016.

Power Investment Company (which holds 80%), the Myanmar Ministry for Electrical Power (15%) and the Myanmar Asia World Company (5%). and an estimated cost of $8 billion. The deal was that Myanmar would get 10% of the electricity for free with further amounts at a contracted price, while the remainder would be for export.[90] Whether the suspension of the project was intended to burnish the regime's reformist credentials or whether it was a genuine response to local objections and environmentalist concerns is unclear. What is certain is that the CPI has continually pushed for the resumption of work (since it is getting nothing for the $1.2 billion already spent and, even if work did resume immediately, it would still take nine years to complete it).[91] So far it has got no more than a promise by Suu Kyi in August 2016, during her visit to Beijing, that the government would appoint a commission to scrutinise the project, and other hydropower sites.[92]

The suspension of the Myitsone dam caused an immediate backlash in China, leading to a sharp drop in FDI. In the four years after the quasi-civilian government took power in March 2011, total foreign direct investment reached just over $19 billion. This is less than the $20bn in the twelve months from March 2010. Before the cancellation China and Hong Kong had accounted for 70% of the country's FDI. Now the share has fallen to less than 15%. Singapore has now become an entry point for FDI, accounting for more than half of the recent foreign investment. Official data do not fully capture Japan's rising commercial interest, backed by the country's development agency muscle. Dozens of companies have signed up for the new Tokyo-backed Thilawa SEZ south-east of Yangon, including car parts makers and garment manufacturers.[93]

---

[90] A Harvard study suggested that these 90/10 contracts represented particularly poor value for Myanmar compared with other types of contract common in South Asia. See D. Dapice, *Hydropower in Myanmar: Moving Electricity Contracts from Colonial to Commercial*, Harvard Kennedy School, December 2015.

[91] Y. Mon and C. Hammond, 'CPI Pushes for Restart of Myitsone Dam', *Myanmar Times*, 5.6.2015.

[92] *The Irrawaddy*, 19.8.2016. In the meantime, China has taken 13 upstream dam projects in neighbouring Yunnan province off the development agenda. T. Fawthrop, 'China's Myanmar Dam Hypocrisy', *The Diplomat*, 28.1.2017.

[93] M. Peel, 'Myanmar Vies to Retain Investor Allure as Golden Land Glow Fades', *Financial Times*, 3.11.2015.

The second blow to China's plans came in July 2014, when Myanmar's Ministry of Rail Transportation abruptly announced the cancellation of the agreement with the Chinese government to build its part of the Kunming to Kyaukpyu railway. The statement attributed the cancellation to public opposition and the fact that the Chinese had done nothing in the intervening three years to start the project. The first excuse held an element of truth. Since the signing of the agreement, political parties and civil society groups in Rakhine state, through which the railway would have passed, have protested against the construction of the oil and gas pipeline, citing environmental and social concerns. This protest may also have concealed an underlying resentment against exploitation of the country's resources. The rail (and possible road) link seem to have become entangled in pipeline protest.[94] The second accusation was a little unfair. The Chinese authorities had been improving the 350 km line from Kunming to Dali (cutting the journey time from seven hours to two) and have since continued to work on the final 340 km to the Myanmar border. In January 2016 work started on the Nu River Bridge which, with a total length of 1,024 metres, will become the longest land bridge in the world.[95] Nonetheless the 'rumour' that the project was being revived was emphatically denied by Myanmar railway officials.[96]

One project that has managed to continue is the highly contested Letpadaung copper mine jointly owned by Wanbao Mining Copper Ltd and a conglomerate owned by the Myanmar military. The mine gained international attention in 2012 when police used phosphorous smoke bombs against protestors who cited pollution, unfair wages for local employees, forced relocations and illegal land confiscations as reasons to suspend the project.[97] In May 2016 it started operation, with hundreds of police protecting the site from demonstrating villagers.[98]

The new post-election government is a worry for Beijing. China

[94] J. Goldberg, 'Myanmar's Great Power Balancing Act', *The Diplomat*, 29.8.2014; Scally, '20 Billion Sino-Burmese railroad Abruptly Cancelled'.

[95] *The Nation*, 25.1.2016.

[96] *Eleven*, 4.2.2016.

[97] P, Parameswaran, 'China's Influence in Myanmar Facing Growing Scrutiny', *The Diplomat*, 7.1.2015.

[98] *Myanmar Times*, 6.5.2016. See also *Frontier*, 14.11.2016. Demonstrations are still continuing against the planned expansion of the site of the mine and the eviction of

supported the military government for much of Aung San Suu Kyi's period of house arrest (in contrast to the USA and to Western powers, which had imposed sanctions on the regime). However, since 2011 successive Chinese ambassadors have courted leaders of the democracy movement. China still wishes to continue its infrastructure and connectivity projects through the country to the Bay of Bengal, but it wants the suspension lifted on the Myitsone dam project and clarity on several others.[99] It is significant that in January 2016 China's CITIC Group Corporation won the contracts to build the Kyaukpyu deep-sea port and the industrial park of the special industrial zone. This had been part of the memorandum of understanding of 2011 that had sanctioned the Kunming–Kyaukpyu Railway, and although the agreement had been allowed to lapse, the government had not lost interest in the project. Giving the green light to the project was a sign that the government was still willing to play an active part in the BCIM project.[100]

Reflections

From the viewpoint of the Pakistani government, the CEPC is a great success. It dovetails with national priorities and all of the projects are proceeding expeditiously. It promises to open up a direct trade corridor with China and to alleviate the country's crippling power shortages. Pakistan also ranks high in the China's Country Cooperation Index[101] (4/64) but it does raise the question of the risks posed. The CEPC originates in the West in the unsettled region of Baluchistan and, in the North, passes through the mountainous tribal region and the contested area of Kashmir. So endemic is the unrest and so prevalent the random acts of terrorism that the Fragile State Index ranks it the most vulnerable (14/174) of all the states we consider in this volume.[102] In addition Table 5.4 reveals that the country poses

more villagers. *Myanmar Frontier,* 10.2.2017, *The Irrawaddy,* 22.2.2017, 28.2.2017, 25.3.2017.

[99] Y. Sun, 'A New Era for China-Myanmar Relations?', *The Diplomat,* 9.12.2015.

[100] S. Tiezzi, 'Chinese Company Wins Contract for Deep Sea Port in Myanmar', *The Diplomat,* 1.1.2016.

[101] PRC, National Development and Reform Commission, 一带一路大数据报告, Beijing, 2016 (One belt One Road. Big Data Report)

[102] http://fsi.fundforpeace.org/

serious financial risks for foreign investors, that is it saddled with a high level of corruption and that it is not easy for private enterprise to flourish.[103] One hopes that the diplomatic and political benefits compensate for the not inconsiderable medium-term risks involved. One also hopes that they compensate for the missed opportunities in failing to construct a closer relationship with India.

Table 6.4 Risk Indicators of China and the Countries of South Asia

	EIU Risk Assessment	Control of Corruption	Ease of Doing Business
	Score 0-100	Score 0-100	Rank 1/190
China	45	50	78/190
Bangladesh	54	81.73	176/190
India	48	55.77	130/190
Myanmar	59	83.17	170/190
Pakistan	63	76.44	144/190

EIU Overall Risk Assessement: http://viewswire.eiu.com/index.asp?layout=RKAllCountryVW3 ; WBI Control of Corruption Indicator; http://data.worldbank.org/data-catalog/worldwide-governance-indicators; WB Ease of doing Business Index: http://www.doingbusiness.org/rankings

India ranks 18/64 on China's country cooperation index which is, quite frankly, astounding considering its position. The country has long positioned itself as a rival for power in Asia, has failed to endorse OBOR's goals and has resisted cooperation with China. It has routinely condemned the CEPC and, as we will see in Chapter Nine, it is also the most suspicious of Chinese naval intentions in the Indian Ocean. It is probable that even without the CEPC, historical rivalries would have made it difficult for India to cooperate in OBOR, but for China it does mean that it is denied access to the opportunities for infrastructural investment and the expanding consumer market of the World's second most populous country. It is also less risky, less corrupt than the other South Asian countries and enjoys a better

---

[103] See also S.Nawaz and N. Iqbal, 'Pakistan can't reap the benefits of CPEC', *East Asia Forum*, 16.11.2016.

entrepreneurial climate. On the other hand, the Indian government is engaged in increasing connectivity but on its own terms rather than China's, and in its own version of win-win cooperation. It is upgrading its own congested freight train network and, in reaching its Eastern states more directly, it is improving connectivity with Bangladesh.

Myanmar's position (13/64) in China's Country Cooperation Index also seems to owe more to the past relationship with the military government than to current realities. It also provides an example of a country whose government thwarted the wishes of the Chinese government, or at least those of Chinese dam builders, and where neither the reality of a collapse of investment or the blandishments of favourable OBOR deals has yet produced a change in policy. As such it provides a good example of the limitations of 'soft power' or of 'geo-economics'.

CHAPTER SEVEN

Mainland ASEAN Countries

With the exception of Thailand, the countries of mainland South East Asia had all been colonies of one or other of the Western European powers.[1] Laos, Vietnam and Cambodia had all formed part of the French Indo-China until the defeat of the French army at Dien Bien Phu in 1954. As we saw in the previous chapter, Myanmar had previously known as Burma and was part of the British Empire until been it was granted interdependence in 1948. Malaysia and Singapore had formed part of the British Straits Settlements until 1957 when they too gained their independence. For a while they formed the Malay Federation, but Singapore became an independent nation when it was ejected from the Federation in 1965.

One event - the Vietnam War - marked their development since independence, depending upon what side the country lay in history's demarcation line.[2] For Vietnam, Laos and Cambodia, the war represented economic dislocation during the fighting and political dislocation afterwards when communist regimes held onto power and perpetuated autarchic policies and strict economic controls. Myanmar's development was also stymied by the military dictatorships that long held power. However Thailand benefitted directly from

---

[1] A Cotterell, *A History of South East Asia*, Singapore, 2014; N.G. Owen (ed.), *The Emergence of Modern South East Asia. A New History*, Honolulu, 2005; A. Reid, *A History of South East Asia: Critical Crossroads*, Chichester, 2015

[2] A. AcharyaJ. *The Making of Southeast Asia: International Relations of a Region*, 2nd edition, Singapore, 2012;J. Elias and L. Rethel (eds.) *The Everyday Political Economy of Southeast Asia*, Cambridge, 2016; World Bank, *The East Asian Miracle, Economic Growth and Public Policy*, Oxford, 1993.

the US financed road building programme, whilst Malaysia and Singapore gained more generally from increased US military expenditure. Later, as Japanese and later Hong Kong foreign direct investment entered the area, economic growth accelerated facilitated by growth promoting economic policies. As they developed, so the perception grew that they were confronted by common challenges that might better be met by adopting common positions.

Figure 7.1 Map of the ASEAN Countries

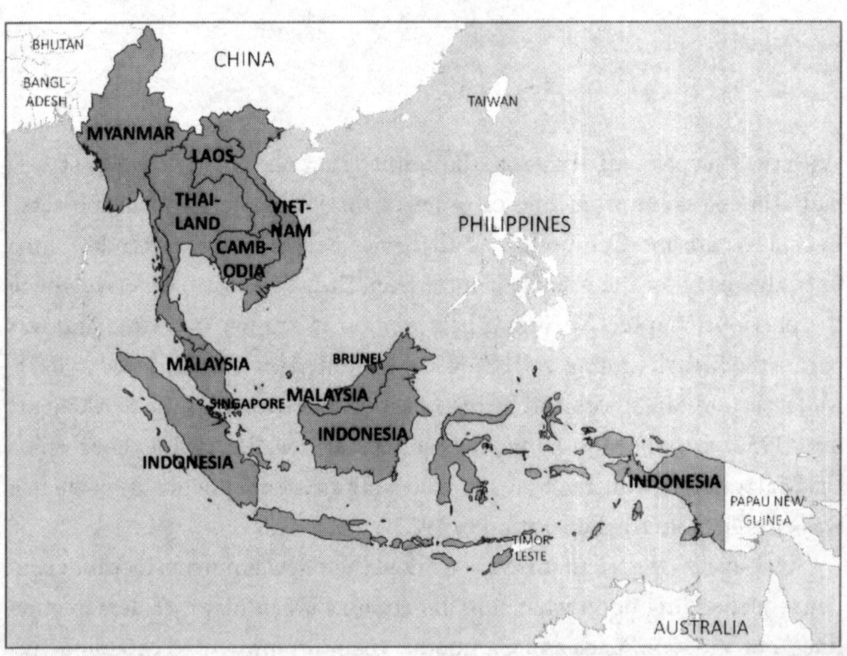

The Association of South East Asian Nations (ASEAN) was created in 1967 by five of America's allies- Indonesia, Malaysia, Philippines, Singapore and Thailand - to form an anti-communist front. The first twenty years of its existence were relatively uneventful. It even took almost ten years before the first summit meeting was held. Its membership was enlarged to include Brunei (1984), Vietnam (1995) Laos and Myanmar (1997) and Cambodia (1999).[3] As economic growth was consolidated, the member states began to

[3] M. Keiling, H.M. Som, M.N. Saludin, M.S. Schuib and M.N. Ajis, 'The Development of ASEAN from Historical Approach', *Asian Social Studies*, 7/7, 2011, 169–89; J. Pelkmans, *The ASEAN Economic Community: A Conceptual Approach*, Cambridge,

countenance steps towards closer economic integration. In 1992 the member states agreed to establish a free trade area amongst themselves, which would effectively establish a tariff preference in intra-area trade. The four later members, all of which were considerably less developed than the rest, were given extra time to fulfil their obligations. Tariffs were indeed lowered and intra-area trade increased in importance, but progress was uneven and non-tariff barriers still proliferated, especially in the less developed member states.[4] In 2007 the members launched an even more ambitious plan for an Economic Community, which would completely eliminate all intra-regional barriers to trade and create a transboundary infrastructure to integrate national markets. Although completion was envisaged by 2015, success is still far off. Two reasons for this are usually given – the uneven levels of development among members states and ASEAN's weak institutional structure. However the scheme stuck more closely at the core of power distribution within and between economies, targeting the positions gained by sectoral protection or by bureaucratic privilege.[5] The question then arises whether the OBOR initiative could act as a catalyst to help realise ASEAN's ambitions or whether it would become mired in the same high rhetoric and slow progress that has characterised much of ASEAN's endeavours to date.

We have already examined Myanmar in Chapter 6 in the context of its links with China and India. Later in this chapter we will focus on its links to Thailand. The area's connections with the maritime Silk Road, as well as the region's maritime disputes with China, will all be dealt with in Chapter 8. Moreover, this chapter will restrict itself to the mainland ASEAN countries, excluding therefore Brunei, Indonesia and the Philippines.

The basis data for the region is shown in Table 7.1. In terms of surface area, China dwarfs all the mainland ASEAN states. Even so the largest of

---

2016; C.B. Roberts, *ASEAN Regionalism: Cooperation, Values and Institutionalisation*, Oxford, New York, 2012.

[4] H. Soesastro, 'The Asean Free Trade Area: A Critical Assessment', *Journal of East Asian Affairs*, 16/1, 2002, 20-53; S.M. Thangavelu and A. Chongvilaivan, A., *Free Trade Agreements, Regional Integration and Growth in ASEAN*. 2009

[5] ASEAN, *A Blueprint for Growth. ASEAN Economic Community 2015: Progress and Key Achiev*ements, Jakarta, 2015;L. Jones, 'Explaining the failure of the ASEAN economic community: the primacy of domestic political economy', *The Pacific Review*, 29/5, 647-670.

these, Myanmar is still the size of France. At the other end of the spectrum, Singapore is more than three times smaller than Luxembourg, which is Europe's smallest state. China also dwarfs all the members of 'mainland' ASEAN countries in terms of population. Vietnam is the largest in the group, with a population that is larger than that of Germany which has Europe's largest population. The list is closed by Singapore which manages to fit with 5.5 million inhabitants into its small space. Turning to per capita income, two of states - Singapore and Malaysia – are richer than China, but if adjustments were made for purchasing power parities, Thailand would also overtake China.[6] One must remember, however, that these adjusted figures only give an indication of spending power as long as that expenditure remains in the country where the income is earned. Step into the real world of current dollars and a Chinese yuan still goes much further than does a Thai baht. The remaining countries are all much poorer and less developed than China.

Table 7.1 Basic details of China and the Countries of Mainland ASEAN

	Area	Population	Per capita GDP
	Million Km2	Thousands	Current US$
China	9,596,961	1,376,049	7,617
Cambodia	181,035	15,578	1,095
Laos	236,800	6,802	1,756
Malaysia	329,847	30,311	10,933
Myanmar	676,578	53,897	1,244
Singapore	683	5,604	55,910
Thailand	513,115	67,959	5,977
Vietnam	331,689	93,448	2,015

Sources: Area http://unstats.un.org/unsd/environment/totalarea.htm;
Population https://esa.un.org/unpd/wpp/Download/Standard/Population/
pc GDP http://data.un.org/Search.aspx?q=GDP+per+capita

[6] World Bank, *Purchasing Power Parities and Real Expenditure of World Economies. A Comprehensive Report of the 2011 International Comparison Program*, Washington DC, 2015.

If we look first at traditional measures of protection Singapore, Myanmar and Malaysia levy tariffs considerably lower than those facing exporters to China. The other mainland ASEAN countries fall broadly into the same pattern as China, with the exception of Thailand's very high tariffs on agricultural imports. Turning to the border compliance indicator which measures the time and cost of importing one container of car parts from the major supplier, only Laos and Myanmar took longer than China to assemble and process all the documentation, while Singapore and Thailand were significantly cheaper as well, as too was Laos.

Table 7.2 Basic Trade Cost Indicators of China and the Countries of Mainland ASEAN

	MFN Applied Tariffs		Border Compliance		Logistics Performance Index
	Non-Agriculture	Agriculture	Time	Cost	n/160
	Simple Average %		Hours	US$	
China	9.0	15.6	158	360	27
Cambodia	10.6	14.9	140	360	73
Laos	8.3	20.1	230	268	152
Malaysia	5.5	9.4	82	381	32
Myanmar	5.1	8.6	280	667	113
Singapore	0.0	1.1	38	260	5
Thailand	7.7	30.7	54	276	45
Vietnam	8.4	16.3	138	575	64

Sources: MFN Tariffs: WTO, ITC, UNCTAD, *World Tariff Profiles*, Geneva, 2016; Border Compliance: Wold Bank, Doing Business, http://www.doingbusiness.org/data/exploretopics/trading-across-borders; LPI: World Bank, LPI Global Ranking (2016) http://lpi.worldbank.org/international/global

To help widen our focus from the border and examining the entire task of organising the entire shipment from its point of origin to its final destination, the World Bank has constructed a Logistics Performance Index. China ranked a respectable twenty-seventh, but it was beaten by Singapore whose fifth position was a reflection of its efficiency as a world trading hub.

At the present time two main international corridors of the UNESCAP Asian Highway Network reach into South-East Asia.[7] The first is the main link of AH2 that starts in Singapore (or, more accurately, in Merak in Indonesia) and travels the length of South-East Asia before heading west towards Iran. The second is an east–west spur of AH3 through Myanmar and Thailand to Chang Rai, on the border with Laos. When these routes are added to those Asian highways of more local importance, the mainland region has a network of 19,691 kms.

Table 7.3 Length and Condition of the Asian Highway in China and the countries of Mainland ASEAN

	Length	Class (per cent)				
	Kms	Primary	I	II	III	<III
China	10847.28	77.8	2.1	17.1	3.0	Neg.
Cambodia	1956.00	-	-	31.2	68.8	-
Laos	2857.00	-	-	8.5	80.7	10.7
Malaysia	1673.00	47.5	3.6	48.8	-	-
Myanmar	4524.99	-	7.1	12.7	37.6	42.6
Singapore	19.00	68.4	31.6	-	-	-
Thailand	5540.13	11.1	74.4	10.8	3.6	-
Vietnam	3121.15	-	31.0	60.0	9.0	-

Source: http://www.unescap.org/resources/status-asian-highway-member-countries

In 2015, 35.1% of these were four-lane highways (Primary and Class I roads) and a further 24.0% were well-surfaced two- or three-lane roads (Class II roads). Two-lane roads with only a bituminous surface (Class III roads) accounted for28.2% and the remainder, all of which were in Laos and Myanmar, failed to meet even this standard.[8]

Mainland ASEAN also has 9245 kms of TAR rail lines. In 1996, the entire mainland ASEAN region used the 1000 mm narrow gauge which is unsuitable for heavy transport movement or long-distance container trains.

---

7 UN, ESCAP, *Intergovernmental Agreement on the Asian Highway Network*, s.l., 2003.

8 UNESCAP Asia Highway Database.

It has light track structures, light axle loads, slow speeds and small vehicle profiles, not suited for large, long-distance container trains. UNESCAP treated the whole region as an almost independent sub-region and not worth bothering to link to the wider international freight network. Within the region, the only upgrading it thought worth investigating were lines between Bangkok and the ports of Kelang and Penang, which would save time and eliminate the need for transhipment via Singapore. The only transport link to the rest of the network was a dual gauge (1000 mm/1435 mm) reaching from China and extending as far as Hanoi. Back in 1996, Myanmar needed 166 km of line to complete the link to Thailand and a further 284 km on the Thai side of the border. Other missing links included 388 km in Cambodia and 145 km in Vietnam. In addition, plans envisaged the construction of a further 2735 km of completely new lines. In 1996 the estimated costs of completing the network, excluding the costs of extra locomotives and rolling stock, was $3.1 billion,.[9]

Within the TAR there were already two regional schemes in development. In 1992 the countries of Cambodia, China (Yunnan province), Laos, Myanmar, Thailand and Vietnam agreed to form the Greater Mekong Sub-region (GMS) as a forum for international cooperation. In terms of transport, the initial focus had been on highway improvement, particularly the routes from Phnom Penh to Ho Chi Minh City and east–west from the Andaman Sea to Da Nang.[10] In 2005 the governments took the decision to widen their priorities so as to embrace rail connectivity. Within this new context, the priority was to complete the Singapore-Kunming rail link (SKRL) that had been approved by the fifth ASEAN summit in 1995 This resulted in a second strategic plan. It concluded that the national networks were burdened by outdated procedures, inflexible schedules and tariffs, and acute overmanning. These required major restructuring if they were to generate sufficient revenues and external funding to be able to expand. The Plan then went on to analyse four options for completing the SKRL, all of which converged on Bangkok before travelling further South.. On the grounds of

---

9 UNESCAP *Trans-Asian Railway Route Requirements: Developments of the Trans-Asian Railway in the Indo-China and ASEAN sub-region*, Volume One, New York, 1996, 3–8, 24.

10 ADB, *The Greater Mekong Subregion at 20: Progress and Prospects*, Manilla, 2011.

projections of potential freight volumes, there was little to choose among the routes, but a route travelling the length of Vietnam to Ho Chi Minh before turning to Phnom Pen (where a new line would need to be laid) and then to Bangkok was by far the cheapest to complete ($1.1 billion), and for this reason it was the one favoured in the report. In terms of potential passenger traffic a route through the Laos and the North of Thailand was by far the busiest, but it was also the most expensive to construct ($6.3 billion). The route through to Laos to Vientiane and then turning into Thailand further South was slightly cheaper to construct ($5.3 billion) but offered the least prospective increase in passenger traffic.[11]

In October 2010 the ASEAN countries adopted the Masterplan on ASEAN Connectivity (MPAC), which was labelled as a 'flagship project' for a closer and more integrated region through enhanced physical infrastructure development (physical connectivity), effective institutions, mechanisms and processes (institutional connectivity) and empowered people (people-to-people connectivity). The plan was designed to tackle the poor transport infrastructure in the region and impediments to movements of vehicles, goods, services and skilled labour across borders. The target for roads was now to upgrade all unsatisfactory Asian Highway roads (under Class III) by 2015, work which had earlier been scheduled to have been completed by 2004. The work still to be done included 1467 km in Myanmar, 391 in Laos and (outside the confines of this chapter) 211 km in the Philippines. For rail infrastructure the intention was to accelerate progress on the SKRL, which had both an eastern and a western route. The eastern route followed the route favoured by the GMS Plan, with a side route from Vung Ang to the Lao capital of Vientiane. However it now carved out a completely new trajectory through Myanmar and crossing onto Thailand through the Three Pagodas Pass (where a new link needed construction). Because this second option was more challenging and expensive, ASEAN also made the completion of the eastern route its first priority. This was a project that had been agreed in December 1995 and had been targeted for completion by 2015, but

[11] ADB, *Greater Mekong Subregion: Railway Strategy Study, Final Report,* TA-7255 (REG), 2011. See also ADB, *Connecting Greater Mekong Subregion Railway. A Strategic Framework,* 2010. The fourth route would ude the existing lines through Vietnam before turning West to Vientiane and into Thailand. This would cost $2.3 billion to construct but offered the second best potential growth in passenger traffic.

fifteen years later 694 km of track were still missing altogether and no work had been done on the 585 km spur from Vung Ang (Vietnam) to Vientiane (Laos). In addition, 2800 km of track required upgrading, including many sections that were still single track.[12]

Progress had been slow since the mobilisation of private investment had been disappointing, and this had contributed to the delays of many connectivity projects. Moreover ASEAN's institutional framework has been deficient, with no clear lines of responsibility, either for national projects or for the border crossings. In addition, the different levels of economic development manifested themselves in uneven technical and financial capacities to manage individual projects. Under these circumstances China's OBOR initiative offered an opportunity to accelerate the ASEAN Master Plan since it would complement existing initiatives. The problem is that China is not negotiating with ASEAN but with individual national (and sometimes regional) authorities, which helps to undermine ASEAN's self-image as the leading driver of regional integration.[13] ASEAN, too, has a dream of its own: 'ASEAN is envisioned as a concert of Southeast Asian nations, outward-looking, living in peace, stability and prosperity, bonded together in partnership in dynamic development and in a community of caring societies ... the need to promote local economic and social development and connectivity, mitigating environmental impacts, and synchronising domestic connectivity with regional connectivity ... The vision of an enhanced ASEAN Connectivity will strengthen the ASEAN motto of "One Vision, One Identity, One Community".'[14]

Vietnam

China and Vietnam[15] have always been wary of each other as neighbours, and as recently as 1979 Chinese forces actually invaded North Vietnam as a

[12] ASEAN, *Master Plan on ASEAN Connectivity*, Jakarta, 2011.

[13] J.A. Toedoro, 'Maintaining ASEAN Centrality in Connectivity through MPAC ASEAN's Connectivity Challenge', *CIRSS Commentaries*, 2/17, June 2015.

[14] ASEAN, *Master Plan*, 5.

[15] M. Gainsborough, *Vietnam: Rethinking the State*, Chiang Mai, 2010; B. Hayton, *Vietnam: Rising Dragon*, New Haven, CT, 2011; T. Jandl, *Vietnam in the Global Economy: The Dynamics of Integration, Decentralization, and Contested Politics*, Latham, MA,

response to Vietnam's invasion of Cambodia the previous year to drive out the Khmer Rouge government.[16] On the other hand, the eastern branch of the SKRL runs through the length of Vietnam before turning west, through Cambodia and onwards to Thailand. In 2015 almost all the country's railway, was electrified including the major sections stretching south from Hanoi. There is dual gauge on the 162 km from Hanoi to Dong Dang on the border with China (and connecting with Nanning) and a short 75 km link from Hanoi northwards to Quán Triều, and this small network is connected by 1435 mm gauge to the port of Ha Long. The 1730 km stretch between Hanoi and Ho Chi Minh City is in the process of being rehabilitated, largely with support of the ADB, which financed the reconstruction of many bridges along the route.[17] There are no mega-plans for high-speed rail. In 2010 the Vietnamese government had already rejected an ADB-backed Japanese proposal for a high-speed rail line linking Hanoi with Ho Chi Minh City. With a price tag of $56 billion (50% Vietnam's GDP), the project was considered too expensive. Instead the government is committed to spending $3.86 billion on upgrading the north–south line to reach speeds of 80–90km/hr (compared to the 50 km/hr on the rest of the network).[18] Looking at the rest of the SKRL, in October 2015 the government agreed, with the help of the Korean International Cooperation Agency, to start studies for the 550 km link between Vung Ang Port and Vientiane.[19] The 129 km section between Ho Chi Minh City and the Cambodian border is stalled at the feasibility study stage.[20]

China has long been investing in Vietnam. Initially much of this was focused on natural resource extraction and processing. However, as China's

---

2015; L. Nguyen, *Guerrilla Capitalism: The State in the Market in Vietnam*, Oxford, 2009.

[16] B. Burton, 'Contending Explanations of the 1979 Sino-Vietnamese War', *International Journal*, 34/4,1979, 699–722; B. Womack, *China and Vietnam: The Politics of Asymmetry*, Cambridge, 2006.

[17] *Presentation on Viet Nam Railway Present Status and its Plan in Railway Connectivity with the GMS and ASEAN*, Ad-hoc Expert Group Meeting on Facilitation of International Railways, Bangkok, 12–13.3.2015.

[18] A.C-H. Lim, 'Recent Developments In Sino-Vietnamese Relations – Analysis', *Eurasia Review*, 16.9.2015.

[19] *Thanh Nien News*, 8.10.2015.

[20] Lim, 'Recent Developments'.

economy slowed down, interest turned to manufacturing investment in order to making use of Vietnam's low price labour. Compared with FDI from other countries, the individual projects were relatively small, and much of it was concentrated in business parks near the Chinese border.[21] The exception to this pattern has been investment in electrical power plants. China is involved in building four of the five power plants in the Vinh Tan thermal power centre, which will generate 6500MW once they are all completed.. In 2012 China Power Investment Cooperation financed 95% of the $3 billion required for the two 1200 coal-fired power plants while the Chinese Development Bank financed a third. However, a Japanese consortium led by Mitsubishi will build Vinh Tan-4.[22]

Laos

With Vietnam showing little inclination to accelerate progress of the SKRL, it was perhaps not surprising that the Chinese authorities turned their attention to Laos.[23] The land-locked country only had one railway line, a short 3.5 km stretch from the Thai border, across the Friendship Bridge to the town of Tha na Lang.[24] Plans to connect it to the capital Vientiane, 20 km away, never materialised. If China were to become involved, it could transform a land-locked country into a hub on an international rail network. The problem was that whatever route was chosen through the country, it would be one of the most expensive alternatives under consideration.

After almost six years of negotiations, in November 2015 China and Laos agreed to build a 417 km single track high-speed railway from Kunming directly to Vientiane. The line passes through mountainous territory[25] and although it is built as a high-speed rail line, because of the terrain passenger

[21] Voice of Vietnam, 22.3.2016; *Vietnam News*, 26.3.2016.

[22] http://www.sourcewatch.org/index.php/Vinh_Tan_power_station.

[23] Y. Bourdet, *The Economics of Transition in Laos: From Socialism to Asean Integration*, Cheltenham, 2000; H. Phimphanthavong, 'Economic Reform and Regional Development of Laos', *Modern Economy*, 3, 2012, 179–86.; V. Pholsena, *Post-War Laos: The Politics of Culture, History, and Identity*, Singapore, 2006.

[24] A. Spooner, 'The First Train to Laos', *The Guardian*, 27.2.2009.

[25] It will require seventy-six tunnels (195 km) and 154 bridges (65 km) along its length.

trains along the line will travel at 160 km/hr and freight trains at 120 km/hr. The cost of the Lao section will be $6.8 billion, 40% funded directly by the two governments (with China taking 70% of that share) and the rest by state enterprises and with low interest loans.[26] The railway itself will cut through the Boten Specific Economic Zone on the Lao–China border. The area has been known as 'Golden City', and a Hong-Kong consortium has built a hotel and casino complex there. This has not been a success and the consortium has since sold 85% of its stake to Yunnan Hai Cheng Industrial Group, which plans to spend $0.5 billion converting the site to include a duty-free centre, warehousing facilities, a bus terminal and a leisure and conference centre.[27] For its part, the Yunnan government has announced plans for a massive pilot economic zone (Mengla SEZ) on its side of the border with Northern Laos, covering 4500 km^2 and with a projected investment of $31.4 billion.[28]

Despite the hype at the opening, after eight months the work on the line in Laos had yet to start, ostensibly because an environmental and social impact study had still to be completed.[29] However, rumour suggested that the deputy prime minister had been sacked because of his soft stance during the negotiations on financing the project, and that the government was beginning to question whether it could afford the terms that it had obtained when the country was already struggling to finance its 30% share of the budget.[30] After a slew of high-level meetings, work was eventually resumed. Forty Chinese railway engineers and technicians arrived in Vientiane to work on the railway and started building on a base camp from which to build the 56 km leg between the Lao capital and Phon-hong to the north.[31] The only remaining hurdle was a last-minute disagreement between Thai

---

[26] *Railway Gazette*, 4.12.2015; T. Kyozuka and T. Abe, 'China Starts Work on Laos Railway, Eyeing Farther Horizons', *Nikkei Asian Review*, 3.12.2015. For more details on the financial implications see 'Laos And China Come to Terms on Loan Interest Rate For Railway Project', *Radio Free Asia*, 4.1.2016 and M. Penna, 'China Starts Controversial Lao Rail Project', *Asia Sentinel*, 7.3.2017.

[27] *Vientiane Times*, 6.1.2016; *New York Times*, 6.7.2016.

[28] *Reuters*, 19.10.2015.

[29] *Reuters*, 29.7.2016.

[30] *The Rayat Post*, 5.6.2016.

[31] The official ceremony marking the start of construction took place on 26 December 2016 in Luang Prabang. *Railway Gazette*, 28.12.2016.

and Chinese engineers over the design of the bridge over the Mekong River to link the line to Thailand. The Chinese wanted a simple 1435 mm guage track, whereas the Thais wanted a second 1000 mm track as well.[32] Time will tell.

Thailand

Thailand[33] is central to the feasibility of the entire SKRL project since it is scheduled to link up with no fewer than four proposed routes still under consideration. One is the link through Laos which we have just been discussing. A second major project involves extending the railway from Bangkok to Chiang Mai northwards to the Chiang Khong on the Lao border. Both of these routes were intended to be high-speed train routes. A third route envisages a link to the west that was originally envisaged to connect with the rail network at Myanmar at through the Three Pagoda Pass but which was later altered to a shorter connection between the projected port of Dawei and Kanchanaburi (but without a connection to the rest of the Myanmar network). And finally, there remained the question of completing the connection to Cambodia and linking to the route that travels north through Vietnam. All these routes converge on Bangkok, and from there the railroad heads south towards Malaysia and Singapore. We will look at plans for this last route at the start of the Malaysia/Singapore section of this chapter.

In May 2014 Thailand's politics were shaken to their core by a military coup that replaced the democratic government. This was intended to end the struggles that often threatened to paralyse the country. The previous government had been supportive of the OBOR initiative, which held out the prospects not only of fast overland links to China but also to the centre of Europe. The immediate issue was whether the military junta would follow this lead. Very soon the question was answered. The junta announced

---

32 *Radio Free Asia*, 26.9.2016.

33 ADB, *Thailand: Industrialization and Economic Catch-Up*, Manilla, 2015; P. Chambers, *Civil-Military Relations in Thailand since the 2014 Coup. The Tragedy of Security Sector "Deform"*, PRIF Report 138, Frankfurt, 2016; R.F. Doner, *The Politics of Uneven Development: Thailand's Economic Growth in Comparative Perspective*, Cambridge, 2009; A.M. Marshall, *A Kingdom in Crisis: Thailand's Struggle for Democracy in the Twenty-First Century*, London, 2014.

plans to build the two high-speed rail lines to Laos with trains travelling on dual-track standard gauge tracks at top speeds of 160 km/hr. It envisaged that construction would start in 2015 and be completed in 2021. After China had agreed to lend Thailand the necessary funds, with the loan repayment backed by deliveries of rice and rubber, the National Legislative Assembly approved the scheme, stipulating only that China would not receive land use rights along the routes. On 19 December 2014 the two countries signed a memorandum to build the railways.[34]

Behind the scenes there were several misgivings and misunderstandings about the deal. For a start, China was still insisting on interest of 2.5% as opposed to the 2% the Thais were demanding, and the 1% that they thought they could squeeze out of the Chinese. There was also a disagreement of the costs. China estimated 540 billion baht ($15 billion) whereas the Thai estimates were 400 billion baht ($11.25 billion). The proposed railway was for passengers only and it would need an unrealistically high 20 million passengers a year at a high ticket prices simply to pay the interest, let alone cover the running costs and make a profit. Moreover, the intention was to have medium-speed trains, but details such as the minimum railway curves suggested that China seemed to be planning for a high-speed track (200 km/hr). Furthermore, it was unclear whether Thai engineers would be involved in maintaining the line and building the rolling stock or whether Thai nationals would be frozen out altogether.[35] However, as the wider financial implications became clearer, the Thais began to push for Chinese involvement in the running of the project in a B-O-T (Build-Operate-Transfer) operation and in sharing any potential losses, in fact sharing most of the potential losses. The Chinese responded by simplifying the specifications – no more dual tracks, slower trains, shorter routes and omitting the spur from the main line down to Mab Ta Phut in the Gulf of Thailand. Against this background, in March 2016, the military government abruptly suspended all projects with China and announced that Thailand would seek its own funding for a less ambitious and costly version.[36]

---

[34] *Chiang Rai Times*, 18.3.2015.

[35] J. Draper and P. Kamnuans, 'Stalled in the Dragon's Tracks: Thailand–China Railway', *The Nation*, 16.3.2016.

[36] K. Chongkittavorn, 'Sino–Thai Railway Negotiations on a Rickety Track', *The Nation*, 2.5.2016.

The two main projects now took two different dirction. The work on the 873 km of high-speed rail links (dual 1435 mm gauge) from the port of Map Ta Phut to Nong Khai on the Lao border and the spur connecting the line to Bangkok was approved by the Thai cabinet in August 2016. However, the only part upon which work would begin was the 252 km section from Bangkok to Nakhon Ratchasima. This was undertaken with funding from the Chinese, but under the agreement Thailand retained ownership rights (and operational risks) for the entire project. The planning (and financial arrangements) for the rest of the line were both pushed into the future.[37] The only open question was whether China would agree to charging 2% on the loans as the Thais had demanded,[38] rather than the 3% originally requested. The fact that difficulties still remain is evidenced by the decision to postpone the call for tenders for four months and by the decision of the military junta in February 2017 to dismiss the governor and the entire board of the Thai State Railway in an effort to accelerate procedures and eliminate 'irregularities' in procurements.[39]

The second route was now redesigned to reach only 699 km from Bangkok to Chiang Mai, but the partner chosen for the planning of the route and the commercial development in the areas surrounding the stations was the Japan International Cooperation Agency (JICA). This has led to the expectation, in Japan at least, that its Shinkansen high-speed system would be adopted. The announcement made in August 2016 anticipated that construction should start before the end of the year and finish by 2020. At the same time the two sides agreed to implement containerised transportation and railroad projects in the Thai section of the so-called Southern Economic Corridor between the borders with Myanmar and Cambodia, via Bangkok.[40] At the time of writing a visit from the visit of the Japanese Emperor to pay his respects to the new King would be an occasion for an offer of a $1.5 billion loan designed to clinch the deal.[41]

---

[37] *The Nation*, 22.9.2016.

[38] *Bangkok Post*, 22.10.2016.

[39] *Bangkok Post*, 3.12.2016, 23.2.2017.

[40] *Japan Times*, 6.8.2016.

[41] *Japan Times*, 3.3.2017 (China's shadow looms large over Japan-Thailand relations).

Myanmar

We examined Myanmar in Chapter 6 as part of the corridor linking India and Bangladesh with China. The discussion in this chapter, therefore, will concentrate on its integration of its western provinces with Thailand, the only ASEAN country with which it shares a border. The ASEAN Master Plan for Connectivity highlighted the need to complete missing rail links between Thanbyuzayat in Myanmar and Nam Tok in Thailand, travelling through the Three Pagoda Pass at the border in order to complete the western route of the SKRL. Of this, 110 km lay in Myanmar and 153 km in Thailand. Completion was envisaged by 2020.[42] This route followed the infamous Burma railroad constructed by prisoners during the Second World War and costing over 12,000 POWs' lives, while 10,000 of the local population were forced to work on the line. Sections of the disused track still survive. In 2011, however, Myanmar and Thai authorities agreed to suspend work on the envisaged railway route and concentrate instead on that part of the line between Dawei and Kanchanaburi, and from there to Bangkok.

Plans to develop Dawei's deep-water seaport facilities and to build an industrial park near the site had been agreed between the Thai and Myanmar governments in 2008 and in 2011 Dawei's was granted the status as a special economic zone. The costs for the whole project were estimated at $10.7 billion and work was entrusted to a Thai-Italian consortium. However, the entire project was dogged by funding problems and delays and by 2012 all work on the project had effectively stopped. In 2015, however, a new agreement to relaunch the project was reached between the original consortium and Japanese investors. The highest priority was to focus on a less ambitious 27 km^2 first phase of the zone's development and to construct a 132 km four-lane road from Dawei to Kanchanaburi in Thailand, with the prospect of a rail link at a later date. The Thai also offered a $130 million loan to fund the completion of the Myanmar section of the road.[43] As late as December 2015 it was reported that the Thai and Myanmar governments were still

[42] ASEAN, *Master Plan.*

[43] *The Nation*, 15.12.2015. The new democratic government took its time to reconsider the project by in 2017 accepted the deal. *Bangkok Post*, 15.2.2017.

undecided over which of the two routes to use as a rail connection between their two countries.[44]

At this stage, according to all appearances the Dawei development was fitting seamlessly into cooperation with Japan in constructing the 'southern corridor'. However, when it came to offering leases on land in the Dawei SEZ, the Chinese companies King Trillion and China Railway Engineering Corporation (CREC) expressed an interest in joining the scheme, taking over the building of the road and some of the port development.[45] A month later, on the very last day in office of the military government, Guangdong Zhenrong Energy Co. was granted a 70% stake in a $3 billion project to build an oil refinery to the south of the port. This would be the largest single foreign investment in the country and, given that China's investment interest had hitherto been concentrated on the Kyaukphyu SEZ, its sudden interest in Dawei was been likened by a Chinese reporter to 'a thunderbolt on a clear day'.[46] At the time of writing, local activists were starting to campaign against the project, especially the oil refinery, and no work had yet begun.[47] For a while the new democratic government had remained silent on its commitment to the project, but in August it agreed to new institutional arrangements to supervise developments.[48]

Cambodia

The connection between Thailand and Cambodia[49] on the SKRL's western route involved, on the Thai side, rehabilitating track from Ban Khlong Luek (near Bangkok) to Aranyaprathet, which is opposite the Cambodian town

---

44 M. Papazoff, 'ASEAN Railway Connectivity: Current Status and Major Issues', Presentation to Joint ESCAP–UIC Seminar on Facilitation and Costing of Railway Services along the Trans-Asian Railway, Bangkok, 11.12.2015.

45 *The Nation*, 7.3.2016.

46 *Myanmar Times*, 8.4.2016; *Myanmar Energy Monitor*, 26.4.2016.

47 For details of the environmental degradation of the area see P. Sukprasert, 'The Dawei dream left high and dry', *Bangkok Post*, 19.3.2017.

48 At the time of writing, the parties were still talking. *Bangkok Post*, 2.2.2017.

49 J. Brinkley, *Cambodia's Curse: The Modern History of a Troubled Land*, New York, 2012; H. Hill and J. Menon, *Cambodia: Rapid Growth with Institutional Constraints*, Asian Development Bank Economics Working Paper, 331, 2013; C. Hughes and K. Un (Eds.), *Cambodia's Economic Transformation*, Copenhagen, 2011.

of Poipet. This involved upgrading and double-tracking the 176 km line. On the Cambodian side it involved reconstructing the 6.5 km missing link between Poipet and the Thai border. The last time trains had run between the two towns had been in the 1970s. Since then Cambodia's rail infrastructure had been allowed to deteriorate under the rule of the Khmer Rouge. The completion of this link would open the prospect of a regular service between Phnom Penh and Bangkok. Work on completing the Cambodian side of the 6 km link was started in July 2014 with the construction of a 43 metre bridge over a stream close to the border with Thailand,[50] but it was not until the end of 2016 that the work was due for completion.[51]

It was as far back as 2006 that it was decided to restore the 48 km line between Poipet and Sisophon, which had been completely destroyed during the civil war – tracks ripped up, bridges blown and wagons burnt. In addition people had since built houses on land that the track had once occupied, especially on the approaches to Poipet.[52] In February 2008, work on restoring Cambodia's railway network was officially started, with priority afforded to the Poipet and Sisophon missing link. Most of the funds were supplied by the ADB and the work was completed in 2012. The final (6 km) part of the project was stalled when an internal investigation was instigated into the accusation that the ADB had breached its own safeguards in the resettlement of families affected by the railways, many of whom were in the vicinity of Poipet.[53]

If the completion of the rail link between Phnom Penh and Bangkok seems tortuous, it is like nothing compared with progress on the eastern section of the envisaged SKRL. Work on the 206 km link between Phnom Penh and Loc Ninh, on the border with Vietnam, has (in December 2015) not even started. In 2010 China had offered to help advance construction of the line, and possibly support some of the $0.6 billion estimated costs.[54] The following year the Chinese had produced a feasibility study on the line

---

50 *Railway Gazette*, 28.7.2014.

51 *Bangkok Post*, 6.12.2016; *Phnom Penh Post*, 7.12.2016. Both sources confirm end of year completion, with only 30 metres of trach needing to be laid.

52 *Phnom Penh Post*, 11.8.2006.

53 IDI News report, 7.2.2014. Ironically it is the issue of compensation for the local community that is still stalling the completion of the line (*Bangkok Post*, 16.3.2017)

54 *Phnom Penh Post*, 31.10.2010; *Railway Gazette*, 4.1.2011.

and a new cost estimate ($0.7 billion, excluding resettlement costs), but nothing seemed to have happened until January 2015, when the government reviewed the report's findings with the intention of asking China to help develop the project.[55]

Malaysia and Singapore

To travel from Bangkok to Malaysia[56], there is an overnight express that will cover the 945 km to Hat Yai in a little over sixteen hours. Upon arrival there is a twice-daily shuttle that takes about an hour to cover the remaining 60 km to the Thai border town of Padang Basar. This service was introduced a little over a year ago. A short walk takes you to the Malay station of the same name where a high-speed electric train, introduced in July 2015, will cover the remaining 420 km in five hours. At the time of writing, the Thai government was about to decide the fate of high-speed lines on two routes south from Bangkok, each covering about 200 km, for a combined cost of $7 billion.[57] The Malay government has upgraded the main line by halving the time taken to reach the border from Kuala Lumpur. It is also considering a new 620 km 'east coast line' to the border town of Tumpat that would halve the time for the journey. In November 2016, the government secured a soft loan from the Export-Import Bank of China to cover the estimated $13.4 billion cost of the project, and appointed China Communications Construction Company to undertake the work.[58]

The most ambitious project involves the building of an advanced rail terminus in Kuala Lumpur, and the construction of a high-speed rail link from

[55] *Khmer Times*, 20.1.2015.

[56] J. Chin and J. Dosch (eds.), *Malaysia Post-Mahathir: A Decade of Change*, Singapore, 2016; B.D. Das and P.L. Onn (eds.), *Malaysia's Socio-Economic Transformation: Ideas for the Next Decade*, Singapore, 2014; H. Hill and T.S. Yean, *Malaysia's Development Challenges: Graduating from the Middle*, New York, 2012; A. Noh, *Small Steps, Big Outcome: A Historical Institutional Analysis of Malaysia's Political Economy*, Asia Studies Centre Oxford, Working Paper 164, 2010.

[57] *Bangkok Post*, 20.10.2016. In February it had approached the Malay government to open talks on constructing a HSR between the two capitals. *Free Malaysia News*, 6.2.2017.

[58] *Straits Times*, 24.10.2016, 2.11.2016.

there to Singapore. The two projects are separate, but they are obviously interlinked in that the developers of the terminus will be in a favourable position when bidding for the HSR link. The terminus will be built on the 196 ha site at Bandar Malaysia, a former airforce base, which is ten minutes away from Kuala Lumpur's city centre. In December 2015 the debt-burdened, scandal-ridden Malay owners of the site, 1Malaysia Development Berhad, were forced to sell a 60% stake in the site to CREC and Iskandar Waterfront Holdings for $1.8 billion. In June 2016, the Ministry of Finance took over the rest. It is intended as a mixed use development zone with factories, offices and 27,000 homes and is to become 'the world's largest underground city', as well as the station for the planned high-speed rail link (HSR) to Singapore. Iskandar Waterfront and CREC's ambitions likely include taking advantage of their status as the majority owner of Bandar Malaysia in competing for the mega-HSR project this year.[59] The Chinese advantage in bidding for the project is reinforced by the award in December 2015 of the $1.7 billion contract for electrifying the 197 km double-track rail line between Gemas and Johor Baru. The operation would raise speeds of trains on the line to hit 160 km/hr and complete the government's programme for double-tracking the entire line to Pedang Besar on the Thai border.[60]

In August 2016 the governments of Singapore[61] and Malaysia announced a joint tender for a dual-track high speed railway (HSR) to connect the capitals of the two countries. The length of the line will be 350 km, with all but 15 km located in Malaysia. The estimated cost of the project is $15 billion and construction is envisaged to be completed by 2024. On completion, the journey between the two cities will be a mere ninety minutes. Although much of Malaysia's rail development is being conducted in cooperation with Chinese firms, Japanese and Korean firms are very much in contention.[62] On a visit by the Singapore prime minister to Japan in September, the two

---

[59] CNBC, 17.6.2016; *Channel News Asia*, 25.10.2016.

[60] *Rakyat Post*, 11.12.2015; *Malaysia Digest*, 6.3.2016.

[61] H. Ghesquiere, *Singapore's Success : Engineering Economic Growth*, Singapore, 2006; L.Y.C. Lim (ed.), *Singapore's Economic Development: Retrospection and Reflections*, Singapore, 2016; K. Siddiqui, 'The Political Economy of Development in Singapore', *Research in Applied Economics*, 2/2, 2010, 1–31; K.P. Tan (ed.), *Renaissance Singapore? Economy, Culture and Politics*, Singapore, 2007.

[62] *Channel News Asia*, 19.8.2016; *Asia One*, 18.10.2016.

countries agreed to establish a high-level committee for bilateral discussions on transport matters, including the HSR link with Malaysia.[63] At the time of writing, the issue is still very much open.

Indonesia's HSR Project

Although we had initially determined that this chapter's remit would only cover the countries involved in the SKRL, it may be instructive to turn our attention to Indonesia, where China and Japan were both in contention to construct the country's first HSR link covering 142 kms between Jakarta and the country's fourth-biggest city, Bandung. After more than five years of feasibility studies and high-level lobbying, Japanese officials thought they were on the brink of bringing bullet trains to Indonesia. Then China showed up. In April 2015, Indonesia's Minister for State-Owned Enterprises Rini Soemarno suddenly announced that the government was considering a Chinese offer to build the railway as part of a $50 billion funding commitment from Chinese state banks. She told reporters that the Chinese proposal was attractive because it did not require any funding guarantees.[64] Then, in September 2015, the government suddenly scrapped the $6 billion plan for a high-speed train because it was no longer considered to be commercially viable. Instead, it wanted a slower train capable of travelling at 200 km/hr and it asked the bidders from China and Japan to submit new proposals.

China's original proposal involved funding through a Chinese loan to Indonesian state companies, whereas Japan's proposal was to be funded through the Indonesian budget and a low-interest loan from Japan.[65] China also managed to shave $0.7 billion from the cost estimate, but the clinching argument was China's business-to-business scheme, without any budget, guarantee or state capital injection.[66] Japan criticised China's proposal as unrealistic. The plan lacked government funding and was likely to end up

[63] *Channel News Asia*, 28.9.2016. This stage was completed in February 2017. *Channel Asia News*, 15.2.2017.

[64] C. Brummit, 'Desperate for Investment, Indonesia Plays China vs Japan', *Bloomberg*, 19.5.2015.

[65] C. Brummitt and N. Chatterjee, 'Indonesia Scraps Bullet Train, Seeks Fresh China, Japan Bids', *Bloomberg*, 4.9.2015.

[66] *Jakarta Post*, 30.9.2015.

making losses as it had to deal with a complex and corrupt Indonesian bureaucracy. Japan then cut the interest on the proposed loan to 0.1%, reduced the size of the Indonesian sovereign guarantee, cut the estimated time to complete the project and offered to transfer some of the technology. However, China responded by putting more money on the table ($5.27 billion, compared to Tokyo's $4.4 billion) and without any government guarantee at all. It offered an even shorter time-frame for the project – completion by 2019, just in time for the 2019 national election.[67]

In January 2016, construction on the line officially began at a tea plantation in West Java that would be the site of one of the stations. A week later, the project stalled because the Transport Ministry had not yet issued a construction certificate to the Chinese/Indonesian consortium, apparently because the consortium had not submitted the files detailing the development design, technical illustrations, field data and specifications needed.[68] In June the certificates still had not appeared, and the continued delay had the knock-on effect that the Chinese would not release funds for preparatory work without the necessary permits. Meanwhile, changes in design specifications were further helping to push up the costs, though they would allow an increase in maximum speeds on some stretches.[69] In February 2017 the project was still stalled. This time the problem was the failure to acquire the final 15% of the land needed for the line, mainly in the neighbourhood of the stations where costs had risen and owners were holding out for better terms.[70]

Once China starts to obtain influence over infrastructural development, it does not automatically mean that it will monopolise the process. In May 2016, the Indonesian government announced that it was cooperating with Japan on increasing the speed of trains between Jakarta and the country's

---

[67] E.A. Syailendra, 'Indonesia's High Speed Rail: A China–Japan Scramble for Influence', *RSIS Commentary*, 269, 2015.

[68] *South China Morning Post*, 19.2.2016.

[69] *Jakarta Post*, 11.7.2016.

[70] *Jakarta Post*, 1.2.2017; *Nikkei Asian Review*, 15.2.2017. In March 2017 it transpired that the crux of the problem lay in the fact that the Indonesian partners could not raise the $150 million required for land purchase and was waiting for profits to be generated from other ventures before completing the necessary transactions (*Tempo.co*, 22.3.2017).

second largest city Surabaya, with the aim of reducing journey times over the 750 km route from seven hours to five. The estimated cost of the project was $1.8 billion.[71] In October 2016, Japan was offered the project, which would involve the elimination of thousands of crossings and constructing a double track line along the railway's entire length.[72]

Reflections

The Chinese are relatively pleased with their cooperation with the nations of ASEAN. Thailand and Indonesia and third and fifth in the Country Cooperation Index with Vietnam, Malaysia and Singapore taking the next three places. Laos is tenth and Cambodia closes the group in fifteenth position.[73] On the basis of the efforts at overland connectivity, the fact that the ASEAN countries are considered so favourably is somewhat surprising as are some of the individual positions. The patience of Chinese companies and their engineers must have been tested to the limit by the continuous delays that have plagued many of the projects. The clearest progress has been shown in dealings with Malaysia which, as will be shown in the next chapter, has also been active in cooperating in port developments. On the other hand Singapore, whose size anyway offers few opportunities for cooperation, actually favours Japan for the prize project – the HSR connecting it to Kuala Lumpur.

---

[71] *Nikkei Asian Review*, 25.5.2016; *Jakarta Post*, 28.5.2016.

[72] *Jakarta Post*, 8.10.2016. In January 2017 it seemed likely that Japanese consultants would be asked to look at the feasibility of building a HSR along the route (*Jakarta Post*, 25.1.2017)

[73] PRC, National Development and Reform Commission, 一带一路大数据报告, Beijing, 2016 (One belt One Road. Big Data Report)

Table 7.4 Risk Indicators of China and the Mainland Countries of ASEAN

	EIU Risk Assessment	Control of Corruption	Ease of Doing Business
	Score 0-100	Score 0-100	Rank 1/190
China	45	50	78/190
Cambodia	58	87.50	131/190
Laos	58	80.29	139/190
Malaysia	30	34.13	23/190
Thailand	46	56.25	46/190
Singapore	12	2.88	2/190
Vietnam	48	60.58	82/190

Source: EIU Overall Risk Assessement: http://viewswire.eiu.com/index.asp?layout=RKAllCountryVW3 ; WBI Control of Corruption Indicator; http://data.worldbank.org/data-catalog/worldwide-governance-indicators; WB Ease of doing Business Index: http://www.doingbusiness.org/rankings

On the other hand, as the data in Table 7.4 shows, Chinese investments in the area are relatively safe, but both Laos and Cambodia have high levels of corruption and a stifling business climate. These are low-wage countries where China is disposed to locate some of its labour intensive manufacturing, but the portents for success are not good.

Overall, the most striking feature of than examination of China's relationship with ASEAN countries is the illustration of the lack of control that China had over the outcomes of its OBOR policies. In Chapter 6 we saw how a change in regime in Myanmar completely overturned the climate towards Chinese investments. In this chapter we have seen how hesitations by governments and inefficiency by ministries have contributed to delays in the implementation of even projects that have already been agreed. To some extent this built-in to the regimes with which China has to deal, but it also raises the question whether bilateral state-to-state approaches are the best way to guarantee success in this particular region. ASEAN already had a connectivity plan that coincided completely with the main priority identified by OBOR, namely the building of the Kunming-Singapore HSR and it had a proven track record of fruitful (though not necessarily painless) cooperation. It is possible to envisage a situation where a new ASEAN plan, incorporating China's finance and expertise as well as that of other potential partners, such as the ADB and the World Bank and Japanese and Korean Development Banks, might not in the long-run have been a more successful strategy. On the other hand, it could be that the choice of ASEAN might have ended in interminable bickering and even longer delays. As it is, we will never know the answer.

CHAPTER EIGHT

The Maritime Silk Route

In October 2013 President Xi announced China's vision of a Maritime Silk Road (MSR), alluding to the seven voyages made by Admiral Zheng He at the start of the 15th century. Subsequently the Chinese authorities released maps of the land and sea routes identifying the ports that it considered to be or should become part of the MSR and drawing lines across the seas between them, as though this somehow represented a maritime route. Before we start, there are two fairly obvious points that we have to make. First, there are many more seaports than those in which China is interested. Second, on land the lines of a map mean something: they represent the roads and railway track along which goods actually travel. On the sea, this is not the case. For decades ships transporting fuel, minerals, dry goods and, more recently, containers have been plying the waters between Europe, the Middle-East and Asia and will undoubtedly continue to do so whether China builds or expands new ports or not.[1] The maritime (silk) route already exists. China does not have to create it.

The lion's share of international transport travels by sea. In 2004 (and there is no reason to believe that the pattern has shifted dramatically) slightly over half of the value of international trade was carried by sea, compared with 31.3% carried overland (27.8% by road and 3.5% by rail) and the remaining 18.4% by air. South Asia and East Asia were even more dependent

---

[1] You can see the maritime traffic in real time in the whole world at http://MaritimeTraffic.com and, if you wish, identify each individual ship.

on maritime trade, with shares of 74.8% and 72.8% respectively.[2] When analysis is undertaken in terms of the weight and distance travelled rather than by value (i.e. tonne/km) the domination of maritime transport in world freight soars to 95%. This is because traders prefer the sea for transporting low-value produce over long distances.[3] This was probably always the case. In 1998 local fisherman discovered an ancient wreck in sixteen metres of water off the coast of the Indonesian island of Belitung. It was an Arabian dhow, remarkably preserved and with its cargo of Chinese goods, ranging from 60,000 earthenware bowls to precious bowls and cups made of gold, still intact. The ship dated from 830 AD and was probably representative of Arabian ships of the era. It had a capacity for carrying 25 tons of cargo.[4] Given that the average load for a camel is about 200 kg, this ship alone carried the load of 125 camels (or twelve large caravans).

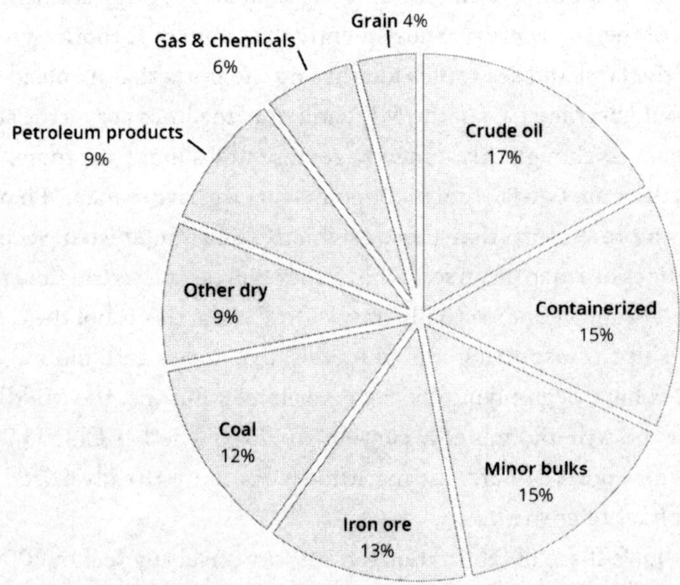

---

[2] Only 35.5% of its international trade travels by sea, with 46.5% travelling by road, 4.5% by rail and 13% by air..

[3] A. Cristea, D. Hummels, L. Puzzello and M.G. Avetisyan 'Trade and the Greenhouse Gas Emissions from International Freight Transport', *Journal of Environmental Economics and Management*, 65, 2013, 153–73.

[4] R. Krahl (ed.), *Shipwrecked : Tang Treasures and Monsoon Winds*, Singapore, 2010.

Figure 8.1 Distribution of Maritime Trade by Cargo

Source: UNCTAD, *Review of Maritime Transport*, 2015

If we return to today's seaborne trade, over a quarter is made up of crude oil and petroleum products. Container traffic, with 15%, is the second largest category. The distribution of the rest of is shown in Figure 8.2. Between leaving Chinese waters and arriving at the coast of Iran there are no fewer than 378 sea ports, some of which serve only local traffic or function as fishing ports. Not all these ports can deal with container ships. In fact there are only fifty-nine container liner ports in the area[5] Chinese interest is involved in less than ten of them. Because of their length or depth, some of these ports can only handle smaller container ships. What tends to happen is that the larger container ships head for the ports that can service them and these ports then become hubs for reloading small ships, which carry the goods to their final destinations. There are even fewer of these in the area. Their number may be ascertained in various ways, one of which is to look at Panamax ports. These are ports that can accommodate (larger) ships capable of passing through the Panama canal and have a maximum capacity of 5000 TEU. There are only nineteen of these in the region and a further six in the planning stage.[6] China is involved in the funding and construction of a handful of these, though because of the recent down-turn in container traffic, Chinese firms are increasing their share in others by mergers and acquisitions as cash strapped companies attempt to liquidate assets. It is the building of these deep sea ports that so worries security experts, since they could also (with modification) be used for servicing larger naval vessels.

China

The core position of Fujian Province on the MSR can be traced back to the Song Dynasty (960–1279). Quanzhou, a city in Fujian, was known as the largest port in Asia during the Song Dynasty and the Yuan Dynasty

[5] World Port Service database. http://www.marinetraffic.com/nl/ais/index/ports/all

[6] https://www.revolvy.com/main/index.php?s=List%20of%20Panamax%20ports. It is interesting that the widening of the Panama canal will soon lead to a revision of the list of ports since the 'new Panamax' definition is for ships with a 13,000 TEU capacity.

(1279–1368). Situated across the Taiwan Straits, the province also has a geographical advantage that can help strengthen ties with Taiwan, Hong Kong, Macao and South-East Asia. The Vision and Action Plan specifically designated Fujian as the core area for the MSR.[7] In April 2015 when the Plan appeared, the authorities announced the opening of an experimental 118 km^2 free economic zone on three separate sites, one of which was specifically based around the port of Xiamen. The zones would benefit from simplified customs clearance facilities and financial incentives to firms choosing to locate there. Foreign firms were invited to invest on equal terms with Chinese concerns (aside from a 'negative list' of businesses reserved for Chinese firms). At Xiamen itself, the zone was split into a 24.4 km^2 Haicang port area, which also incorporated an airport and facilities for cruise ships (a unique combination for China), and a 19.4 km^2 Cross States Zone to exploit the trade and investment opportunities offered by proximity to Taiwan.[8]

When Fujian province produced its Implementation Plan, Xiamen was named as the main international port for the MSR. It was certainly not the largest available. Measured in terms of the capacity of container ships docking at ports (the usual way of counting), there were eight busier container ports in China. However, it does have the advantage that it is able to handle the post-Panamax container ships. In February 2016, the *Benjamin Franklin* with a capacity of 18,000 TEU and a length of nearly 400 metres left Xiamen destined for Seattle, where it would take five days to unload.[9] It can not only handle these mega-ships, but it is also rather good at doing so. Measured by the number of containers that can be moved for each hour that the ship is at berth (berth efficiency), Xiamen,, Shanghai, Shenzhen and Tianjin are the most efficient in the world.[10]

---

[7] PRC, National Development and Reform Commission, *Vision and Actions*.

[8] HKTDC Research, 'China (Fujian) Pilot Free Trade Zone', 29.6.2015.

[9] *Fortune*, 1.2.2016.

[10] *International Transport Forum*, 2015.

South China Sea

From the ports in the south of China, the MSR enters the disputed waters of the South China Sea.[11] It is perhaps no surprise that aside from civil and military installations on some of the islands claimed as its own, China has had difficulty in establishing substantial maritime assets in the ports and harbours located in the area. Part of the reason is that China's claim to the islands, and therefore to the waterways and to the underwater resources, are disputed by every one of the states bordering the seas and by the United States and other Western powers as well. It is easy to see why.

Claims to international water stem from territorial claims to land. Islands are always problematic, and in this case especially so. Many of the so-called islands are submerged during high tides, and might better qualify as reefs. In addition, the islands to which China lays claim are a long way from the mainland and are closer to other neighbouring countries than they are to China itself. The Spratley Islands, for example, are nearly 2000 km from the Chinese mainland. China's claims rest on two foundations. The first is that the islands, and the seas around them, belong to the traditional jurisdiction of China as is evidenced by their inclusion in ancient maps of the Empire. Lines on old maps are comforting, but of little relevance in modern territorial politics. But nor, for that matter, is proximity to other masses of land, as the UK and Argentina know in the case of the Falklands/Malvinas. The legitimacy of a claim rests more firmly on the country occupying and ruling the territory, and the legitimacy of that jurisdiction. This is the basis of China's rejection of any attempts to move to arbitration using the United Nations Convention on the Law of the Sea, since at issue is the question of sovereignty over land (i.e. the various reefs, atolls and islands) over which the Convention has no jurisdiction. From the rights to the land, under current international law, countries can claim territorial control to 12 nautical miles of adjacent waters, and 200 nautical miles of economic activity (such

[11] Paul Gewirtz, *Limits of Law in the South China Sea*, Brookings East Asia Policy Paper, 8, Washington DC, 2016; R.D. Kaplan, *Asia's Cauldron. The South China Sea and the End of a Stable Pacific*, New York, 2014; X. Liu, *China's Perspectives on the South China Sea Verdict*, Chatham House Transcript, London, 2016; N. Roy, *The South China Sea Disputes: Past, Present, and Future*, Lanham, MD, 2016; I. Storey and C-Y. Lin, *The South China Sea Dispute: Navigating Diplomatic and Strategic Tensions*, Singapore, 2016.

as fishing, mining and drilling). China claims to control 80–90% of the 3.5 million km^2 of waters that fall within the lines of the map drawn by the Kuomintang government back in 1947. In rejecting any arbitration procedure or judgement of an international tribunal, China's resolution lies in bilateral negotiations. In fact, in 2006 it specifically excluded itself from any recourse to the UN's Convention.[12] However, with China's starting position that its territorial claims are irrefutable, and with new assets (and feet and armaments) changing the position on the islands almost daily, it is difficult to see how such disputes can easily be resolved. This is where the soft power rhetoric of the MSR faces the hard facts of 'realist' status-quo politics. None of this is supposed to affect shipping. Even warships can pass through territorial waters as long as they are engaged in 'innocent passage'. In addition, in 2002 China signed an agreement with ASEAN on a 'Code of Conduct in the South China Sea', which it reaffirmed ten years later,[13] itself, unfortunately, evidence of the lack of progress on the issue.

The rejection of China's claim by the Court of Arbitration in The Hague may be a moral victory for the Philippines, which brought the case, but that, by itself, had no effect on the situation. What did alter the situation was the election of President Duterte in June 2016 and his decision to set aside the ruling and deal directly with Beijing over the issue.[14]

Vietnam

Vietnam has responded to China's land reclamation works in the South China Sea by reclaiming land and constructing buildings at West London

[12] Ministry of Foreign Affairs, PRC, *Summary of the Position Paper of the Government of the People's Republic of China on the Matter of Jurisdiction in the South China Sea Arbitration Initiated by the Republic of the Philippines*, 2014.

[13] ASEAN, Declaration on the Conduct of Parties in the South China Sea, 4.11.2002 and 17.10.2012; http://asean.org/?static_post=declaration-on-the-conduct-of-parties-in-the-south-china-sea-2.

[14] *Forbes*, 4.1.2017. However, at time of writing it was unclear whether he was hardening his country's stance once more (R. Robles, 'Duterte plays a dangerous game in the South China Sea', *South China Morning Post*, 27.2.2017) or whether he was holding out an olive branch by suggesting that the two countries could cooperate in exploiting the mineral resources in the disputed area (A. Alimario, 'Duterte hits U.S. inaction in South China Sea dispute', *CNN Asia*, 24.3.2017)

Reef and Sand Cay in the Spratly archipelago. Of the rival claimants to the Spratly archipelago, it is Vietnam that has established the greatest number of outposts on the disputed islands: forty-eight as of May 2015, compared with eight each for China and the Philippines.[15] The only Chinese influence in the country is the 70% that Hong Kong's Hutchison Port Holdings has in the new Saigon International Terminal Vietnam (SITV) situated in Phu My, 80 km south-east of Ho Chi Minh City, which started operations in 2010.[16]

When, in July 2015, the Vietnam government announced that it would build a new $2.5 billion deep-water seaport in the Mekong delta on Hon Khoai Island, 15 km off the coast of Vietnam's southernmost province, it turned to the USA for assistance. The US Export-Import Bank would finance 85% of the costs. The province is pivotal in the country's rice exports and provides much of its fruit harvest and fish catch, which would otherwise have to be exported via Ho Chi Minh City. Progress, however, has not been fast, and one year later there was no sign of progress.[17] The feasibility study for the port, with twelve transhipment berths, has been undertaken by Bechtel Corporation, the largest US construction and civil engineering company.[18]

Indonesia

It was surely no accident that it was before the House of Representatives in Indonesia [19], a nation composed of thousands of islands, that President Xi Jinping unveiled his vision of a MSR. And almost a year later newly

---

[15] A. C-H. Lim, 'Recent Developments In Sino-Vietnamese Relations – Analysis', *Eurasia Review*, 16.9.2015.

[16] http://www.sitv.com.vn/Home.aspx?Cul=En; Drewry, *Global Container Terminal operators. Annual review and Forecast, 2016*, 52.

[17] *Thanh News*, 21.7.2015; *VNExpress International*, 23.8.2016.

[18] G. Ong-Webb, 'Thailand's Kra Canal: Is Vietnam Angling In?', *The Establishment Post*, 28.9.2015.

[19] E. Aspinall and M. Sukmajati (eds.), *Electoral Dynamics in Indonesia: Money Politics, Patronage and Clientelism at the Grassroots*, Chicago, 2016; H. McDonald, *Demokrasi: Indonesia in the 21st Century*, Melbourne, 2015; A. Nasution, Macroeconomic Policies in Indonesia: Indonesia Economy since the Asian Financial Crisis of 1997, Oxford, New York, 2015; A.J.S. Reid (ed.), *Indonesia Rising: The Repositioning of Asia's Third Giant*, Singapore, 2012; D.E. Weatherbee, 'Understanding Jokowi's Foreign Policy', *Trends in South East Asia*, 12, 2016, Singapore.

elected President Joko 'Jokowi' Widodo mirrored this ambition by positing Indonesia as an independent 'global maritime fulcrum' between the Indian and Pacific Oceans. The oceans, he explained, were part of Indonesia's identity as well as a source of his country's prosperity. It was necessary to maintain maritime resources, to develop the maritime infrastructure and connectivity and to combine with other nations to eliminate sources of conflict at sea.[20] Indonesia has been careful to take a 'non-claimant' position in the South China Sea dispute.[21]

China had been interested in developing the port facilities in Jakarta. Jakarta and Surabaya are the only two ports capable of handling large international cargo vessels; other goods need to be transhipped from Singapore or Malaysia. The overcrowded port of Tanjung Priok (Jakarta) handles over half of Indonesia's foreign trade, but was desperately in need of expansion and improvement. It had not had a significant upgrade for 130 years.[22] Hong Kong investors had been interested in the project, but in 2013 the $2 billion contract to build a new container terminal and a petroleum terminal (the first phase of the work) was awarded to the Japanese construction firm of Mitsui and Co. The whole project, which opened in 2016 will increase the capacity of the port from 5 million TEU to 18 million and will also have equipped it to handle the post-Panamax container ships. Hutchison Port Holdings has a 51% stake in the operating company of the main terminal and a 45% stake in the operating company of the (smaller) Koja terminal.[23] At the time of writing, no decision had been taken on the contracts for the further expansion.

A second project with which Japan has also been involved is the new deep-water seaport that will replace the scrapped Cilamaya port in Karawang (West Java). The first phase of construction would cost $1.2 billion and give the port a capacity of 3.75 million TEU. The initial study for the project was financed and conducted by the JICA and Japanese firms were expected to

---

[20] R.A. Witular, 'Jokowi Launches Maritime Doctrine to the World', *Jakarta Post*, 13.11.2014.

[21] R.A. Supriyanto, 'Out of Its Comfort Zone: Indonesia and the South China Sea', *Asia Policy*, 21, 2016, 21-28.

[22] C. Dodd, 'Indonesia Launches Massive Port Expansion', *Finance Asia*, 28.2.2015.

[23] *Port Technology*, 22.4.2012; *World Maritime News*, 13.9.2016, Drewry, *Global Container Terminal Operators. Annual Review and Forecast*, 2016, 52.

win the construction contract. Suddenly, in April 2015, the project was cancelled and an announcement made that it would be relocated to an unpublicised location further along the coast. The reason given for cancellation was that the port would interfere with oil and gas exploitation in the area, and the reason for non-disclosure of the new site was to deter land speculators. In December, the transport minister assured the Japanese counterparts that Japan was still the preferred partner for the project. However, the cancellation allowed criticism to be made over the involvement of government funding rather than private capital, (the same argument that had derailed Japan's bid to construct the Jakarta–Bandung HSR). A brave reporter suggested that the decision reflected manoeuvres among the governing elite to cosy up to the president, who was known to favour the Chinese, and to secure personal (political gains).[24] In May 2016, the government announced that the new port would be built in Patimbang. When completed, it would have a capacity of 7.5 million TEU and would have cost $3.2 billion. The first phase, scheduled for completion in 2019, would have a capacity of 1.5 billion TEU and will be funded by the JICA.[25]

Malaysia

The next port of call on the MSR is the Port Kuantan and its industrial park in Pahang, on Malaysia's East Coast. The $3.4 billion scheme dates from 2013. It was seen as a counterpart of a joint industrial park in the port city of Guangxi in Southern China. The Chinese side of the deal was to expand the port facilities ($0.9 billion) and to develop a steel plant, an aluminium processing facility and a palm oil refinery in the park ($1.6 billion).[26] In September 2015 the Malay Federal government committed itself to ploughing a further $375 million into the project in the form of supporting infrastructure (roads) that would be necessary if the port were to succeed in doubling its capacity.[27] It would later ask for Chinese help in funding an

[24] R.A. Witular, 'Insight: Japan at Risk of Losing the Next Big Thing', *Jakarta Post*, 12.1.2016.

[25] *Jakarta Post*, 2.5.2016; *Maritime News*, 3.5.2016, *Detik Finance*, 4.1.2017.

[26] M. Ramasamy, 'China, Malaysia Plan $3.4 Billion Industrial Park in Kuantan', *Bloomberg Business*, 5.2.2013.

[27] *FMT News*, 20.9.2015.

east coast rail route that would (also) link the port to Kuala Lumpur.[28] Whilst everything in the park seemed to be developing on schedule, the state authorities threatened to stop bauxite mining in the area, and therefore closing the processing plant, if no solution were found to the pollution from the transport and storage of bauxite ore, and the failure of filters inside the plant, with the result that the dust was literally turning the sea red.[29]

On the Western coast side of Malaysia lie the Straits of Malacca. This has a significant chokepoint at the Phillip Channel with the canal narrowing down to a width of 2.8 km and runs for a length of just over 2 km. When one considers that 200 vessels per day pass through the channel, this risk profile presents problems when taking account of the potential for collisions, delays and piracy. For China this is a particular concern, since 85% of its imports and 70% of its oil and gas imports pass through the Straits.[30] In addition, if differences with China were ever to escalate to the point of imposing sanctions, its dependence on free passage through the Straits represents a serious security risk as well.

The main port in the region is Port Kelang, 38 km from Kuala Lumpur and the eleventh largest container port in the world. It comprises three separate ports. Hutchison Port Holdings has a 24% stake in the Westport, which accounts for 75% of the revenues of the entire port complex and is expecting to further expand its container terminal capacity. It already boasts a capacity of 11 million teus.[31]

Melaka Gateway is a port development on one natural and three artificial islands off the coast of Malacca. The aim is to build a cruise ship terminal and all the retail and entertainment facilities to keep the passengers happy. The whole project was launched in 2014 and became known as the Melaka Gateway. Its projected costs are $7.4 billion. In 2016 discussions began on cooperation with China for the construction of a deep sea port. This part of the project is estimated to costs $1.9 billion. The construction would be a joint venture of the state-owned KAJ Development (holding a 51%

[28] *Channel News Asia*, 31.10.2016.

[29] *Asia One*, 15.2.2015; *Malaysia Insider*, 5.6.2016.

[30] F. Umaña, *Transnational Security Threats in the Straits of Malacca*, Foundation for Peace, Washington, 2012; A. Wheeler, 'The New China Silk Road (One Belt, One Road): Changing The Face Of Oil & Gas In SE Asia', *OilPro*, 28.7.2015.

[31] *New Straits Times*, 27.9.2016; 2.10.2016; Drewry, *Global Container*, 52.

Stake) with three Chinese partners (PowerChina International, Shenzhen Yantian Port Group and Rizhao Port Group). The port is designed as a liquid cargo terminal and will house containers for petroleum, chemicals and vegetable oil. The agreement has raised both military and commercial concerns. Militarily, will it serve China's strategic interests in the region? Commercially, will it challenge the position of Singapore. Perhaps more pertinently, will it make the expansion of Port Kelang redundant? Further in the distance, would China's investment on overland trade and pipeline routes, make the Melaka Gateway itself redundant?[32]

Then, in July 2016, the Malay government proposed a joint China–Malay construction of a new port on Carey Island between Malacca and the Port Kelang, while stressing that the administration of the port itself would remain in local Malay hands.[33] The $45 billion port-city project is designed to complement the developments at Port Kelang and to become integrated into the Port Kelang free trade zone. However, with a planned capacity of 30 million teu's (about the same the traffic passing through Singapore) the new complex would have to attract considerable trade from Singapore if it was not to end up by exacerbating overcapacity in the region.[34]

Singapore

Singapore is suffering from a decline in world container traffic and is losing market share to Malaysia. The only Chinese interest is the 49% share of the Chinese Ocean Shipping Company (COSCO) in two berths, with a capacity of 2 million teus at Singapore's Pasir Panjang Terminal.[35] In March 2016, the operations moved to three brand-new mega-berths and to expand operations further in to develop a new phase of the terminal some time in 2017.[36] When completed, COSCO's container line will shift its operations from Port Kelang to the new facility[37] shifts and consolidations in ownership among

[32] *Nikkei Asian Review*, 3.9.2016; *Port Strategy*, 25.10.2016; *Free Malaysia Today*, 14.11.2016.

[33] *China People's Daily*, 5.7.2016.

[34] *Malaysiakini*, 1.2.2017; *The Independent*, 20.2.2017.

[35] Drewry, *Global Container*, 82.

[36] *Straits Times*, 29.3.2016; *Nikkei Asian Review*, 31.3.2016.

[37] *JOC.com*, 9.6.2016.

the major international chipping lines have served further to consolidate Singapore's leading position as the main international hub in the region.[38]

Thailand

One way of avoiding the problems inherent in using the Straits of Malacca and, at the same time, cutting 1200 km off the journey between the Indian and Pacific Oceans would be to cut a canal through the isthmus of Thailand at its narrowest point, just beneath the southernmost tip of its border with Myanmar. In fact, a look at history would suggest that using the Malacca Straits had long been regarded as an inefficient transport corridor. Already at the end of the 17th century French engineers had conducted a feasibility study for the Kra Canal and advised against its construction as being technologically unfeasible. The British East India Company also considered the option but rejected it because of the costs. In the late 19th century, when the interests of Singapore became paramount, the Thai and British governments agreed not to construct such a canal (it was obvious who had the biggest warships), and this undertaking was reinforced in the Anglo-Thai Treaty of 1946. The idea has repeatedly been suggested since, but without ever moving towards realisation.[39]

In May 2015, the idea of building the Kra Canal, as it had become known, resurfaced when rumours appeared that the Thailand Infrastructure Investment Development Company and its Chinese counterparts had signed a memorandum of understanding in Guangzhou for the construction of the canal. It would have two parallel shipping lanes of 50 km each (400 metres wide and 20 metres deep), and would be able to take the Postpanamax ships and supertankers. The project would cost $28 billion and would take ten years to complete.[40] The rumours were almost immediately denied by both governments, but never really died. In January 2016, the Thai prime minister was forced publicly to disavow any intention to build the Kra Canal by arguing that his government's priority lay in a massive deep-water seaport,

---

[38] *Lloyd's List*, 22.2.2017.

[39] A. Panda, 'How a Thai Canal Could Transform Southeast Asia' *The Diplomat*, 1.12.2013. *The Independent*, 2.10.2016.

[40] L.H. Liang, 'Thailand, China Sign Agreement to Construct a New Strategic Kra Canal', *Seatrade Maritime News*, 19.5.2015.

oil refinery and industrial estate in the town of Dawei in Myanmar, and that the Dawei project, which spans nearly 200 km^2, was set to be Thailand's new gateway to the Indian Ocean in three decades' time.[41] But the denial does not mean that the idea is dead. In China a spate of articles have speculated that this could 'become an international golden waterway'. Military analysts have argued that it would make a future blockade less tempting because freight routes would be more diffuse. Academic commentary suggested that such a canal would benefit the whole region.[42] It has also resurfaced as an opinion piece in *The Nation* in the context of combating piracy in the Straits[43] and there a rumours that the new King is more favourably inclined towards the project than his late father.[44]

Myanmar

As early as 2008, Chinese authorities had started to take an interest in Myanmar's off-shore gas reserves. Although their contribution to China's energy needs would be small, the pipeline required to ship the energy straight through to South-West China would also enhance energy security by shortening the journey and avoiding the Malacca Straits.[45] By 2011 the scheme, devised by China's CITIC Group, had expanded to include a large deep-water seaport and an airfield at Kyaukpyu, as well as a 200 km/hr railway connecting Kyaukpyu to Dali, in Yunan Province. The history of the entire scheme has been a troubled one. The gas pipeline, designed to transport gas from Rakhine's coast, began construction officially in August 2011. Of the 1700 km, 800 km were located in Myanmar and the completion date of June 2013 was met on time.[46]

The deep-water seaport was intended to allow the export of containers to China. The construction of the port and the 20 acre special economic

---

41 *Channel News Asia*, 13.1.2016.

42 L.J. Goldstein, 'Could This Be China's Panama Canal?' *The National Interest*, 30.5.2016.

43 *The Nation*, 13.8.2016.

44 *Executive Intelligence Review*, 16.1.2017.

45 J. Goldstein, 'Communist China aims for a Pipeline in Burma', *New York Sun*, 15.1.2008.

46 *Ramree.com*, 31.5.2011.

zone was expected to cost $2.4 billion.[47] Meanwhile, environmental concerns and local opposition had contributed to delaying the construction of the refinery in Kunming. The refinery had been supposed to receive nearly half of the 22 million tons of crude oil that could be sent through the pipeline each year, and oil from Africa and the Middle East was scheduled to start flowing soon. Reports suggested that that the receiving refinery might have been abandoned and a new refinery project started elsewhere. Doubts were also raised in China over whether the oil pipeline project was viable at all. The CNPC–Burma pipeline is the first that pumps oil into China that is not directly linked with an oil field. The cost of transhipping the oil first, storing it (in twelve tanks with a total capacity of 5.3 million barrels) and then pumping it into the pipeline would all serve to push up costs. The CNPC is required to pay Naypyidaw $13.6 million a year in rent for the pipeline as well as $1 per ton of crude that flows through it. That would be $22 million if the pipeline operates at full capacity — and nothing if it doesn't operate at all.[48] The project received a second setback when, in July 2014, Myanmar's Ministry of Rail Transportation cancelled the agreement with the Chinese government to build a railway to Kunming, blaming the cancellation on public opposition to the project. Political parties and civil society groups in Rakhine state, through which the railway would have passed, have protested at the construction of the pipeline as well as the railway, citing environmental and social concerns. Groups in Rakhine state also oppose the practice of exporting local natural resources out of Rakhine territory.[49] Nevertheless, by January 2015 the oil terminal at Kyaukpyu was ready to welcome its first (small, 100,000 ton) oil tanker.[50]

With the oil terminal and pipeline back on track, in January 2016 the Myanmar government awarded China's CITIC Group Corporation the contracts to build Kyaukpyu's deep-water seaport and the accompanying industrial park. The cost would be shared on a 51:49 basis by China and Myanmar respectively. By eliminating the need to travel via the Straits of Malacca, Kyaukpyu Port would save about 5000 km in sailing distance for

---

47 *Ramree.com*, 23.12.2012.

48 *Ramree.com*, 22.11.2013.

49 J. Goldberg, 'Myanmar's Great Power Balancing Act', *The Diplomat*, 29.8.2014.

50 *Ramree.com*, 30.12.2014.

shipments travelling to China from India and points beyond.[51] The port, which is designed eventually to have a capacity of 7 million teu, is ideally situated for export-minded food processors, sewing companies and other businesses looking to capitalize on the large local supply of inexpensive labour. In addition petrochemical and heavy machinery companies are expected to build facilities there in the future.[52]

Bangladesh

The construction of a port in Bangladesh would have provided some cover if things went wrong in Myanmar since both countries enjoy the same locational advantages. The government also wanted a deep-water seaport of its own, There had been no new seaport built in the country since independence and, since then, Bangladesh had become the world's second largest exporter of garments (which contributed 15% to its GDP). The waters surrounding Chittagong and Mongla, Bangladesh's two existing main ports, were so shallow that vessels had to wait for the tides to berth and to leave and they could not accommodate bigger vessels, which had to transfer their loads to smaller vessels. All this undermined the ports' competitiveness compared with those in neighbouring countries.[53]

The original OBOR maps had identified Chittagong as a target of Chinese interest, but instead attention turned to two other alternative sites a mere 25 km apart, Matabari and Sonadia Island. Although Japan had conducted the initial feasibility study for the Sonadia Island port, the Myanmar government had turned to China to help construct it, but no contracts had been signed at the time. Meanwhile Japan had turned its attention to Matabari, upscaling its ambitions and offering financial support. The port would still fill its role as a coal port, and would host four 600 MW coal-fired power stations, but it would also be able to handle other cargoes. The project now also included an industrial corridor and the construction of roads, rail

[51] S. Tiezzi, 'Chinese Company Wins Contract for Deep Sea Port in Myanmar', *The Diplomat*, 1.1.2016.

[52] M. Matsui, 'Industrial Parks Seek Life Beyond Yangon', *Nikkei Asian Review*, 3.2.2016.

[53] N.O. Pearson, 'Japan Beating China in Race for Indian Ocean Deep-Sea Port', *Bloomberg*, 23.6.2015.

and electricity infrastructure. The JICA offered 80% of the funding ($3.7 billion) at 0.1% interest for thirty years, with no payments for the first decade.[54] In June 2015 Japan was given the go-ahead for the construction of the 18 metre deep-seaport at Matarbari with work scheduled to start in January 2016. The planning minister also suggested that pressure from both the USA and India might have been behind the decision,[55] but the interest rate on China's loan for Sonadia Island was 2% p.a. and, in addition, China was insisting that commodities, services and equipment be procured from China.

As if to confirm this suspicion of Indian influence, the Bangladeshi authorities announced that they were working with India to construct a new deep-water seaport at Payra, near Chittagon. In order to make it fully functional engineers would need to cut a deep channel through the heavily silted port to allow access for larger vessels. Initially the port would handle food grains, fertiliser and cement, but eventually it would operate as a large container port. Situated near the Indian border, in the initial stage the port would serve Indian trade as well. Bangladesh hoped to start fully fledged port activities, with a capacity to deal with 75,000 containers, by 2023.[56]

Sri Lanka

Sri Lanka[57] where China has two maritime ventures running, was not on the original OBOR map. However, its position, commanding the oceans at the southern tip of the Indian sub-continent, could scarcely seem more strategic. The country's involvement in Sri Lanka dates from the final stages in the civil war when the government was facing Western sanctions for war crimes. With the screaming need for investment on the one hand and a withdrawal of original backers on the other, the stage was set for China to arrive. All that was needed was a scale of ambition to match the fund avail-

[54] S. Miglani and R. Paul, 'Bangladesh Favours Japan for Port and Power Plant, in Blow to China', *Reuters*, 10.9.2015.

[55] Pearson, 'Japan Beating China'.

[56] *BDNews*, 4.6.2016; *Dhaka Tribune*, 5.10.2016.

[57] International Crisis Group, *Sri Lanka: Jumpstarting the Reform Process*, Asia Report 278, 2016; P. Lowe, *The Causes and Consequences of Separatist Conflict in Sri Lanka: Tamil Separatism and Civil War*, Wallingford, 2014; N. Wickramasinghe, *Sri Lanka in the Modern Age: A History*, Oxford, 2015.

able. The then president, Mahinda Rajapaksa, was determined to restore the country's fortunes and large-scale infrastructural projects seemed to be the way to proceed, and ones familiar to his potential Chinese backers. Two projects emerged. One was to upgrade the city port of Colombo into a first-class regional hub (later expanded to Port City). The other was to turn the small coastal town of Hambantota, 250 km to the south-east of the capital, into Sri Lanka's second major city. It is one of the poorest parts of the island and, coincidentally, it happened to have been the president's home town.

The Colombo Port Expansion Project (CPEP) to develop the south port area was initiated in 2008. The two-phase project was estimated to cost $1.2 billion. The first phase, costing $0.3 billion and financed by the ADB, involved the construction of a new breakwater, the dredging of the harbour and the rerouting of oil pipelines, all of which was undertaken as a joint venture between the Port Authority and the Korean Hyundai Engineering and Construction Company.[58] The second phase, which involved the construction of three new terminals capable of handling Panamax (and post-Panamax) container ships, was started in 2011 as a joint venture with the China Merchants Holdings Company and a Sri Lankan consortium. The first of the three terminals opened for business in August 2013, and all three are now fully operational.[59] In 2011, so the story goes, on a tour of the project the president observed the land adjacent to the construction site and saw the potential for the creation of a new financial hub. And so was born the $1.4 billion Colombo Port City project. This was to be built on an 233 ha artificial island next to Colombo's main port and included apartments, shopping malls, a water sports area, a golf course, hotels and marinas. The whole enterprise, funded by Chinese loans, was entrusted to the China Harbour Engineering Company (a subsidiary of China Communications Construction Company Ltd). Work on the project began in September 2014.[60]

As the work began on expanding the port in Colombo, so plans were revived for a second harbour (also known as the Ruhunu Magampura International Port) in Hambantota to relieve congestion in Colombo. The

[58] *Sunday Observer,* 13.2.2011.

[59] *Live Mint,* 5.8.2013; *Shiptechnology.com.*

[60] *Roar.lk,* 26.1.2016.

whole port area was to be 16 km^2 and to have a capacity of 20 million TEU a year (which, if translated into reality, would make it the fifth largest container port in the world). The first phase started in 2008 and involved the construction of basic port and ship repair infrastructure. It was entrusted to a joint venture between Sinohydro Corporation and China Harbour Engineering Company. The \$361 million cost was financed for 85% by a loan from China's Export-Import Bank[61] with a fixed interest rate of 6.3%.[62] The installation of fuel tanks and bunkering facilities cost a further \$76.5 million and was completed by the Han Quin Engineering Construction Company of China. The second phase of the project started in 2011, and involved the new long quays and wharfs, a container oil terminal, harbour basin, handling yards roads and a flyover. The contract was awarded to China Communications Construction Company and a loan from China's Export-Import Bank covered the \$810 million costs. In addition, adjacent to the port, a tax free zone was built, with a price tag of \$550 million.[63] While all this was going on in the harbour, the building of a new international airport was started 18 km north of the town. Most of the \$209 million spent in its construction was covered by a loan from China's Export-Import Bank and the construction work was undertaken by Chinese firms. The airport can handle 1 million passengers a year, and it opened for business in September 2013.

It was inevitable that such grand schemes would attract criticism. Environmentalists expressed concerns about pollution and the degrading of Sri Lanka's unique nature. Small businesses feared being squeezed out by larger multinationals. Fishermen regretted their reduced access to traditional fishing grounds. But most important were the questions raised over the viability of projects, the ability to sustain the level of debt incurred and the lop-sided dependence on China. In 2014 the new airport at Hambantota made a loss of \$20 million, while the port was only able to operate by taking funds from Colombo and recorded a loss of \$5 million.[64] In the January 2015 presidential elections Maithripala Sirisenan, candidate for the opposition

[61] *Shiptechnology.com*

[62] S.S. Pattanaik, 'Controversy over Chinese Investment in Sri Lanka', *East Asia Forum*, 5.6.2015.

[63] *Shiptechnology.com.*

[64] Pattanaik, 'Controversy'.

New Democratic Front, deplored the rising corruption in his country, which he attributed to foreign interests paying huge bribes to a handful of top officials and burdening future generations with the debts so incurred. 'If this trend continues for another six years', he argued, 'our country would become a colony and we would become slaves.' He promised to tighten controls over corruption, to expose the true state of loans, to reassess all mega-projects and to rebalance relations with the country's neighbours.[65] And on that programme, and a raft of other promises, he won the election.

In March 2015 work on Colombo Port City was suspended while the grounds for approval of the project were investigated and another report was commissioned on the environmental impact. If this fell somewhat short of his followers' expectations,[66] worse was to follow. After a visit by China's assistant Minister of Foreign Affairs Liu Jianchao, the government announced that the port project would still go ahead, once its security issues had been resolved (this as a sop to Indian sensitivities).[67] In January 2016, faced with claims of $380,000 a day in penalty clauses, the government signalled its readiness to resume the project, but under new conditions.[68] Lying behind those conditions was a government concern to reduce the weight of the cumulative $8 billion debt it had incurred. What this involved was to convert any of these ventures to public–private partnerships involving debt for equity swaps,[69] which boiled down to giving the Chinese title to the land (since foreigners could not own land, this meant giving them rights to ninety-nine-year leases) and operational responsibility (and profits) from some of the ventures. Trying to salvage something from the wreckage, the prime minister explained that the arrangements would make room for new loans for social projects. The distaste for mega-projects had also been lost. Colombo Port City would become part of a megapolis of 8 million people in the country's western province, with plenty of opportunities for development for all.[70]

---

65 M. Sirisena, *Manifesto. A Compassionate Maithri, Governance, A Stable Country*, 2014.

66 Pattanaik, 'Controversy'.

67 D. Mudalige, 'Port City Construction to Recommence, with Slight Changes to Initial Agreements', *Daily News*, 11.12.2015.

68 *Reuters*, 12.1.2016.

69 *Asia Times*, 15.4.2016.

70 *Sri Lanka Sunday Times*, 10.4.2016.

China Merchant Holdings International acquired an 80% stake in port at Hambantota in return for absorbing $1.1 billion of Sri Lanka's debt to China. At least the deal seemed to offer some hope the Chinese might actually finish the scheme[71] but it was greeted with violent protests, ironically led by the former president, Mahinda Rajapaksa. In addition, the land acquisition for the industrial park had not been completed and so, in January 2017, the Chinese suspended all work on the project and halted the financial transfers that had been agreed.[72] The government now wanted to revise the original deal. While agreeing to the land concession, it wanted Sri Lankans to be allowed to acquire a majority holding in the entire venture. The Chinese offered only prepared to divest 20% of their share (bring their share down to 60%) and that only in ten years' time. At the time of writing, a cabinet subcommittee is examining the proposals.[73]

Pakistan

Pakistan has two main ports, in Karachi and Port Quasim. However, since 2002 the government has been developing a new deep-water seaport in the small town of Gwadar in the remote province of Balochistan on the western side of the country. It is in Gwadar that China has its main focus as far as the MSR is concerned. The Pakistani government began the construction of the port in 2002, with China providing 80% of the $248 million for the first phase of the project, which involved the construction of three berths and supporting facilities.[74] Despite considerable Chinese involvement, the management of the container port since it started operation in 2008 was entrusted to the Singaporean firm, PSA International, possibly because of the government's sensitivity to US concerns. However, in February 2013, frustrated by its slow development (possibly because of its poor road links to Karachi), the government handed the running of the port to the China Overseas Ports Holding Company (COPHC). At this point, China began considering plans that would develop the port not simply for containers,

[71] *Economy Next*, 28.10.2016; *Forbes*, 28.10.2016.

[72] *Forbes*, 21.2.2017.

[73] *BdNews24.com*, 22.3.2017.

[74] *Port Strategy*, 10.2.2011.

but as an oil and gas terminal to transport some of the 60% of its crude oil imports from neighbouring Gulf countries overland to China.[75] When the Action Plan appeared in 2015, Gwadar featured as the anchor of the CPEC. Among the fifty-one memoranda of understanding signed at the time between the two governments were commitments (and concessional loans) for further port expansion, the construction of a new highway, the building of a new international airport and a framework agreement for a terminal and pipeline project.[76] In June 2016 work began on a 10 km^2 free trade zone next to the harbour. The $2 billion for providing the infrastructure is provided by China,[77] and the project is undertaken and managed by COPHC. Firms moving into the zone are granted ninety-nine-year leases and a twenty-three-year tax holiday.[78] On 29 October 2016 a convoy of 45 containers left Kashgar for Gwadar. Having travelled almost 9000kms in China, it crossed the border at Sust and travelled under heavy security along the newly constructed roads of the Western corridor that passes through Balochistan, arriving at Gwadar 870kms away on 12 November. The following day, amid much speechmaking and self-congratulation, they were loaded onto two ships as part of a consignment of 250 containers of Chinese and Pakistani goods, destined respectively for Africa and the Middle East.[79]

Work on the oil and gas terminal and the pipeline were moving more slowly. By the middle of 2016, there had been no response to the (Chinese) bid for the $2 billion contract, despite the fact that China was offering soft loans (Libor rates plus 2.25%) to fund 85% of the cost (the remainder to come from a levy on consumers). The reason, it transpired, was the finance ministry's reluctance to release the necessary funds, apparently because they had already been spent on other projects.[80] Finally, irked by the continuous delays, China withdrew its BOT offer and opted instead simply to be the

[75] *Port Strategy*, 28.2.2013; F. Yousaf, 'Is Gwadar Worth the Theatrics?' *The Diplomat*, 22.8.2013.

[76] *Dawn*, 20.4.2015.

[77] *Express Tribune*, 20.6.2016.

[78] *Daily Times*, 1.9.2016.

[79] *Pakistan Observer*, 5.11.2016; *The Nation*,14.11.2016.

[80] *Express Tribune*, 3.5.2016.

contractor. It would still underwrite the initial construction costs on the same basis as before.[81]

Pipelines are not Pakistan's strong suit. The 'Peace pipeline' had originally been conceived as one linking Iranian oil fields to Pakistan and India. When India withdrew from the project in 2009, the two other countries continued alone, with the intention of completing the project by December 2014. Whilst Iran completed its side of the deal at the cost of $2 billion, progress in Pakistan was non-existent.[82] The new date for completion has been set as December 2017, but work in Pakistan has still to start.[83] Into this vacuum stepped India. Although President Xi was one of the first heads of state to visit Iran in 2016 after the lifting of sanctions (and signing a raft of bilateral agreements), and although the Iranian goods arrived in China along the overland Silk Road a few days later, it was India that seized the initiative. In May 2016 President Narendra Modi visited Iran and secured a deal to develop the port of Chabahar, a mere 76 km from Gwadar. India committed $500 million to the port project and a further $16 billion to an eventual free trade zone adjoining the port. The development would not only give India access to Iranian markets and resources, but also offer a route to Central Asia that bypasses Pakistan.[84] Six months later a visitor noted 'a single ship floated at the main jetty. Most of the cargo containers scattered in an asphalt lot bore the logo of the state-owned Islamic Republic of Iran Shipping Lines. In an adjacent harbour, a dozen wooden dhows, or traditional fishing boats, bobbed in the water.'[85] In an even more striking development, in August 2016 India and Iran announced an agreement to build a 1400 km underwater gas pipeline between the two countries at the cost of $4.5 billion, again circumventing Pakistan.[86]

---

81 *Express Tribune*, 21.10.2016.

82 *Presstv.iran*, 12.6.2016.

83 *The International News*, 6.9.2016.

84 *Quartz India*, 24.5.2016.

85 *Bloomberg*, 5.10.2016.

86 *Reuters*, 8.8.2016.

Suez Canal

The second choke point on the sea road from China to Europe lies at the entrance to the Red Sea. Opposite, on the African coastline, lies Djibouti. In January 2013 the China Merchant Holdings International took a share in the management of the main Port of Djibouti. Already Chinese firms were awarded the contract for building the new 756 km electrified railway link from the port to landlocked East African countries. Djibouti's new port expansion programme will include work at the Doraleh Multipurpose Port, which will be upgraded to four terminals for the handling of vehicles and rolling cargoes. The investment, jointly provided by Djibouti Port SA and China Merchant Holding will amount to $590 million.[87] Chinese naval vessels, alongside those of other countries, had been active in the area guarding tankers and cargo ships from the pirates operating there. In many respects China's decision to acquire a naval base was late in coming. In May 2016, the country leased a plot of land upon which to build a naval base.[88]

From the entrance to the Red Sea, the MSR turns northwards towards the entrance of the Suez Canal. Built originally by British and French engineers, the canal has remained little changed (though often fought over) for much of the subsequent 150 years. In 2015 the Egyptian government opened the 'New Suez Canal', which deepened the existing canal over 37 km of the existing 164 km length and added a second 35 km parallel canal to allow ships more easily to sail in both directions. It reduced waiting times and almost doubled the capacity of the canal. The total cost of the project was $8.2 billion.[89] Even at the time, questions were raised over whether the expansion was needed. One year later, and there is no evidence that traffic has actually increased, although this may simply be a reflection of the slowdown in world trade in general.[90]

While work was progressing on the canal, Chinese firms were engaged in expanding their interests at both ends. At the canal's southern entrance, China Harbour Engineering Company (CHEC) had already in 2009

[87] *Port Strategy*, 7.9.2015.

[88] *Financial Times*, 31.3.2016; *Global Post*, 3.5.2016.

[89] *Bloomberg*, 4.8.2016; *Economist*, 8.10.2015.

[90] *AL Monitor*, 6.8.2016.

invested $1 billion in building a new quay at the al-Adabiya port, and in 2012 work began on the construction of a new container terminal. At the northern end of the canal at Port Said East Port, COSCO Pacific had already taken a 20% stake in a joint venture to operate the container terminal since 2008. In 2012 CHEC won the contract to construct a new quay.[91] For the rest, there is little evidence that China is seeking to expand its interest in the area.

Greece

Although Greece is not officially one of the OBOR countries, we will nevertheless examine developments since it anchors the MSR's route in Europe. COSCO's involvement in Piraeus began in 2009, when it obtained a thirty-five-year concession from the Greek government to operate two of the three piers of the port's container terminal. To increase the volume of container traffic, with the aim of converting Piraeus to a major hub in the Mediterranean, COSCO extended the piers and built a railway link to connect the terminal to the national network.[92] In 2013, as Greece was reeling under the austerity measures imposed on the country in the wake of the financial crisis,[93] Beijing agreed to invest $258 million in further developing the port. At the same time it also invested $6.7 billion in upgrading Athens Airport, $1 billion in the construction and management of Crete's airport. It also proposed the construction of a railway line connecting Piraeus port with Central Europe.[94]

In January 2016, COSCO became the sole (and successful) bidder for a 67% stake in the remaining pier (for passenger traffic). It eventually offered

---

[91] E. Scott, 'China's Silk Road Strategy: A Foothold in the Suez, But Looking To Israel', *China Brief*, 14, 19, 10.10.2014.

[92] F-P. van der Putten, *Chinese Investment in the Port of Piraeus, Greece: The Relevance for the EU and the Netherlands*, Clingendael Report, The Hague, 2014; F-P. van der Putten and M. Mijnders, *China, Europe and the Maritime Silk Road*, Clingendael Report, The Hague, 2015, 9–14.

[93] M. Galenianos, *The Greek Crisis: Origins and Implications*, Crisis Observatory Research Paper 16/2015; G. Papaconstantinou, *Game Over: The Inside Story of the Greek Crisis*, Charleston, SC, 2016.

[94] G.A. Atzori, 'Can China's New Silk Road Save the Greek Economy?', *The Diplomat*, 21.1.2016.

$410 million for the remaining shares that it did not already own. This implied the valuation of the company as $611 million, to which had to be added the $33.5 million of debt that COSCO inherited with the purchase. Given the fact that current gross earnings were only $28 million, it would take twenty-seven years simply to recoup the initial investment; thirty years if maintenance is taken into account. For the investment to make a profit would require either a large increase in traffic or a considerable increase in efficiency.[95] In April 2016, as part of the government's privatisation scheme, COSCO acquired 51% of the Greek state-owned Piraeus Port Authority (PPA), making it the controlling shareholder and giving the corporation management and operation rights until 2052. COSCO paid $420 million to secure its majority percentage stake. As part of the deal, in five years' time it would be able to acquire a further 16% stake for $88 million—once it has completed investments worth $350 million. These include expanding the infrastructure of the cruise port, upgrading the shipyard repair zone and the construction of a multi-storey garage in the RO-RO (or 'roll-on, roll-off') vessel port.[96] The new cruise terminal, capable of accommodating ten cruise ships at a time, was opened in October 2016.[97]

Reflections

The development of the MSR offers examples of developments that are similar to those we have seen throughout this volume on the overland development corridors. Changes in governments and changes in priorities serve to delay and even thwart Chinese ambitions. The main difference lies in role played by super-power politics and by security threats. In the South China Seas the United States still plays the role of a protector of navigation rights that China has never actually challenged. To underscore its regional alliances it has urged members in disputes over reefs and islands and under-water resources to adopt a rigid stance on international law and multilateral dispute settlements. It is my hunch that China will be compliant on (shared) access to fishing rights and underwater energy and mineral

[95] *Port Strategy*, 27.1.2016; 28.2.2016.

[96] E. Sellier, 'China's Mediterranean Odyssey', *The Diplomat*, 19.4.2016.

[97] *Maritime Journal*, 19.10.2016.

rights if it serves to remove a bone of contention standing in the way of its greater commercial and financial ambitions. At the time of writing there are two potentially conflicting developments in progress. On the one hand, the increased militaristic rhetoric emanating from the Trump Administration may harden the positions of the ASEAN nations in the dispute, and lead to their search for other partners in harbour developments. On the other hand, the withdrawal of the USA from the TTP implies a setback in hopes for improved overseas markets for Asian developing states which.in their search for compensatory advantages from China, may impel them to soften their stance in the dispute. It is still too early to tell.

The other area where security issues are a cause for concern are in the Indian Ocean or, more specifically, in India. I have seen maps where the Chinese harbour developments are presented so as to 'surround' India and that there are little Chinese warships dotted around the ocean. As an exercise, I played with the data in Drewry's review of container ports and operators. The Review measures the container traffic passing through each port in 2014, and then adjusts the holdings of each firm according to the share of the equity it holds. In that year Chinese firms (including Hutchison Holdings, which is a Hong-Kong firm) held an equity adjusted share of 5.9% of the ports in South East Asia and 10.7% of the ports of South East Asia. If these percentages represent a security concern, then we have some real problems because in Northern Europe Chinese firms hold 21.2% and in Southern Europe 9.8%.

CHAPTER NINE

Final Reflections

Anchoring the Western end of OBOR lie the countries of the European Union. Aside from the countries that joined the EU in 2004 and later, none of them are recognised as part of the OBOR initiative. Before we recap on some of the positions adopted in the previous chapters, I would like to address one final question. How should the EU react?

The many of the regular rail freight routes from Chinese cities end their journeys in European terminals and the Chinese containers ships travelling the MRS dock in Greece, to continue their journey overland. Indeed, in January 2017, the first dual 'land-sea express route' on the Silk Road.by a freight train carrying Chinese goods from Piraeus to Budapest[1] The train had travelled on conventional track but towards the end of 2016 a $3 billion deal was concluded to build a HSR between Belgrade and Budapest, eventually intended to extending south to Piraeus.[2] The EU response was not long in coming. The European Commission (the executive arm of the EU) has started investigations into whether the project is in compliance with EU rules on competitive public procurement. Given what we know about Chinese financial assistance being tied to Chinese contractors, it is highly unlikely that it does comply, thereby plunging any potential cooperation between China and the EU immediately into a crisis.[3]

This would be an unfortunate outcome since the EU has had plenty of

---

[1] *CCTV*, 7.2.2017

[2] Global *Construction Review*, 12.9.2016, *Xinhuanet*, 6.11.2016, *CCTV* 6.11.2016.

[3] *Financial Times*, 20.2.2017.

time to make a positive response, and plenty of reason to as well. Europe has a connectivity plan of its own. No famous names or legends have been attached to its conception. Outside the circles of the policy makers involved, a handful of academics and the commercial interests hoping to benefit, few people even know of its existence. [4] When the Plan was announced in November 2014 it was not short of ambition. Its aim was to improve Europe's transport infrastructure but the unique element, so it was claimed, lay in that it had been designed for the first time on a truly European scale. This change in perspective, so the story continued, had created a new momentum.[5] At the same time the European Commission proposed creating a European Fund for Strategic Investments (EFSI) with a focus on infrastructure and innovations. The EU itself committed €21 billion seed capital to the Fund, with the intention of eventually mobilising as much as €315 billion over the following three years).[6] Presenting the Plan to the European Parliament, Claude Juncker proclaimed that "Christmas has come early". He continued by asserting ""This is the greatest effort in European history to mobilise the EU's budget to trigger additional investment," said Juncker, "Europe is back in business. This is not the moment to look back. Investment is about the future. We are offering hope to millions of Europeans disillusioned after years of stagnation. Yes, Europe can still become the epicentre of a major investment drive. Yes, Europe can grow again." The President of the European Parliament called it a "turning point" after years of slow growth

---

[4] Typed into Google the "EU infrastructure investment plan" registered 2340 results, in Google Scholar (where academic articles can be found) the result was four. Even under its more popular title of the "Juncker Plan", named after the President of the European Commission, the results of the searches were 80,000 and 454 respectively. By comparison "OBOR" recorded 15,800,000 and 110,000 using the two search engines (Google search conducted 1.3.2017).

[5] European Commission, *Building Infrastructure to Strengthen Europe's Economy,* 2014. The scheme envisaged constructing nine freight and passenger 'corridors' connecting Europe from North to South, East to West. It identified thirty priority areas of which no less than eighteen are railway projects, three are mixed rail-road projects and two involve inland waterway transport. In addition one project for a 'motorway of the sea" seems to resemble a European version of the maritime Silk road..

[6] European Commission, *An Investment Plan for Europe,* COM(2014) 903 final, Brussels, 2014. It was only in June 2015 that the scheme secured the backing of the European Parliament (*EurActiv*, 25.6.2015)

and austerity. The head of the European Investment Bank suggested that it represented a paradigm shift in the use of the EU budget. [7]

Here surely was a scheme that matched the scale and scope of China's belt and road initiative. Separated on opposite sides of by the Eurasian landmass, Beijing and Brussels seemed to share the same vision. All that was needed would be to trumpet its creation at the EU-China summit in July 2015, point out similarities with the Chinese intentions and express some words of mutual admiration and support. Instead the final joint statement merely expressed the intention of both sides to explore the synergies between the two plans and to establish a technical Connectivity Platform with the specific intention of promoting "seamless traffic flows and transport facilitation" and identifying opportunities for joint projects and joint funding".[8] In the event, it was China that sought to link the two projects in a meaningful way, with officials suggesting Chinese investments of between €5 billion to €10 billion in the European Fund.[9] The problem with that proposal was that China wanted to tie the investments to projects that Chinese firms would execute, a condition that the EU was disinclined to accept. After a full year of negotiation, China conceded the point, but by now the sum under discussion that now dropped to €2 billion.[10]

Why was the opportunity lost? Part of the reason lay in the complicated decision-making process within the EU itself. Such an announcement would have required the approval of the member states and of the European Parliament. Several member states had an interest in stalling a joint position towards China on this and other matters on the agenda (especially agreements over investment and trade) in order to real the potential advantages of separate bilateral agreements. The European Parliament would also have had to approve, and it would doubtless have attached various clauses on human rights and working conditions that would rather have deflated the

---

[7] *The Guardian*, 26.11.2014.

[8] European Council, *EU-China Summit joint statement. The way forward after forty years of EU-China cooperation*, Brussels, 2015.

[9] *EurActiv*, 6.10.2015.

[10] Reuters, 10.7.2016. M. Makocki,'The EU Level: 'Belt and Road' Initiative Slowly Coming to Terms with the EU Rules-based Approach' in F-P. van der Putten, J. Seaman, M. Huotari, A. Ekman and M. Otero-Iglesias (eds.) *Europe and China's New Silk Roads*, ETNC Report, December 2016, 67-71.

celebrations.[11] Another reason may have lain in the fact that the European Plan was not as solid as was presented. Observers looked for the source of the billions of euros in seed money and discovered that much of it was either in the form of guarantees or from cuts elsewhere. Others questioned the enormous leverage that the Plan envisaged and doubted that an investment by the EFSI would be capable of unlocking private investment fifteen times in size.[12] A further explanation may have lain in the vagueness of Chinese plans and intentions in the middle of 2015, but that excuse is surely long passed and still there has been no unified European response. This has prompted one observer to ask whether Europe was no in danger of missing the train altogether.[13]

This last question misses the mark since it conflates the EU with its individual member states. There is nothing to prevent a member state government from using its foreign assistance budget to support OBOR. In 2015, of the $25 billion in foreign assistance, the EU member states give $6.2 billion to countries in Asia, so there is plenty of scope for shifting the geographical balance and for shifting the balance of that aid towards infrastructural projects.[14] In addition EU private investors placed abroad a total of $521.8 billion in the form of FDI[15] which also leaves sufficient resources for engaging more actively with OBOR, without having to wait for help from national governments. Indeed Europe is responding to OBOR. They are already investing in China and have long been active in the Middle East (all of which fall under China's definition of OBOR countries). The Hague-based APM Terminals has a stake in five ports in China (including) Shanghai as well as in Jakarta, Bangkok,Vung Tau (Vietnam), Mumbai and Colombo, to name

---

[11] See for example K. Kinzelbach, *The EU's human rights dialogue with China: quiet diplomacy and its limits*, New York, 2015. (Vol. 7). Routledge.

[12] D. Gros, *The Juncker Plan: From €21 to €315 billion, through smoke and mirrors, CEPS Commentary*, 27.11.2014.; J.D. Schneider, *Growth for Europe–Is the Juncker Plan the answer.* EPC Discussion Paper, 20, 2015.

[13] A. Arduino, *China's One Belt One Road: Has The European Union Missed the Train?* RSIS Policy Report, March 2016.

[14] http://www.oecd.org/development/stats/oecdstat-faq.htm

[15] http://www.oecd.org/corporate/mne/statistics.htm

only the largest.[16] The first block container train from China to Europe was a joint venture between Deutsche Bahn and RZhD and the group is about to open ta direct route between China and Iran.[17]

So, OBOR is developing, and we can safely conclude that European firms are participating in its development even if their national governments are generally modest in their response. OBOR is not a line on a map joining China and Europe. It offers opportunities of engaging in a unique development program, aimed at raising income in the less developed countries along its path and in the Southern tributaries. Since sixty years of Western-led models of development assistance have yielded only disappointing returns, it might be worthwhile considering the Chinese model of a combination of soft infrastructure loans accompanied by private, 'for-profit' direct investment. This chimes well with the more recent accent on income transfers (from whatever source, and not just from governments) in Western development thinking and the stress on the relationship of aid with trade. The official Chinese rhetoric for the 'belt and road initiative' is for *mutual* benefit for the parties involved. This would hold for European investors as well, and these gains would be easier realised if European governments and the European Union were involved from the start rather than following from behind.

So, what has this volume contributed to the discussion?

It is very difficult to capture the essence of OBOR. It is a loose network of roads, rails, pipelines all of which link China with various parts of Asia and Europe. It includes a portfolio highways, railroads, power stations and ports in which Chinese firms have an interest. and it embraces some other projects, most of which involve power generation and distribution. Chapter One argued that OBOR deserved to be analysed in these terms and not simply relegated to a realist/institutionalist discourse to be judged largely on its potential geo-political implications. It also argued that OBOR had at its heart a powerful metaphor that conflated a Chinese and an Asian dream. I have often asked at conferences, what does Europe have to match? I am usually answered by suggestions including democracy, transparency and

16 Drwery, *Global Container Terminal Operators Annual Review and Forecast*, 2016, 58-64.

17 *Technology Review*, 3.2.2017.

human rights. This rely may play well in Europe, but it looks very different from the perspective of countries that, within living memory, had been the object of formal Western imperialism.

Chapter Two made clear that whatever the outcomes of academic discussions, we are unlikely ever to know for certain what originally motivated OBOR and what has subsequently driven it forward. It will have economic consequences and these will create dependencies that can alter the balance of power and influence within the region. Later in the volume, we observed that not all these developments pointed in the same direction and that pre-existing rivalries could easily forestall China's ambitions.

Chapter Three argued that OBOR differed from current Western models of development assistance – that it made no demands of standards of governance and that the provision of loans in place of grants could improve responsibility and that the accent of connectivity and energy provision addressed bottlenecks in the path of development. Recent ADB calculations suggests that Asian countries require $1,500 billion annually if it is to continue on its current growth trajectory; $1700 billion if the impacts of climate change is included. That is double the current amount that the region is investing.[18] The region is also blighted by cumbersome administrative procedures at its borders that raise the costs of international trade and hinder economic development. If we take these factors together – development support, institutional arrangements to remove trade barriers and improve connectivity and the success of integration in defusing intense regional rivalries, then the European Union does have a dream to share.

The country chapters that followed showed how the fractured nature of international relations, coupled with domestic rivalries, regime changes, local opposition and inefficient governance repeatedly thwarted OBOR's progress. The largest fissure lies between China's financial muscle and infrastructural penetration which potentially can unravel at any time. Currently Russia is in no position to challenge OBOR's impact but by fostering security and promoting regional integration, it has managed to stay in the game. The other rupture in the region is that between Pakistan and India which has cost China any influence in the latter and access to its infrastructural programmes. It is difficult to imagine an alternative approach that could

[18] ADB, *Meeting Asia's Infrastructural Needs*, Mandaluyong City, 2017.

have appeased India's sensibilities, but it is worth reflecting that only five years before France and Germany embraced the idea of a supranational community, the two countries had been at war with each other, In Myanmar we saw how a political transition could completely undo the previously close cooperative relationship whilst in Mongolia we saw how a dependence on China for financial support could force a humiliating climb-down by the government there. In South-East Asia we saw China trying to implement a regional scheme with which all the parties agreed, but negotiating it bilaterally with countries one-by-one. In opting for a route through Laos, the government was choosing for expediency over commercial rationality. The point to bear in mind is that, for all the rhetoric and for all the alarmist geo-strategic predictions, China does not have complete control over OBOR or over its wider implications. Multilateral operations on this scale are always unpredictable and carry unintended consequences to which China, and the rest of the world will have to adapt.

I realise that throughout this book I have not confronted the realist, power-fixated analysis of China's rise. This is partly because of the choice of focus of the book, but it is partly out of frustration of the deterministic focus of much of the analysis, also in the context of OBOR. In our discussion of the MSR we come closest to the strategic literature. Basically it suggests that deep-sea harbours are potentially dual-purpose and can also be used for the basing, repair and supply of naval vessels, including submarines. This is true, but it is true of any deep-sea port. What matters is not the facility itself, but the intention and the capacity to use it for military purposes. Port construction and management is a multinational business. There is no 'wreath of tulip' literature about APM Terminals interests in ports in Asia and China, nor anything similar about those of the Singapore-based PSA International or the Dubai-based DP World or even the interest of Hutchison Holdings and COSCO in ports in Europe. When the international situation deteriorates and there is a build-up of offensive weaponry, it might be time to revisit the security threat posed and time to take appropriate measures to deny naval access to such facilities. Meanwhile OBOR's port initiatives should be taken at face value – as a means of shortening trade routes to southern China, as a means of streamlining alliances with Chinese shipping companies and as part the competition for commercial 'hub and spoke' traffic.

Recommendations

The Dutch pride themselves for being 'clear-headed' in their approach to problems ('nuchter' is the word in Dutch) and consider that this gives them the right to lecture to others less gifted in this respect. As a long-term resident of the country, I feel obliged to follow the tradition and suggest a few improvements. Fortunately, I am not the first to do this, so I would like to start with an analysis made by the research team at Renmin University (Beijing). They make five recommendations which can be summarised as follows

- Improve internal planning and coordination mechanisms,
- Ensure that long-term progress is consistent and encourage innovation,
- Promote a consistent message to the OBOR partners,
- Use the expertise of the global Chinese diaspora,
- Improve the assistance to Chinese companies operating in OBOR countries.[19]

All of these recommendations are looking inward and are designed to improve the efficiency of the operation as directed from China. To these I would add the following suggestions to improve its operation externally

- Decide that OBOR is a/the major foreign policy priority and act appropriately.
    - Be fair and generous in resolving bilateral disputes.
    - Avoid disproportional responses that can create new resentments.
- Recognise that it is the goal of OBOR that is important, not the means.
    - Always choose appropriate technological solutions, dictated by local circumstances and not by Chinese capacities.

[19] The Belt and Road Progress Research Team, Renmin University of China, Adhering to the Planning, Orderly and Pragmatically Build the "Belt and Road". The Belt and Road Progress Report, Beijing, 2016, 33-35.

  - Avoid the temptation of giving local elites opportunities for 'show-boating' with mega-projects.
  - Consider the debt burden for recipient countries and their capacity for debt service and repayment.
- Treat OBOR as a multinational effort, albeit one led by China.
  - Contribute the data that will allow an accurate analysis of the Chinese effort.
  - Recognise and incorporate the efforts made by national governments and other foreign participants.
  - Consider coordinating and aligning all the investments within OBOR into an understandable and sequential framework.
- Keep the focus on trade expansion.
  - Continue the work on improving the operation of BCPs.
  - Initiate more efforts for bilateral and multilateral trade pacts, remembering that it is easier for countries with a trade surplus to make concessions than those with deficits.
- Prepare for failures.
  - Realise that transplanting development models has never been easy.
  - Remember that all complex projects have unintended consequences (not always bad).
  - Recognise that any project impacts hardest with the locals, and accept that local opposition may be justified even if a project makes sense at a national level.
- Stay adaptable
  - Be prepared to modify policy instruments to take account of experiences learned during the OBOR initiative and changes in external circumstances.
  - Remember those unintended consequences? They might offer new synergies to be exploited.

China's belt and road initiative has the potential to change the lives of millions of people living on the Eurasian continent and beyond. Broadening its scope and anchoring it in within a more international context will help engender the trust that is necessary for it to succeed.

INDEX

C

D

S

T

U

V

W

X

Y

Z

* 708507-970940 *   30